NEWCOMERS' LIVES

Newcomers' Lives

The Story of Immigrants as told in Obituaries from *The Times*

EDITED BY
PETER UNWIN

B L O O M S B U R Y

LONDON • NEW DELHI • NEW YORK • SYDNEY

First published in Great Britain 2013

Obituaries copyright © The Times
This selection and editorial material copyright © Peter Unwin, 2013

The moral right of the author has been asserted

A Continuum book

Bloomsbury Publishing Plc
50 Bedford Square
London WC1B 3DP

941.004

www.bloomsbury.com

Bloomsbury Publishing, London, New Delhi, New York and Sydney

Published with the kind support of the Pears Foundation

pears
foundation

www.pearsfoundation.org.uk

A CIP record for this book is available from the British Library.

ISBN 978 1 4411 5917 5
10 9 8 7 6 5 4 3 2 1

Typeset by Fakenham Prepress Solutions, Fakenham, Norfolk NR21 8NN

Printed and bound by CPI Group (UK) Ltd, Croydon, CR0 4YY

Contents

Foreword

Dr John Sentamu, Archbishop of York

I am delighted to contribute a foreword to this book. In it are assembled fifty-five obituaries of immigrants to Britain that have been published in *The Times* over the last 150 years. The first, which appeared in 1861, records the death of Prince Albert, Queen Victoria's consort and counsellor, the second that of Karl Marx. At the other end of the scale come obituaries, both published in 2011, which describe the careers of two very different immigrants, one of them Lucian Freud, who was when he died Britain's foremost artist, the other Basil D'Oliveira, the cricketer of colour whose exclusion on apartheid grounds from the England team due to tour South Africa in 1968 led to an international scandal and the abandonment of the tour.

These four men, and the other men and women whose lives are recorded in this book, have two things in common. All were born outside this country but decided, for an immense variety of reasons, to make their homes here. And all of them achieved through their lives and work the distinction that an obituary in the pages of *The Times* denotes. Lady Randolph Churchill, for example, gave birth to Britain's greatest prime minister. Basil Issigonis designed the Mini. The music of Georg Solti and Yehudi Menuhin delighted millions. Lord Sinha became the first Indian to sit in the House of Lords. Air Chief Marshal Sir Keith Park defended London and Malta from air attack in the Second World War. Freddie Mercury set the pop scene alight. Melanie Klein pioneered child psychiatry and Ludwig Wittgenstein logical positivism. Joseph Conrad settled in Britain to write some of the greatest novels of the twentieth century in what was not his native tongue.

One can identify three sources in particular for this flow of talent into Britain. Many of the people whose obituaries appear here came from what was the British Empire and is now the modern Commonwealth. Several others exchanged their American citizenship for residence in this country. But the most pressing reason that brought immigrants here in the early decades of the twentieth century was fear of what awaited them at the hands of tyrants on the European mainland. By no means all were Jews but many were, bringing a particular kind of central European genius and intellectual sophistication with them.

Immigrants are rarely popular; they steal jobs, hide their faces, bring unfamiliar cooking smells into British suburbs; and some are thought to harbour dangerous extremists, even terrorists. These are fears which deserve to be given due weight. But beside them we need to put other considerations. Migration has always been with us. Britons settled or occupied half the world, but there has always been traffic in the opposite direction. An infinitesimal proportion of the population apart, all the inhabitants of this country have immigrant blood in their veins. Medieval England witnessed Jewish pogroms. Queen Elizabeth I ordered that 'blackamoors' should be removed from the country. In the late seventeenth century the persecution of the Huguenots brought many thousands of Frenchmen and women to Britain. The Dutch came with William of Orange, Germans with George I. French aristocrats crossed the Channel to escape the guillotine. Uncounted Irishmen and women came here in the hungry 1840s; dispossessed Belgians in 1914. Polish soldiers and their families who feared to go home to communist Poland made their homes here, so did Hungarians after the 1956 revolution. And now, licensed by European Treaty, Poles, Lithuanians and Bulgarians earn their keep and make their homes, temporary or permanent, in Britain.

All these people bring skills as well as problems with them. This book celebrates the contribution of just a few of them. It provides salutary documentation of the ability, wisdom and sometimes even genius that strangers can bring to us, and of what they can do for Britain.

+ *Sentamu Ebor*

List of plates

Acknowledgments

As editor, I am indebted to the true authors of this book, the many anonymous men and women who between 1861 and 2011 contributed the individual obituaries which make it up. I am grateful also to the Archbishop of York for agreeing to provide the foreword; to Ian Brunskill, the Obituaries Editor of *The Times*, and his colleagues, especially Fiona Wilson and Melissa van der Klugt, for their work in tracking down individual obituaries in their archives; to Kim Storry, David Defew and Robert Bullard, who prepared the text for publication; and to Robin Baird-Smith and Nicola Rusk at Bloomsbury for bringing the whole project to completion.

Prince Albert

Queen Victoria's consort and counsellor
December 16, 1861

The news of the serious illness of the late Prince Consort alarmed and amazed all England on Saturday. To the attentive readers of the Court Circular it was only known that his Royal Highness was slightly indisposed, and the bulletin which on Saturday announced that his illness had taken an unfavourable turn spread dismay and astonishment throughout the country. Then, all at once, the fearful affliction which threatened Her Majesty was seen, and on every side information as to the state of his Royal Highness's health was sought for with the most intense eagerness. The announcement which we published in our third edition of Saturday, that a change, slightly for the better, had taken place in the illustrious patient's condition, was welcomed as almost a relief from the state of feverish anxiety under which all had waited for news. Unhappily, this slight improvement, which raised such ardent hopes wherever it was known, proved to be but a precursor of the fatal issue. During Saturday morning – at least in the early part – his Royal Highness undoubtedly seemed better, and, notwithstanding that his condition was in the highest degree precarious, the change, though sudden, was marked, and almost justified the strong hopes which were then entertained that he would recover. This change was but for a short time, and, in fact, but one of those expiring efforts of nature which give delusive hopes to the mourners round so many death-beds. Soon afterwards his Royal Highness again relapsed, and before the evening it became evident that it was only a question of an hour more or less. The Prince sank with alarming rapidity. At 4 the physicians issued a bulletin stating that their patient was then in "a most critical condition," which was indeed a sad truth, for at that time almost every hope of recovery had passed away. Her Majesty, and the Prince of Wales (who had travelled through the previous night from Cambridge), the Princesses Alice

1

and Helena, and the Prince and Princess of Leiningen, were with their illustrious relative during all this mournful and most trying period. The approach of death from exhaustion was so rapid that all stimulants failed to check the progressive increase of weakness, and the fatal termination was so clearly foreseen that even before 9 o'clock on Saturday evening a telegram was forwarded from Windsor to the city, stating that the Prince Consort was then dying fast. Quietly and without suffering he continued slowly to sink, so slowly that the wrists were pulseless long before the last moment had arrived, when at a few minutes before 11 he ceased to breathe, and all was over. An hour after and the solemn tones of the great bell of St. Paul's – a bell of evil omen – told all citizens how irreparable has been the loss of their beloved Queen, how great the loss to the country.

During yesterday the intelligence was received everywhere with a feeling so painful that it would really be difficult to exaggerate the amazement and grief manifested. The first fear – a wide, deep, and general fear – was, that the great and keen affliction with which it has pleased Heaven in its wisdom to visit the Royal Family might prove too much for the strength of Her Majesty, and that she herself might sink under her irreparable bereavement. A bulletin, however, posted at Buckingham Palace, stating that the Queen, though overwhelmed with grief, bore her loss with calmness, and had not then suffered in health, was soon known everywhere – such was the eagerness with which news of the Queen at such a heavy time was sought for.

Prince Albert died on December 14, 1861. He was born in 1819.

Karl Marx

Prophet of the collapse of capitalism

March 17, 1883

Our Paris Correspondent informs us of the death of Dr. Karl Marx, which occurred last Wednesday, in London. He was born at Cologne, in the year 1818. A the age of 25 he had to leave his native country and take refuge in France, on account of the Radical opinions expressed in a paper of which he was editor. In France he gave himself up to the study of philosophy and politics. Indeed he made himself so obnoxious to the Prussian Government by his writings, that he was expelled from France, and lived for a time in Belgium.

In 1847 he assisted at the Working Men's Congress in London, and was one of the authors of the "Manifesto of the Communist Party". After the Revolution of 1848 he returned to Paris, and afterwards to his native city of Cologne, from which he was again expelled for his revolutionary writings, and after escaping from imprisonment in France, he settled in London. From this time he was one of the leaders of the Socialist party in Europe, and in 1866 he became its acknowledged chief.

He wrote pamphlets on various subjects, but his chief work was "le Capital", an attack on the whole capitalist system. For some time he had been suffering from weak health.

Karl Marx died on 14 March, 1883. He was born on 5 May, 1818.

Sir Moses Montefiore

Financier, philanthropist, protector of his Jewish co-religionists and centenarian

July 29, 1885

Sir Moses Montefiore passed away peacefully yesterday afternoon at his house of East Cliff, near Ramsgate. It would be out of place to use the conventional terms of regret with regard to one who has died so full of years and honours. His life has gradually and painlessly waned away since his neighbours and friends, the latter to be found in the most diverse ranks, religions, races, and climates, celebrated on October 28, 1884, the completion of the 100th year of his singularly prolonged and memorable existence. He retained intermittently to the last great mental clearness and activity which he enjoyed alternately with long periods of passive expectancy waiting for the end; and it is satisfactory to know that he was cheered and positively sustained by being told from time to time how the good works he had set on foot prospered, and by learning the universal interest felt in his health and the long continuance of his days.

He was, in particular, greatly cheered to hear Dr. Hermann Adler's good report of the well-being of the tenants of the dwellings which he had promoted in and about Jerusalem; and he was much occupied with the wedding present which he was privileged to present to Princess Beatrice. On this he caused to be engraved the verse from Proverbs, "Many daughters have done virtuously, but thou excellest them all," which he had never tired of applying to his own wife. When he no longer possessed the energy for conversation he was sometimes heard repeating under his breath verses in Hebrew from the Psalms, and it may truly be said that his last thoughts were occupied with the duties of piety, loyalty, and benevolence, which it had been his aim during the century to fulfil. To the Jews it may well seem as if with him the central pillar of their temple had fallen; but those who calmly contemplate his life will understand that the example of his useful and benevolent career has done its work.

Moses Montefiore was born, the eldest son of a not very wealthy merchant, on the 24th of October, 1784. His ancestors had dwelt in Ancona and Leghorn, cities in which by special, and then exceptional legislation, Jews had been permitted to trade. His grandfather, Moses Haim Montefiore, had settled in England, where he had nine sons and eight daughters and was a near neighbour and associate of Benjamin Disraeli, the grandfather of Lord Beaconsfield.

Joseph Elias, fourth son among the 17 children, married a daughter of the house of Mocatta, a family of Moorish or Spanish Jews, who had left their tombs in the Lido at Venice and in the graveyard of Amsterdam. Joseph Montefiore's wife accompanied him to Leghorn whither he went to buy for the English market, and there in the Via Reale she gave birth to the first of her eight children, Moses Haim, the subject of this notice, whose name was registered as born on October 24 (the eve of Heshvan 9th), 1784, in the books of the synagogue.

Returning to England with his parents, Moses Montefiore was educated privately, articled to Mr. Robert Johnson, a wholesale tea merchant in Eastcheap, and afterwards entered the Stock Exchange, where his uncle purchased for him for £1,200 the right to practise as one of the 12 Jewish brokers. No greater number than that was permitted by the City of London, although a more enlightened body than most of the English communities of that day, to compete with the stock-brokers of the orthodox confession.

Moses Montefiore joined a Surrey volunteer regiment (he lived at Kennington Terrace), and rose to the rank of captain. He became very popular on the Stock Exchange, and much consideration was shown for him when, in consequence of the default of another person, he had to ask for a few days' time, which was cheerfully accorded him, to deliver some Exchequer Bills. He began the publication of a regular price-list of securities, was joined in business by his brother Abraham, and became connected in business and by marriage with Nathan Mayer Rothschild, whose name is still signed on the cheques of the great house in New Court.

The two friends married sisters, daughters of Levy Barent Cohen, a merchant of Dutch descent, greatly respected for his wealth and benevolence. Abraham Montefiore wedded Henrietta Rothschild, sister of the great financier, and thus established another bond of union between the families. It is fitting that in Sir Moses's will this time-honoured connexion is still recognized. Lord Rothschild, whose elevation to the peerage during the last few weeks of Sir Moses's life was a sign of the completeness of the emancipation for which the Rothschilds and Montefiore battled so long, is named as one of the executors, the others being Mr. Joseph Sebag, Mr. Arthur Cohen, Q.C., and Dr. Loewe. Mr. Joseph Sebag, the senior surviving nephew, is the senior executor; Mr. Arthur Cohen is a nephew of the late Lady Montefiore; and Dr. Loewe is the linguist and Orientalist who accompanied Sir Moses and Lady Montefiore on their journeys to the East.

Moses Montefiore married in 1812. It was in 1813 that Mr. Rothschild brought out the British loan for £12,000,000 for warlike operations against Napoleon Bonaparte; and henceforward the brothers Montefiore were associated with the transactions of the house of Rothschild. He lived next door to Mr. Rothschild, and has himself described how "N. M. Rothschild," as Sir Moses was wont to call his brother-in-law in speaking of him to other persons, roused him at 6 o'clock in the morning to give news of the escape from Elba, which Mr. Rothschild was able to communicate to the Ministry. The carrier, on being told the message he had brought in a sealed despatch, cried "vive l'Empereur" and his interlocutors were able to frame from his enthusiasm a shrewd estimate of the temper of the French.

In 1824 Mr. Montefiore had retired from business and settled in Park Lane, Mr. Rothschild removing at about the same time to Piccadilly, where he long occupied a house now the property of the Savile Club. "Thank God, and be content," was his wife's behest to Mr. Montefiore, and he was henceforth only occupied with duties of a semi-public nature, as in founding, in conjunction with his friends, the Alliance Fire, Life, and Marine Insurance Office, the Imperial Continental Gas Association, and the Provincial Bank of Ireland. The Alliance Office was successful from the first, profiting as it did in its life department by the greater average of longevity among its Jewish clients, who were admitted at the ordinary rates, based on actuarial calculations embracing both Jew and Gentile. The Gas Association, though its shares stand now at a high premium, had as hard a struggle for existence as the electric light companies which are now striving to soften the heart of the Board of Trade.

In connexion with the Irish banking business Sir Moses went twice round Ireland, and was presented with the freedom of

Londonderry. He was for a short time a director of the South-Eastern Railway, and in memory of this connexion received in 1883 from the then directors a gold pass, a purely honorary distinction in the circumstances.

It was in 1827 that Mr. Montefiore undertook the pilgrimage which coloured the whole of his future existence. He had been known as a pious and benevolent man, and as one who, while reverent of tradition, controlled it by good sense, as in seeking his wife from among the "German" Jews, although himself a member of the Sephardic or Spanish synagogue. But his life-long devotion to the cause of his oppressed brethren in the East dates from his visit to Palestine in 1827.

The way to Palestine then lay through Egypt, as that to Cairo now passes by Constantinople. The record of the journey, as told by Mrs. Montefiore in her diary, is interesting. Mr. and Mrs. Montefiore drove to Dover, had their travelling carriage placed on the Boulogne steamer, and posted to Turin. At Radicofani Mr. Montefiore, a man of 43, and ignorant that he himself would exceed a century of existence, gave the curate a dollar for the oldest person in the place, who, writes Lady Montefiore, "had only the heavens for his covering and the earth for his couch." They were rowed from Messina to Malta, and took in their convoyed ship which they chartered for Alexandria three poor Greek women, whose husbands had fallen at Missolonghi.

The meeting with Mehemet Ali laid the foundations of a lasting friendship, but Mr. Salt, the British Consul, warned the travellers strongly against proceeding to Palestine. They would be sold for slaves; he trembled to think what would become of Mrs. Montefiore. This pair of travellers, however, were not easily frightened. They sailed to Jaffa and rode into Jerusalem, "a fallen, desolate and abject" city, as Lady Montefiore describes it. They found the Jews very poor and miserable, dwelling like conies in the clefts in the rocks, oppressed by officials, paying £300 a year for the melancholy privilege of weeping at the wall which is called the Wailing Place of Jerusalem.

After administering bountiful alms, and making still more fruitful inquiries into the possibility of a permanent amelioration of the condition of the people by stimulating industry, the Montefiores returned to Alexandria, where they heard Arab women lamenting in the street the defeat of Navarino. Afterwards they themselves brought home some of Codrington's despatches.

Immediately on his return from this visit to the East, Mr. Montefiore joined the Board of Deputies of British Jews, a body of representatives elected by the synagogues, and this council for many years afterwards under his direction took a lively interest in the welfare of its foreign brethren. The English Jews had, however, on their own part a struggle to maintain for political emancipation. Wealthy, well-educated, and often honoured socially, they were excluded by their religion from sitting in either House of Parliament and from most public offices. The battle for the privileges and duties of citizenship had to be won by showing themselves conspicuously worthy of these rights and able to fulfil these duties.

David Salomons, the friend of Montefiore, being a candidate for the shrievalty, was told that if a criminal were reprieved from hanging on a Saturday, his Sabbath, his religion would prevent him from announcing the commutation of the sentence. He refuted so absurd a charge and was elected sheriff of London and Middlesex, but was unable to take the qualifying oath, and accordingly exercised but an imperfect jurisdiction, till Lyndhurst passed a Bill to relieve him.

This was in 1835; in 1837 Montefiore came forward and became the second Jewish sheriff. A year before, he had been elected a Fellow of the Royal Society. As sheriff at the Coronation Moses Montefiore was knighted by the Queen, to whom as Princess Victoria he had already been enabled to offer the courtesy of the use of his grounds at Ramsgate, the agreeable gardens attached to his house at East Cliff at which he lived for over 60 years and at which he ultimately died.

By his energy, popularity, and his own munificence, Sir Moses Montefiore made unprecedentedly large collections for the City charities during his year of office as sheriff. He was also able to secure the pardon of the only criminal whom it would have been his duty to cause to be put to death.

Immediately after he had served his year Sir Moses and Lady Montefiore departed on their second pilgrimage to the Holy Land. They visited on the way the seven synagogues of Rome, making benefactions to the congregations; and while they fulfilled the responsibilities of life did not forget its graces. They met Prince Coburg and the Duchess of Sutherland at a reception at the Duke of Torlonia's, saw Severn's pictures, Gibson's statues, and the museums, bought works of art, entertained a Papal monsignor and a French abbe, and sent Passover cakes to their friends.

At Malta, where Prince George of Cambridge (now his Royal Highness the Field-Marshal Commanding-in-Chief) arrived during their stay, news met them that the plague was raging at Jerusalem. Sir Moses accordingly proposed to proceed alone. "This", writes Lady Montefiore, "I peremptorily resisted, and the expressions of Ruth furnished my heart at the moment with the language it most desired to use: 'Entreat me not to leave thee, or to return from following after thee ; for whither thou goest I will go, and where thou lodgest I will lodge.'" This time they were received in Jerusalem with the most brilliant ceremony as the friends of the Egyptian ruler, and the benefactors of all.

After distributing funds entrusted to him by the Chief Rabbi, Sir Moses returned to Beyrout impressed with the necessity of introducing agriculture among the Jews of the Holy Land. He obtained from Mehemet Ali a decree authorizing the Jews to acquire land, and was preparing an extensive scheme for farming the soil of Palestine by the descendants of those who anciently possessed it, when political disturbances overturned all the plans formed, and rendered valueless the privileges acquired. The Sultan sent his armies against Syria, Acre was bombarded, and the rule of Mehmet Ali was destroyed.

In 1840, the blood accusation, the terrible and lying charge that the Jews offer up human sacrifice, was stirred against them in Rhodes and Damascus. In both these places the populace demanded the blood of the Jews, and the local authorities were not averse to imprisoning such as could afford ransom. Some of these victims perished in captivity. Sir Moses Montefiore called upon his fellow-citizens to express their disbelief in the charge and their sympathy with the oppressed Israelites. The Lord Mayor presided over a public meeting at the Mansion House, Lord Palmerston received a deputation, Sir Moses Montefiore proceeded to Alexandria and Constantinople to demand a fair trial for the accused. Political complications made a public hearing at Damascus impossible, but the surviving prisoners were released; the Rhodian charge fell to the ground; and the Sultan, in response to Sir Moses's appeal, issued the firman of 12th Ramazan, 1256, which discusses the inveterate calumny, refers to the Biblical maxim which prohibits Jews from using the blood even of animals, and dismisses as groundless the charge that they employ human blood. The firman goes on to declare the equality before the law of the Jewish nation with the other subjects of the Commander of the Faithful, and forbids any molestation of them in their religious or temporal concerns.

During his visit to Constantinople Sir Moses found that few of the Jews could read or write the language of the country, although they were by no means illiterate so far as concerned Hebrew and the strange dialect compounded of Spanish and Hebrew which their ancestors had brought away in exile from the Iberian Peninsula. He conferred with the leaders of the congregations, and suggested that the Turkish language should be taught in their schools. "I am quite satisfied" he writes "it will be greatly useful, as it will fit our people for employments and situations from which they are now excluded." This expectation has been signally fulfilled. At that time no Jew was in the public service. Now many have attained high military or civil rank.

The result of the mission of 1840 was felt to be so momentous that it was proposed in Germany to institute a new Purim in its honour. In England the Queen granted to her Knight-errant, who had ridden abroad redressing human wrongs, the right of bearing supporters, an honour usually reserved to peers and the knights of orders.

Sir Moses Montefiore's next mission was to Russia. In the wintry weather of February and March, he travelled to St. Petersburg to induce the Czar to recall a ukase which he had issued ordering the removal into the interior of all Jews living within 50 versts of the frontier. With the good offices of the Court of St. James, and the commercial results of the measure being foreseen, it was recalled. Great risks had been run from wolves and ice during this journey. And the eloquence, or rather the sincerity of Sir Moses Montefiore, and the effect of his bearing as a representative Israelite, and at the same time an English gentleman of high standing, had entirely prevailed. On his return several members of the Royal House attended a reception given in his honour by the late Charlotte Baroness de Rothschild, at Gunnersbury, and the Queen conferred upon him a baronetcy.

In 1858 Sir Moses travelled to Rome and had his unsuccessful encounter with Cardinal Antonelli, who refused to give up the child Mortara, surreptitiously baptized by a nurse and stolen from his mother, who died of grief. The refusal, perhaps, hastened the fall of the temporal power.

In 1860 Montefiore headed the subscription for the relief of the misery of the Christians of Syria, who had been attacked by the

Druses of Mount Lebanon. His letter appeared in our columns on July 12, and resulted in the collection of more than £22,500.

We cannot describe all his journeys to the Holy Land, which he visited seven times in all, on the last occasion when he was more than 90 years of age. Whole cities went out to meet him on the way, sermons were preached, odes composed in his honour. In Palestine he endowed hospitals and alms-houses, set on foot agricultural enterprises, planted gardens, built synagogues and tombs. Besides his own benefactions he was often chosen to administer the charities of others, as, for example, by Juda Touro, of New Orleans, who left large sums at his disposal for improvements in Jerusalem. He pleaded with a later Czar (Alexander II) in St. Petersburg and with the King of Romania at Bucharest for his brethren, "crossed the great desert on a litter to the city of Morocco" and procured a milder treatment for Jews tortured by barbarians.

From his bedroom at East Cliff he sent letters to every member of the Hungarian Legislature exposing the iniquity of the false blood accusation at Tisza Elsa, and corresponded with Lord Beaconsfield and the present Prime Minister on the subject of the Jews of Roumania, whose condition he believed in vain to have been permanently regulated and improved by the Treaty of Berlin.

Judith, Lady Montefiore, the dear companion of his travels died in 1882. He built in her memory a college at Ramsgate, where rabbis maintained by his benevolence pass their days in prayer and study of the law. He also founded in her memory scholarships and prizes for girls and boys. The mausoleum at Ramsgate in which she at present lies alone is a model of the building called the tomb of Rachel on the road from Bethlehem to Jerusalem, which he had often visited with her who was as dear to him as Rachel was to his ancestor.

Sir Moses's entry into his 100th year on the 8th of November, 1883 (corresponding with 8th Heshvan, 5643), was celebrated as a public holiday at Ramsgate, where his liberal but discriminating charities, administered by the local clergy of all denominations, and his unfailing courtesy and hospitality, had made him most popular, The occasion became, by reason of the widespread public interest aroused, one of national significance, and the Queen herself telegraphed, "I congratulate you sincerely on your entering into the hundredth year of a useful and honourable life." The Prince of Wales, the Duke of Edinburgh, the City of London, and hundreds of representative bodies sent similar messages. At

Jerusalem and among the Jewish congregations throughout the world special prayers were offered up and services hold. The Lord Mayor attended the special service held last year (October 20, 1884) in London on the completion of Sir Moses's century of existence, and the commemorations at Ramsgate and throughout the country and the world in churches and synagogues were still more striking than that of 1883.

The excitement of receiving so many congratulations was great for a centenarian, but on the whole it had a beneficial effect upon his health. Sir Moses had ardently desired to see his hundredth year, and that wish had been fulfilled. We have since then chronicled in Dr. Woodman's bulletins his gradual and peaceful decline. He passed away without a struggle yesterday at 4. 30 p.m. His nearest relations had been summoned by telegraph early in the morning. The funeral has been appointed to leave East Cliff Lodge, Ramsgate, precisely at 2 on Friday for the mausoleum already described, where Sir Moses will be laid beside the body of Judith, his wife.

Sir Moses Montefiore was born on October 28, 1784. He died on July 28, 1885.

Jenny Lind

"The Swedish Nightingale"
November 3, 1887

We regret to announce the death, early yesterday morning, at Malvern, of Madame Lind-Goldschmidt, who is better known and will be remembered in history by the name of Jenny Lind. Her health had been failing for some time, and she was compelled not long ago to resign her post as professor of singing at the Royal College of Music – the last link still connecting her with the practice of an art which she had loved from girlhood and in which her successes had been equalled by few.

From the stage she had retired at a comparatively early age and while still in the zenith of her power, and her last important appearance on the concert platform abroad took place in 1870, when she sang the soprano part in her husband's oratorio, Ruth, at Düsseldorf. Since then she was occasionally heard at charitable concerts and in private; but to the present generation of amateurs she had become a stranger and an honoured name. Seventeen years of retirement are apt to dim the brightest fame of an executive artist in the minds of living men. If Madame Goldschmidt had died 30 or 40 years ago, when the Jenny Lind "fever" was at its highest, the news would have sent a thrill through musical Europe. As it is, the loss will be felt chiefly by the large circle of friends who loved and esteemed her in private life.

Jenny Lind was born on October 6, 1820 at Stockholm, and is said to have evinced musical talent and a beautiful voice in her fourth year. Mlle. Lundberg, the famous dancer, heard the child in her ninth year, and induced her parents to send her as a pupil to the school of singing attached to the Court Theatre of her native city. Berg and Crolius were her first masters, and she made her debut as Agatha in Der Freischutz at Stockholm in 1838, playing also Euryanthe, Alice in Robert le Diable, and Spontini's La Vestale with signal success. But although she pleased the public she failed

13

to satisfy herself, and in 1841, when her engagement at Stockholm had expired, she went to Paris, to place herself under Manuel Garcia, with whom she studied for several months, and appeared once at the Grand Opera in 1842, but without success. It is said that this disappointment induced her to make a vow never to sing in Paris again, and this she strictly kept, although tempting offers were not wanting at a later period when her fame had become European. In another sense, however, her stay in Paris was to have important consequences. Meyerbeer heard her, and discovered the rich promise which the Parisian public had failed to see, and it was through his means that she obtained the engagement at the Berlin Opera, from which her international celebrity may be said to date. This was in 1844, when Jenny Lind appeared in Meyerbeer's The Camp of Silesia, the principal soprano part of which had been specially written for her. Here success was instantaneous.

The public greeted her as the "Swedish Nightingale" and Moscheles, who happened to be in Berlin, and later on in London, became one of her warmest friends, speaks of her in a letter to his wife: "Jenny Lind has truly enchanted me. She is unique of her kind, and the air with two obligato duets is perhaps the most incredible thing in the way of bravura that can be heard anywhere." This testimony from a highly competent musician may be supplemented by that of a still greater one, Mendelssohn, who wrote: "in my whole life I have not seen an artistic nature so noble, so zeanine, so true as is that of Jenny Lind. Natural gifts, study, and depth of feeling I have never seen united in the same degree; and although one of these qualities may have been more prominent in other persons, the combination of all three has never existed before."

The posthumous fame of a singer could not rest on a safer basis than such words from such men. It is true that other contemporary critics are not always equally favourable. The author of "Musical Recollections of the Last Half Century," who witnessed Jenny Lind's debut in London, declares that "to my ear she invariably sang somewhat sharp, and I could by no means consider any prima donna to be a great artist who was only positively successful in four operas – Roberto, la Sonnambula, La Figlia del Regimento, and Le Nove di Figaro, her Norma having been a complete failure." The charge of the lady's continually singing sharp may be safely dismissed in the face of ample evidence to the contrary, but the fact of her Pertotie being somewhat limited cannot altogether be denied. Jenny Lind as a stage singer was a vocal artist rather than the interpreter of great dramatic emotions. It is true that her acting as Alice in the scene at the Cross is spoken of as a carefully-studied performance, but some competent witnesses whom we have consulted agree in saying that Jenny Lind belonged to the class of soprani leggieri who sing first and act afterwards. It is quite true that her and the public's favourite operas required more singing than acting; at the same time it is an interesting subject for speculation how Jenny Lind and some of her famous contemporaries would have acquitted themselves in the more dramatic style which has since come into vogue.

That her own bias was not really for the stage is sufficiently proved by the fact that she left the opera as early as 1849, her last appearance "on any stage" as Alice in Robert le Diable taking place on March 18 of that year. Henceforth she confined herself exclusively to the concert platform, and there she gained laurels even greener and more lucrative than those of the earlier stages of her career. Her singing of Swedish songs was in its way unequalled; these simple ditties became the rage of the town, and Loscholes and other fashionable composers of the day transferred them to the piano. But still greater triumphs were in store for the artist in oratorio. Her singing in Mendelssohn's Elijah still lives in the memory of those who heard it. The first performance in England of Schumann's Paradise and the Peri, with Jenny Lind as the principal soprano, which was given at the Hanover-square Rooms in the presence of the Queen (July, 1856), was also a memorable incident in the great artist's career.

Jenny Lind's first appearance on the London stage took place at Her Majesty's Theatre on May 4, 1847, and was preluded by every art of reclame then in fashion. Two rival managers, Lumley and Bunn, went to law over her, and one of them recovered heavy damages, afterwards reduced, in the Court of Queen's Bench. The lady's Continental successes and her private virtues, her charity, and her childlike innocence, were canvassed by the newspapers with a fullness of detail which would do credit to modern journalism of a certain class. No wonder that on the eventful evening the house was crowded, and the tickets were retailed by the agents at fabulous prices. The "Jenny Lind fever," already alluded to, raged during that and the following season with unabated violence, taking the form of portraits printed on handkerchiefs, fans, and similar objects. One chronicler even mentions "Jenny Lind potatoes," called so from the blue specks on their skins, because the prima donna had blue eyes. Mr. Chorley, the well-remembered critic, says from the first moment till the end of that season (1847) nothing else was thought about, nothing else talked about, but the new Alice, the new Sonnambula, the new Maria in Donizetti's charming comic opera – his best. Pages could be filled by describing the excesses of the public. Since the days when the world fought for hours at the pit door to see the seventh farewell of Siddons nothing had been seen in the least approaching the scenes at the entrance of the theatre where Mlle. Lind sang. Prices rose to a fabulous height. In short, the town, sacred and profane, went mad about "the Swedish Nightingale." The fame of Sweden as the home of operatic song-birds has, it may be parenthetically stated, been fully sustained since then by such artists as Madame Nilsson and Mlle. Arnoldson, the promising debutante of last season.

In 1850 Jenny Lind went to America under the auspices of Mr. Barnum, and accompanied by Mr., afterwards Sir, Julius Benedict. Here she remained for two years giving concerts under Mr. Barnum's management, and later on her own account, and the profits realized by her were fabulous, being variously stated as £20,000 and $3,000,000. It was at Boston, on February 5, 1852, that she married Mr. Otto Goldschmidt, the well-known composer, whom she had previously known at Hamburg, and who assisted her at her concerts. Readers of Mr. Bayard-Taylor's autobiography will remember the amusing incident of the ode written in connexion with Mlle. Lind's triumphs and conferring upon the poet a celebrity the reverse of agreeable. Returned to Europe, the young couple settled first at Dresden and afterwards at Wiesbaden and Hamburg.

In 1856, however, Jenny Lind once more appeared on the English concert platform; and England she finally made her home. Living in comparative retirement from society, the great artist gathered round her a circle of admiring friends, and never lost her interest in the two chief objects of her life, music and charity. A writer in "Grove's Dictionary" states that the whole of her American earnings was devoted to founding and endowing art scholarships and other charities in her native Sweden; while in England, the country of her adoption, among other charities she has given a whole hospital to Liverpool and a wing of another to London. The scholarship founded in memory of her friend Felix Mendelssohn also benefited largely by her help and countenance; and it may be said with truth that her generosity and sympathy were never appealed to in vain by those who had any just claims upon them. Of late years Madame Lind-Goldschmidt was actively interested in the Bach Choir, as long as it was conducted by her husband, and she was seen at the head of the soprani at each of the concerts given by that institution. She also held, as already mentioned, a professorship of singing at the Royal College of Music. Her holidays she loved to spend at a house bought by her on the slope of the Malvern Hills, and it was here that she died, surrounded by her husband and her family.

Jenny Lind was born on October 6, 1820, and died on 2 November, 1887.

Baron Paul de Reuter

Creator of Europe's first modern news agency

February 27, 1899

A Reuter telegram from Nice states that Baron de Reuter died there on Saturday morning in his 83rd year.

Baron Paul Julius de Reuter was the founder of the great international telegraphic news agency which bears his name. He was born at Hesse-Cassel in 1816. Entering commercial life when only 13, he remained for some years in the office of his uncle, but during this time he made the acquaintance of the telegraphic experimentalist Professor Gauss, whose influence upon the young man was destined to have great results. In this manner young de Reuter became associated with the beginning of practical telegraphy, and when the first line on the Continent – that between Aix-la-Chapelle and Berlin – began operations in 1849, he opened an office in the former place for the collection and transmission of news by telegraph, thus starting in humble fashion the organization which now has agents in every portion of the world.

Difficulties at first were, of course, numerous, but by steady persistence and indomitable energy, Reuter speedily overcame them. Means had to be devised in order to establish regular communication between places not already connected by telegraph, and swift couriers, carrier pigeons, and the services of the railways were among the agencies by means of which the news was sent from one centre to another. The Press censorship and vexatious laws, which at that period handicapped newspaper development on the Continent, naturally hampered the enterprising spirit of the late Baron, and the fact that Great Britain was alone among the European nations to enjoy a free Press, coupled with the laying of the Dover and Calais cable, in 1851, decided him to transfer his chief office to London, where it has ever since remained.

At first his efforts were chiefly centred on commercial intelligence; but the inadequacy and incompleteness of the foreign news then published by most of the English papers afforded de Reuter an excellent opportunity to utilize his organic system – as yet only a few years old – in order to remedy this deficiency, and in 1858 he undertook to supply some half-a-dozen London morning newspapers with foreign telegrams. This was the day of small things, but the extension of the telegraph system at home and abroad was followed by a corresponding enlargement in the scope and methods of Reuter's Agency. His clientele gradually increased, and the public soon came to depend upon the agency for prompt and trustworthy information of occurrences all over the world. Among the earliest of de Renter's "hits" was the telegraphic account of the momentous interview between Napoleon III and the Austrian Ambassador which plainly indicated war between the two empires.

It is difficult to realize the days when all American news had to come by mail. At this time everything possible was done by de Reuter to accelerate the transmission. Fast sailing yachts met the incoming steamers off the Irish coast and received on board the despatches, packed in hermetically-sealed boxes, which were immediately conveyed to Crookhaven, the nearest point on the Irish coast. Thence the news was telegraphed by way of Cork over some 60 miles of wire laid down by de Reuter himself in order to obtain the most rapid transmission to London. When President Lincoln was assassinated by Booth the mail had already left New York, but Reuter's correspondent chartered a swift steamer, overtook the mail boat, and got the news on board. It was a Reuter telegram which first gave England the tidings of the disaster at Isandhlwana in the Zulu war, and our defeat at Majuba Hill by the Boers was likewise first learnt in this country through the same agency. But, in addition to so extensively using the telegraph system, de Reuter was himself instrumental in laying new lines. In 1865 he obtained from the Hanoverian Government a concession for the construction of a submarine telegraph link between England and Germany which enabled a through telegraphic communication to be made direct between London and the principal towns of his native country. He also acquired from the French Government the right to construct and lay a cable between France and the United States. This was worked in conjunction with the Anglo-American Telegraph Company.

Twenty-four years ago Baron de Reuter converted his agency into a limited liability company, retaining, however, the managing directorship. In 1878 he retired from this position, though he still continued as an ordinary member of the board. He was succeeded in the post of managing-director of the company by his son, Sir Herbert de Reuter, another son, Baron George de Reuter, having also a seat on the board.

The untiring energies of Baron de Reuter were not exhausted by his labours in connexion with the news agency. In 1872 he was granted an important concession by the Shah of Persia, which gave him the exclusive privilege of constructing railways, working mines and forests, and making use of all the other natural resources of that country, as well as of farming the Customs. The Baron endeavoured to make this gigantic monopoly subservient to British interests, though without excluding other nations, but in consequence of difficulties placed in his way as the result of various intrigues the British Government interposed in his favour and the concession was annulled, de Reuter receiving instead the concession of the Imperial Bank of Persia.

Baron de Reuter's title was conferred upon him in 1871 by the then Duke of Saxe Coburg and Gotha, in recognition of his public services. He married, in 1845, Ida, daughter of Dr. S. M. Magnus, of Berlin.

Paul Julius Reuter was born on July 21, 1816. He died on February 25, 1899.

Carl Rosa

Impresario who brought the singing of opera in English to Britain

May 1, 1889

The name of Carl Rosa, as this obituary states, will always be associated with the cause of English opera. He was responsible for the first production in English of The Flying Dutchman, Lohengrin and Aida.

The death of Mr. Carl Rosa at the early age of 46 is a loss which will be felt severely by all who are interested in the success of English opera. The deceased impresario, whose real name was Carl August Nicolas Rosa, was born at Hamburg, on March 22, 1843. When still young he exhibited decided musical talent, and in 1859 entered the Leipsic Conservatorium, where he made such progress as a violinist that in a short time he achieved a position that justified his appearing at the Crystal Palace, on March 10, 1866, as a solo player. In the same year he went to America where he met the well-known soprano, Madame Parepa, to whom he was married, at New York, in February, 1867.

It was mainly owing to his wife that Mr. Rosa abandoned the career of a violinist for that of an opera manager. The Parepa-Rosa Opera Company, which for four years won a great reputation in the United States, was for a time dissolved by the illness of Madame Parepa, who, with her husband, returned to England in 1871. Madame Parepa died in January, 1874.

In the following year, Mr. Rosa resolved upon carrying out his idea of producing standard operas in English in London. From the beginning of September until the end of October he carried on a brief but brilliant season, in which he proved satisfactorily that opera in English, if adequately performed, could be made a pecuniary as well as artistic success. From this time until his death, Mr. Rosa continued to carry on the undertaking, which, from a small beginning, resulted two years ago in the formation of a limited liability opera company, which was formed to carry on Mr Rosa's successful enterprise.

Mr Rosa, who occasionally wielded the baton as conductor, was always ready and eager to encourage the composers of his adopted country. Besides his conspicuous ability as a manager, he was a musician of no ordinary talent. His loss will be severely felt, but it is to be trusted that the work to which he devoted the greater part of his life is now so well established that it will remain as a memorial to his energy and ability.

Sir George Grove, in his "Dictionary of Music and Musicians," gives a long list of the operas introduced by Mr. Rosa to the English public. The last of these was Paul Jones, which was brought out with great success at the Prince of Wales's Theatre, where it reached its hundredth night on Easter Tuesday last. Mr. Rosa was not present at the celebration, as he had gone to Paris. It was in that city, at the Grand Hotel, that he died yesterday morning, after a short illness. He appears to have caught cold during the journey from London to Paris last week. Peritonitis followed, and almost before his friends in London had heard that he was dangerously ill the news came of his death. The Court Theatre at Liverpool, where one of his opera companies was playing Paul Jones, was shut last night.

Carl Rosa was born on March 22, 1843. He died on April 30, 1889.

James Abbott McNeill Whistler

A great but quarrelsome artist
July 18, 1903

We regret to learn that Mr. Whistler, the artist, died yesterday afternoon at Chelsea. James Abbott McNeill Whistler was American by birth and French by artistic training and sympathy; and French-American he remained to the end, in spite of his long residence in London. He liked to wrap a certain veil of mystery about his early years, but there seems no doubt that he was born in Lowell, Massachusetts, in the year 1834, or a little earlier. His father was Major George Washington Whistler, an engineer, and his mother a lady of the Baltimore family of Winans – this southern strain of blood helping us to explain the extraordinary unlikeness of the most volatile of painters to the staid and serious stock of Puritan New England.

In Whistler's boyhood his father accepted a position as railway engineer in Russia, and in that country the future painter appears to have spent some years. In 1851 he returned to America and entered as a student at West Point Military Academy, where he remained four years; and for a short time afterwards he seems to have been in Government employment – whether military or civil does not appear – as a maker of maps and charts. There is a story of a spoilt plate, the young artist having scratched some fancies of his own upon it; of confiscation, a reprimand, a Whistlerian repartee, and of consequent departure to Paris and to the free life of the studios of the Quartier Latin.

This was about 1857, and some time afterwards, in Gleyre's studio (then the meeting-place of all the clever young artists of the day), Whistler met Du Maurier, making upon him the impression which is well remembered by all readers of the first and unexpurgated edition – the Harper's Magazine edition – of "Trilby." At that date it was that Whistler began to etch; the earliest of the 268 etchings which Mr Wedmore has catalogued so carefully belongs to that year.

Two years later appeared the group of 13 etchings, known to collectors as "The French Sot," which were published by Delatre, and which at once made a considerable mark. Some time afterwards Whistler came to London, and took up his quarter among the group of artists who had lately discovered the beauties of Chelsea and Cheyne Walk. He lived here for several years, and one of the oddest episodes in the history of modern art is to be found in his comradeship, almost friendship, with Rossetti. Differing in all points but one, they agreed in being artists and in accepting that position with a completeness which seemed to them thoroughly logical. To both the world was divided into two classes only – the artists and the not artists; and the latter was a class whose chief function was to provide for the wants of the former, to accept in a grateful spirit what the artists were pleased to give it, and to be heartily despised in return. A crowning instance is to be found in the relation of both artists to the late Mr Leyland, of Prince's-gate, shipowner, collector, and "patron." Rossetti's letters to him were published some years ago in the Art Journal by Mr Val Prinsep; and most instructive reading they are. Whistler painted for Mr. Leyland the famous "Peacock Room" – a wonderful scheme of decoration, peacock's eyes on a gold ground, the whole leading up to a fantastic full-length picture, the "Princesse du Pays de la Porcelaine" – then quarrelled with him, and took a savage revenge by painting a life-size portrait of him as a devil with horns and hoofs. This picture is still in existence. An American admirer, Julian Hawthorne, once wrote, "there is an immense and sweet good nature in Whistler." Mr Layland's experience of it was the picture in question.

The best fruit of the long residence in Chelsea was the series of Thames etchings which Whistler produced at intervals during the sixties, and which were first collectively published by the late Mr F. S. Ells in 1871. As collectors know, the plates afterwards changed hands more than once, and the later impressions are not so good as those in Ellis's or the still earlier (partial) issues. "Each one of them," writes Mr Pennell, himself one of the best etchers of the Whistler school, "is a little portrait of a place, a perfect work of art." The "Limehouse," the "Custom-house," and many others of this series from the first moment were enthusiastically admired by a very large number of artists, collectors, and humble lovers of art, and it is mere rhetoric to say that they and their author have triumphed through "the courage of a great artist, which has enabled him, through a whole lifetime, to fight through the insults and abuse that have been hurled at him unceasingly".

People who talk in this way forget that Whistler was not only an innovator – we speak of his paintings, not of his etchings – but an extremely irritating controversialist. His sharp tongue and caustic pen were always ready to prove that the man – especially if he happened to paint or write – who did not fall at once into line as a worshipper was an idiot, or worse. For the most part the public only laughed; but if now and then someone who was not quite a nobody, like Ruskin or Burne-Jones, became annoyed and spoke sharply, what wonder? The painful thing was that Whistler, who did not mind how much his own epigrams might hurt others, could not himself stand criticism. The famous instance is the libel action brought by him against Mr Ruskin in 1878, the eminent writer having denounced a certain "Nocturne" shown by Whistler in the Grosvenor Gallery as "a pot of paint flung in the public face."

The trial was painful to many, amusing to more; in the end Mr Whistler obtained one farthing damages. He relieved his soul by publishing a pamphlet on "Art and Art Critics," and the public laughed still more. But Mr Ruskin brought no libel action. This, however, is to anticipate matters. While he was producing the beautiful Thames etchings the young Whistler was also painting a few pictures, and some of them he exhibited at the Royal Academy. Among these were "The Little White Girl" (1865), the "Symphony in White" (1867), "The Balcony" (1870), and the famous "Portrait of the Artist's Mother" (1872). One of the earliest was the work commonly known as "The Piano Picture"; this attracted the admiration of the well-known colourist John Phillip, who asked the price. Whistler left it to him and received a cheque for 30 guineas, with which he was well satisfied. The value is now perhaps a hundred times that sum, so that the Scotch painter had a bargain. "The Little White Girl" had been rejected at the Salon of 1863, sharing the fate of many a Rousseau and Corot in those unregenerate days; but 21 years later the " Portrait of My Mother" obtained a gold medal at the same Salon, and in 1891 was bought for the Luxembourg. This same picture, it is said, had been almost refused at the Academy in 1872, but Sir William Boxall threatened to withdraw from the council if it were not accepted.

As to the general reception of Whistler's works in those days, it cannot be said that they aroused any strong feelings on one side or the other. The "insults and abuse" of which Mr Penmell speaks, and which had really been "hurled" at the Pre-Raphaelites 15 years earlier, were not forthcoming. Some artists were greatly interested, some shook their heads, and the public – who, of course, do not count – were mildly puzzled. One wonders what might have happened if the Academy had chosen at that time to elect Whistler an A.R.A. The irreconcilable might have been reconciled; he might have encountered what a rival wit called "the last Insult – popularity"; and we might never have chuckled over that crowning production of a big man's small vanity – "The Gentle Art of Making Enemies."

But it was not to be, and in 1877 Sir Coutts Lindsay opened the Grosvenor Gallery with Whistler for one of his chief attractions. Here were shown not only the too celebrated "Nocturnes,", but those really considerable works the " Miss Alexander," the "Carlyle" the "Lady Archibald Campbell," and several other portraits, which at least proved to a doubting world that the painter was somebody to be reckoned with. In all the years that have followed Whistler never reached the same level as here. The "Carlyle" – which some time afterwards was bought for the Glasgow Corporation Gallery – ranked the highest level of his achievement, and the point in which he came nearest to his master, Velasquez.

Not even in 1885-86, when he showed the "Sarasate" at Suffolk-street, did he succeed in making so deep an impression, though to be sure the libel action and the gossip of friends and foes had in the interval made him one of the most talked about men in London – a fine preparation, as everybody knows, for artistic fame. That Suffolk-street episode was perhaps the oddest of an odd career. The most mediocre and middle-class of all the artistic societies of London's in low water, and the thought occurred to some revolutionary members to make Whistler president. It was like electing a sparrow-hawk to rule a community of bats. Some of the bats moved out; some followers of the sparrow-hawk came in; but the interesting new community did not last long. The suburban ladies who had been the support of the Society of British Artists were shocked at the changes; they found no pleasure in the awning stretched across the middle of the room, the battened walls, the spaced-out "impressionist" pictures, and the total absence of the anecdotes and bright colours which they loved. A few hundreds of visitors of another sort came and were charmed, but the commercial test of success was not satisfied; before long Whistler ceased to be president, and the society, under a more congruous chief, "relapsed to its ancient mood."

At various dates after this Whistler held small exhibitions, sometimes of etchings and sometimes of paintings, in London. A set of "Venice" etchings vas published in 1880, a series of "Twenty-six Etchings" in 1886, and he held a small loan display of "Nocturnes, Marines, and Chevalet Pieces," accompanied by an amusing catalogue, in which, by quotations from his critics, he easily showed how the different voices of the public may contradict each other in the matters of art. Early in 1885, too, he delivered a lecture in London before a very fashionable audience, attracted as much by his reputation as a merciless sayer of sharp things as by the fame of the painter. This was the so-called "Ten O'clock," afterwards reprinted with a multitude of less worthy and more personal arts and scraps of the Whistlerian philosophy In "The Gentle Art."

The lecture had a little of Heine in it, a little of the Book of Ecclesiastes, a good deal of Walt Whitman and the residue pure Whistler, the moral being – that mankind is divided into artists (about one in a generation) and the rest; that the rest should on no account presume to talk, think, and, least of all, write about art; that art is "for the one, not for the multitude"; that she neither progresses nor decays, but comes where she will and when; that she depends not on virtues or vices; that the Master appears and disappears in obedience to no law. "Art happens," that Whistler "happened" too was the corollary; and, indeed, there is no known law, no known condition of race or society, that can account for him. A few years afterwards he more or less withdrew from London to his rooms in the Rue du Bac, where a certain number of very rich people, chiefly Americans, came and bought his pictures at high prices. The date of his great vogue, if one may use that word in a semi-commercial sense, began with the exhibition of his pictures at the Goupil Gallery, when such pictures as the "Symphony" were brought back to the notice of a generation that had been prepared for them by the habit of seeing, over and over again, the best works of modern Continental art, "impressionist" and other. The exhibition had a prodigious success, and Whistler's belief in the idiocy of the many received a severe shock.

Since then he took a leading part in organizing the rare exhibitions of the International Art Society at Knightsbridge, of which he was the president. His contributions, however, were not of much relative importance, nor were the works of recent date which he showed in the American section of the Paris Exhibition of 1900. They gave him a medal, of course, but his success was a success d'estime, a success based on his previous reputation.

Whistler's book is full of evidence of his colossal vanity, and the stories of his quarrelsomeness are many. But with these he had other and more lovable qualities. His marriage with the widow of E. W. Godwin, the architect, was extremely happy; and to the last he kept real friends. As an artist, none can deny that he had the root of the matter in him, and that in the search after what to him was the beautiful he was indefatigable. Inspired, more than he would ever admit, by Velasquez and the Japanese, he was set upon the exclusive task of painting and etching what he saw, with no ulterior thought of utility, or popularity, or what would advance him in position and esteem. He did not invent the phrase "Art for art," but if it means anything it means the doctrine that Whistler professed and practised to the end. Speaking in his lecture of Rembrandt and Tintoret, he says: No reformers were these great men – no improvers of the way of others! Their productions alone were their occupations, and, filled with the poetry of their science, they required not to alter their surroundings – for as the laws of their art were revealed to them they saw in the development of their work, that real beauty which, to them, was as much a matter of certainty and triumph as to the astronomer the verification of the result, foreseen with the light given to him alone.

This, indeed, leaves us as far as ever from a definition of beauty; but it at least lays down two propositions that can scarcely be disputed to-day – that the great artist is one who finds beauty in the actual world, the actual generation, in which his lot is cast; and that the artist and the moralist or reformer are different persons with different activities. Whistler's whole work is laid out on these lines. He was a portraitist of persons and places to whom modern costume and the fogs of London offered no terrors; and from his pictures there is no lesson to be drawn except the lessons of art alone.

Whistler was born on July 10, 1834. He died on July 17, 1903.

Lady Randolph Churchill

A "brilliant and high-stepping" American who became the wife and mother of British statesmen

June 29, 1921

The sudden death yesterday morning of Lady Randolph Churchill is announced on another page. Those who have known London life for three or four decades will realize that in Lady Randolph Churchill a once brilliant and high-stepping figure has passed away.

Jeannette, daughter of Leonard Jerome, of New York, had all the dash and her full share of the various talent for which American young womanhood is remarkable. She flung herself ardently into many occupations and amusements: Literature, hunting, drama, politics, marriage. And sometimes she combined two or more of them, as when, after reading Renan, she named her black mare (by Trappist out of Festive) L'Abbesse de Jouarre. She was 19 when, in 1873, at a dance given by the officers of the cruiser Ariadne in honour of the Cesarevitch, she first met Lord Randolph Churchill. Three days later he proposed to her. In the following year they were married.

She was already a woman of the world. Some of her childhood had been spent in Trieste, where her father was American Consul; some of her girlhood in Paris, whence she escaped in the last train that left before the siege of 1870 began. Lord Randolph was a man of many interests, and she shared most of them. She hunted with him; she entertained with him, the charm of her society, her wit, and her French cook making her dinner table grateful to King Edward (then Prince of Wales) and many another good judge. On Lord Randolph's visits to Russia and to Germany she "went down" notably well at the Imperial Courts. At electioneering she shone. In 1885 she helped her husband so dashingly that Lord James of Hereford wrote to her: "But my gratification is slightly impaired by feeling I must introduce a new Corrupt Practices Act, tandems must be put down, and certainly some alteration, a correspondent informs me, must be made in the means of ascent and descent therefrom; then arch looks have to be scheduled, and nothing must be said 'from my heart'. The graceful wave of a pocket-handkerchief will have to be dealt with in committee." And in later years, while canvassing for Mr. Burdett-Coutts, she made a famous repartee. When a waverer observed slyly, "If I could get the same price as was once paid by the Duchess of Devonshire for a vote, I think I could promise." "Thank you very much," she replied, "I'll let the Baroness Burdett-Coutts know at once."

Behind all this brilliance lay a power of hard and steady work. Lady Randolph was a woman of solid ability as well as of dash and daring. In his meteoric political career, and especially, perhaps, in the Primrose League, she helped her husband "Like a man"; and history, perhaps, will never have the chance of revealing how much the early career of her son, Mr. Winston Churchill, owed to his mother's intellect and energy.

Anglo-American Amity

Outside the field of strict politics, the dearest wish of this American wife of one Cabinet Minister and mother of another was to render the United States and Great Britain intelligible to each other. During the Boer War she equipped the Maine as a hospital ship with American money, sailed in it to South Africa, and headed the executive committee which controlled it. And the same purpose underlay her most solid contribution to literature – the Anglo-Saxon Review, which she founded, owned, and edited. The idea was permanence. "Articles full of solid thought and acute criticism, of wit and learning, are read one day and cast into the waste-paper basket the next." To issue them in a more costly form would be to lengthen their existence; buyers would preserve a book they had paid highly for, and contributors would write the better for that expectation. No pains were spared in the production; a new cover was to be designed for each issue; and each was to be a facsimile of some celebrated binding of the 16th, 17th, and 18th centuries. The price was fixed at a guinea for each quarterly number. Among the contributors were Swinburne, Henry James, Mr. Max Beerbohm, and Mrs. Craigie (John Oliver Hobbes). But permanence cannot be guaranteed; and the Anglo-Saxon Review's career was brief.

Lady Randolph could write, as well as edit. Her "Reminiscences" (1908) were discreet, but interesting. Her book of essays, "Small

Talks on Great Subjects" (1916) was readable. Her love of the drama was expressed not only in her passion for attending first nights, but in the authorship of two plays, His Borrowed Plumes (1909) and The Bill (1914). The latter was a political play, and proved rather too discreet to be entertaining. The men in it (wrote a critic) were humdrum, but she was far more successful with her women, the naughty little roguey-poguey and the elderly cats. These say and do amusing things, because Lady Randolph knows her sex, and does not hesitate to let her lively sense of humour play freely over it. She had been beautiful; she had been brilliant; she filled her life with work and play. She had her worldly rewards – the Order of the Crown of India, the Order of the Royal Red Cross, the Ladyship of Grace of the Order of St. John of Jerusalem; not to mention great social success.

It came to her to be called upon to fit her vigorous, daring personality to a narrower mould than that which it had once filled. But to the last no illness nor social change could dim her courage and her kindliness. To Lord Randolph Churchill (who died in 1895) she bore two sons, Mr. Winston Leonard Spencer Churchill and Mr. John Spencer Churchill. In 1900 she married Mr. George Cornwallis West, whom she divorced in 1913. In 1918 she married Mr. Montagu Porch, who survives her.

Lady Randolph Churchill died on June 28, 1921. She was born on January 9, 1854.

Joseph Conrad

Sailor, novelist and philosopher of literature
August 4, 1924

Mr. Joseph Conrad (whose death is announced on another page) must ever remain one of the most remarkable examples in literary history of a writer who has adorned a language that was not by birth or upbringing his own. His proper name was Joseph Conrad Korzeniowski, and he was born in the Ukraine in 1857 of a Polish landed family. His father, a man of letters who translated Shakespeare into Polish, became involved in the Polish rebellion of 1863, and was banished to Vologda. He returned, however, for the last year and a half of his life to Cracow, where his son Joseph passed his boyhood. At an early age his passion for literature disclosed itself. "I was a reading boy," he recounted later in life; "I read, what did I not read!" But he not only read; he dreamed. His dreams were of the far spaces of the globe; there is a tale that he pointed, when he was ten, to the unmarked tracts in Central Africa on an atlas of the time, declaring, "When I grow up I will go there." But it was the sea that became an ever stronger lure as he approached manhood; he must be a sailor, and an English sailor, too. He was 19 when he found his way to Marseilles and made his first voyage to the Gulf of Mexico. He worked on two French ships, and then, having joined the crew of an English steamer on her voyage to the Azov Sea, came back with her to Lowestoft, and thus reached his second fatherland.

In the British Service

His grand aspiration was now to be realized. He became an A.B. on board a British ship and was raised to second officer. By 1884 he was a master in the British merchant service, and had reached the goal he had set himself. Before another ten years had passed he had tasted all the varieties of sea-life and steeped himself in the enchantments of the tropical lands that had haunted his imagination from childhood. Together with this hoarded knowledge, he had learned English seamanship and also, of necessity, the English language. Only the spark was needed now to fire in creative energy this triple acquisition. In some biographical notes that received his sanction he is said to have "dropped somewhat casually into the literary life, partly as a result of illness, partly through his friendship with John Galsworthy and the prompting of Edward Garnett." That "casually" can only refer to the occasion. It was, perhaps, a chance that this or that stimulus sent Conrad to pen and paper. But that there lay deep in him the compulsion to expend himself in writing he confessed in his book "Some Reminiscences," published in 1912. He speaks there of "a hidden, obscure necessity, a completely masked and unaccountable phenomenon" - a force as imperious and inexplicable, in short, as that which had drawn him to the sea and England. He speaks, too, revealingly of "a sentiment akin to piety which prompted me to render in words assembled with conscientious care the memory of things far distant and of men who had lived."

As these words remind us, his earliest books were made directly, from the stuff of his sea-experience. The first story he published was "Almayer's Folly," in 1895. How it was written he has laconically noted: "Commenced in September, 1889, in London, then laid aside during voyages to Congo and Australia. Taken up again in 1893, and finished on May 22, 1894. Submitted to T. F. Unwin on June 2 1893. Accepted in August same year. Published in May, 1895." The author worked at the manuscript at sea, and it was nearly lost in the wreck of a boat on the Congo. The tragic hero of this tale of the Borneo coast had his original in the author's own observation. "I had seen him for the first time some four years before from the bridge of a steamer moored to a rickety little wharf forty miles up, more or less, a Bornean river." The manuscript, as it accompanied him on his wanderings, grew slowly, with the laborious effort that never ceased in one who found composition a toil and a strain. "Line by line," he recorded, "rather than page by page, was the growth of 'Almayer's Folly.'" It was the mental fruit of Conrad's experience as first officer of the Vidar, trading between Singapore, Borneo, Celebes, and Sumatra.

When the book was finished, Edward Garnett kept its dubious author to his vocation by a skilful suggestion. "You have the style, you have the temperament; why not write another?" The modesty of the demand for just one more prevented Conrad (he has recorded) from feeling scared; and "another" came – "An Outcast of the Islands," in 1896, the scene of which is laid on the same coasts as "Almayer's Folly."

"The Nigger of the Narcissus"

After that there could be no real question of turning back. In 1897 appeared "The Nigger of the Narcissus," based on a voyage made by the author from Bombay to England in a sailing-ship; it is a study of sea-types from the British merchant service, and was, in its writer's opinion, "the story by which, as a creative artist, I stand or fall, and which, at any rate, no one else could have written." "Lord Jim" (1900), the tale of a young sailor who, after incurring disgrace as a seaman, becomes a wanderer in the East and a ruler in a savage Malayan village; "Typhoon" (1903), a collection of four short stories, with its sinister introductory storm-piece; and " Nostromo: a Tale of the Seaboard" (1904), with its picture of an imaginary state in South America, may be selected from the group of works that mark Conrad's first period, and find in "The Mirror of the Sea" (1906), with its blend of fable, reminiscence and reflection, a kind of epilogue. Here we find the sea pictured as those only know it who have formed their manhood battling with it.

"For all that has been said," writes Conrad, "of the love that certain natures (on shore) have professed to feel for it, for all the celebrations it had ever been the object of in prose and song, the sea has never been friendly to man." And again:- "It seems to me that no man born and truthful to himself could declare that he ever saw the sea looking young as the earth looks young in spring. But some of us, regarding the ocean with understanding and affection, have seen it looking old, as if the immemorial ages had been stirred up from the undisturbed bottom of ooze. For it is a gale of wind that makes the sea look old."

"The Secret Agent" (1907) opened up a different vein of memory and imagination. In this grim tale of the anarchist and criminal underworld (suggested by an attempt on Greenwich Observatory during the 'nineties) we are conscious of the son of an insurrectionary intellectual, who had seen at close quarters and felt the grip of Tsarist police methods. Yet here, as in the ghastly stories of crime and violence contained in "Within the Tides" (1915), we discern a harsh stoicism in facing the malignancies of life and nature, which leaves more room for irony than compassion.

The year before, in "Chance," Conrad had painted in Mr. Smith, once known as "the great de Barral" of the "Orb Bank," the "Sceptre Trust," and other bubble enterprises, a subtle figure of the financial adventurer. In the same year as "Within the Tides" came "Victory," a return to the background of Celebes and Java; and in 1919 "The Arrow of Gold," a romantic fiction dated "about the middle years of the 'seventies, when Don Carlos de Bourbon, encouraged by the general reaction of all Europe against the excesses of Communistic Republicanism, made his attempt for the throne of Spain, arms in hand, among the hills and gorges of Guipuzcoa."

Conrad's last novel, "The Rover," published last December, was also a historical tale, with its scene laid on the peninsula between Toulon and Hyeres, and Nelson himself appearing for a moment. In 1905 the Stage Society produced a play by Conrad entitled "One Day More". It was described in these columns as "a heart-breaking little piece," but "the rugged strength and unflinching sincerity" of it were acknowledged. In 1919 "Victory" was dramatized by M. B. Macdonald Hastings, and in 1922 Conrad himself drew a replay from "The Secret Agent," which just fell short of repeating the success of the novel. The year before a volume called "Notes on Life and Letters" revealed the rare critical capacity that accompanied Conrad's creative and imaginative power in letters. About the same time appeared a book by Captain J. G. Sutherland, "At Sea with Joseph Conrad." The author had commanded a "Q" ship in 1916 for trapping submarines, and told how Conrad, who had been caught in Austrian Poland at the beginning of the war, and had already since then experimented with minesweeping and flying, sailed with him on what proved a disappointing voyage.

A Literary Ideal

In the work just mentioned, "Notes on Life and Letters," Conrad gives expression, in passing, to the ideal that ruled all his literary life. Readers of that book, he remarked, would find in it "Conrad literary, Conrad political, Conrad reminiscent, Conrad controversial." The one thing they would not find would be "Conrad en pantoufles." In fact, he never took his slippered ease with the language that he had been compelled to woo as a lover and had never romped with in the nursery. He never came to that point of familiarity with it that permitted neglect or disrespect: – It is only through complete, unswerving devotion to the perfect blending of form and substance; it is only through an unremitting, never-discouraged care for the shape and the ring of sentences that an approach can be made to plasticity, to colour; and the light of magic suggestiveness may be brought to play for an evanescent instant over the commonplace surface of words: of the old, old words, worn thin, defaced by ages of careless usage. The sincere endeavour to accomplish that creative task, to go as far on that road as his strength will carry him, to go undeterred by faltering, weariness, or reproach, is "the only valid justification for the worker in prose". That was the strenuous and exacting creed that Conrad reaffirmed, in every piece he published. It is, perhaps, the only creed that can be extracted from the long row of his volumes with their shifting glamour of mystery and beauty. The horror seems always close at hand, like the foul things crawling at the roots of the glowing jungle, or the swooping typhoon that ravages tropical calms.

And Conrad was ready to accept the spectacle with the stubbom courage of the storm-beaten sailor: "The ethical view of the universe involves us at last in so many cruel and absurd contradictions, when the last vestiges of faith, hope, charity, and even of reason itself, seem ready to perish, that I have come to suspect that the aim of creation cannot be ethical at all. I would fondly believe that its object is purely spectacular – a spectacle for awe, love, adoration or hate, if you like, but in this view – and in this view alone – never for despair! Those visions, delicious or poignant, are a moral end in themselves. The rest is our affair – the laughter, the tears, the tenderness, the indignation, the high tranquillity of a steeled heart, the detached curiosity of a subtle mind – that's our affair."

Joseph Conrad was born on December 3, 1857. He died on August 3, 1924.

John Singer Sargent

The greatest portrait painter of his age
April 16, 1925

The death of Mr. John S. Sargent, R.A., which we announce with great regret on another page, has closed an epoch in English painting. For all his unfailing desire to learn and his constant freshness of spirit and method, this man of genius was the last supreme figure in a period in the history of English painting which is now past. His harsher critics said of him that he was of his age, not for all time. Admiration is not likely to be denied to his masterpieces at any future moment, but, in spite of the strong individuality of his genius, he belonged to his own age; and the passing of the great painter drives home the truth that the age which he so brilliantly and shrewdly depicted is also past.

John Singer Sargent, by common consent the greatest portrait-painter of his time, was of American birth, but English by virtue of long residence. His father was Dr. Fitzwilliam Sargent of Boston, Mass, a descendant of William Sargent, of Gloucester, England, who emigrated to Massachusetts before 1650. His mother had been Miss Mary Newbold Singer, a member of an old Philadelphia family. The accident of his birth in Florence, on January 12, 1856, has often been referred to as in a manner prophetic, so appropriate it seemed that a great painter should see the light in the capital of art, arid that an artist of a truly cosmopolitan outlook should be born far beyond the boundaries of his parents' home in New England.

His youth was spent in Europe. No stories of infant precocity are told of him, but we know that he rapidly acquired mastery in drawing and painting, to which he early devoted himself. He studied first in the Florence Academy of Fine Art, and at the decisive moment went to Paris, to put himself under Carolus Duran. Cheered by the encouragement and guided by the technical skill of this admirable painter, young Sargent soon reached the

point of high perfection shown in the portrait which he inscribed
"A Mon Cher Maitre, Carolus Duran, 1877." At once spontaneous
in design and mature in workmanship, this portrait met with
immense success – helped, we can readily believe, by the personality of the big and genial young painter, just 21 years old.

But it was not his first work; indeed, he had already visited
America in 1876 and become known as a painter of great promise.
In 1879 he paid his first visit to Spain, where the country, the
blazing sunlight, and the pictures of Velasquez combined to inspire
the most famous of his early pictures, the full-length portrait of
a Spanish dancer, "Carmencita," now in the Luxembourg. The
picture, suggested by Spain, took form in Paris, where Sargent held
a studio from about 1880 to 1884, when he definitely made London
his home, settling in Chelsea, near his fellow American and fellow-
artist Whistler. What the two men thought of each other is not
recorded: but one is at liberty to guess that the little "Gadfly of
genius" while he may have admired, did not like his rival's instant
success, and that Sargent, the most unselfish of men, smiled and
passed on.

Portrait Painting

Many, but not all, of Sargent's clients in the early eighties were
Americans, wealthy men and handsome women clamouring to
be painted by the Boston man who had conquered Paris. Perhaps
the chief picture of that date was one which was presented to the
Boston museum by the family in 1919. This is "The Children of
Edward Darley Boit," a well-known Boston man, a large canvas
portraying with delightful simplicity four little girls in black frocks
and white pinafores in a large nursery. Other American portraits,
to name a few out of many, covering some 25 years, are those of
President Roosevelt, Mr. Rockefeller, and Mr. H. G. Marquand; of
Mrs. Endicott, an elderly lady, with an expression of great dignity
and charm; of the beautiful actress, Ada Rehan; and of three ladies
who married eminent Englishmen – Mrs. Joseph Chamberlain,
Miss Leiter, and Lady Randolph Churchill. In 1899 an exhibition
of his works was held in Boston. It included 120 pictures, of
which some 50 were portraits; and the interest of the collection,
which drew visitors from all parts of the United States and fixed
Sargent's reputation in his parents' country at a very high level; was
enhanced by his mural paintings in the Sargent Hall of the Boston

Public Library. These famous paintings – famous alike for their merit and for the violent opposition which they have from time to time aroused from more than one religious body, represent, in the painter's own words, "a pageant of religion – a mural decoration illustrating certain stages of Jewish and Christian history".

But after the artist settled in London (he was elected A.R.A. in 1894 and R.A. in 1897), it was on the walls of the London galleries that, during the remainder of the eighties and down to about 1910, the public first saw his works. They form a long and noble series, marvellous in their vitality, direct and yet free, dazzling in their representation of textures, and for the most part vividly true as likenesses. Take, for example, the portrait of the late Lord Wemyss, the delightful aristocratic optimist; or by way of extreme contrast, that of Asher Wertheimer, the great Bond Street art dealer. We should be inclined to rank the "Wertheimer" highest among all Sargent's portraits of men, its grasp of character is so complete. But there are also, for example, the "Coventry Patmore" and the "Henry James." The figure of the poet is one of command. He had attained to dogmatic certainty; if others do not share it, so much the worse for them! But to Henry James certainty is no such simple matter: it can only be seen through the hundred facets of a cut diamond, and the man of letters sits there, mentally turning the diamond, so to speak, till he gets the gleam of which he is in search.

Sargent was eagerly sought after by fair ladies in those days, for to be painted by him soon began to be recognized as a high distinction. Nobody wants to see a lady's character analysed quite so mercilessly as this fine painter analysed his men. But if Sargent's faces of young women were treated rather more slightly than those of the other sex, they were wonderfully vivid, while the attitudes and the dresses were always amazing in their freedom and essential truth. The full-length of the Duchess of Portland, though (like the Lord Ribblesdale of the National Gallery) it is too tall, is a picture which future generations will rank with the best Gainsboroughs. So with such half-lengths as "The Duchess of Connaught" and "Mrs. Chamberlain"; so, still more, with the three or four magnificent groups in which Sargent, late in the century, brought back and filled with a much more real life a type of art which had been dead since the days of Lawrence. "The Three Ladies Acheson," the Tennant-Elcho-Adeane group which was painted for Mr. Percy Wyndham, and more than one of the pictures of Mr. Wertheimer's family are at once marvels of decoration and vitally true.

After about 1910 it was difficult to induce Sargent to paint portraits. He was quite rich enough for an unmarried man; why should he go on with work of which he was tired, and which bound him too much to other people, sometimes no doubt rather trying people ? So he travelled, lived a good deal in Venice, and amused himself by painting rapid, vigorous sketches of landscape, architecture, and incident. Many photographs of these are contained in the big folio volume of Sargent's works which appeared with a preface by Mrs. Meynell.

When the Great War came Sargent placed his services as war artist at the disposal of the Government. His terrible picture, called "Gassed," was a chief feature of the Academy exhibition of 1920, and is now in the War Museum.

The Man and his Art

In person Sargent was a tall, burly, bearded man with a full face of sanguine complexion, dark hair, and strongly marked eyebrows. He gave the impression of great strength combined with great nervous sensibility. A friend of his student days with Carolus Duran described him as then a "very tall, rather silent youth," who, though rather shy, could "upon occasion express himself with astonishing decision." These characteristics were preserved in maturity, and to the casual acquaintance Mr. Sargent appeared silent and shy. Hating pretence and affectation, he was extremely generous in his encouragement of less successful artists whose work he admired, his encouragement often taking the practical form of buying their pictures.

He was a great reader, knowing French, Italian, Spanish, and some German, and an enthusiastic musician, being a brilliant performer on the piano. In the biography of the late E. A. Abbey, R.A., by Mr. E. V. Lucas, there is a letter from Abbey, dated September 28, 1885, on his first visit to the Cotswolds, which deserves quotation, not only as giving the genesis of one of Mr. Sargent's most poetical pictures, but also as throwing light upon his tastes, methods of work, and personal characteristics: "We are all as busy as bees in Broadway. Sargent has been painting a great big picture in the garden of Barnard's two little girls in white, lighting Chinese lanterns hung among rose trees and lilies. It is 7ft. by 5ft., and as the effect only lasts about 20 minutes a day – just after sunset – the picture does not get on very fast. We have lots of music – Sargent plays, and Miss Gertrude Griswold sings to us like an angel.... Sargent nearly killed himself at Pangbourne Weir. He dived off the same and struck a spike with his head, cutting a big gash at the top. . . . It was here that he saw the effect of the Chinese lanterns hung among the trees and the bed of lilies." The picture, "Carnation, Lily, Lily, Rose," was bought for the nation out of the Chantrey Bequest Fund in 1887 and placed in the Tate Gallery.

Abbey's letter brings out clearly that close dependence upon "the thing seen" which was at once the strength and the limitation of Mr. Sargent's art. He had acute visual sensibility to the facts and effects of Nature, and extraordinary power of recording them in characteristic terms of the medium he was using; but, though his pictures were generally well composed, he was not remarkably alive to the purely aesthetic significance in form and colour of what he saw. He composed in facts rather than in forms. In this respect, and allowing for individual genius, he may be said triumphantly to close a period, for it is unlikely that we shall ever again have a great painter on the same lines. Painting has, in a sense, gone deeper, both as regards the facts of Nature and the means of their representation, and the thing seen is exchanged for the thing felt by the whole organism, including the unconscious mind. This, however, is not to say that Mr. Sargent was insensible to poetry when it was inherent in the facts or the mood of Nature represented, as in the picture named above, or in the human personality, as in the extremely beautiful portrait of his niece, "Marie Rose," exhibited in the Academy of 1913. It might be claimed, too, that in his later works, particularly after the shock of the war, without greatly changing his methods, Sargent did respond to the time-spirit, restraining the effect of "immediacy" and suppressing his more obvious skill in execution, in the effort to allow the more permanent values to shine through the facts. His portrait of "Sir Philip Sassoon," exhibited in the Academy of 1924, is a case in point. Nor, though Mr. Sargent was not in the special sense a decorative painter, was he deficient in decorative ability. His work in the "Sargent Hall" of the Boston Public Library, including the coloured relief of "The Crucifixion," shown in the Academy of 1901, is proof to the contrary; and his much-criticized group of "Some General Officers of the Great War," in the Academy of 1922, presented by Sir Abe Bailey to the National Portrait Gallery, showed in its very restraint a much deeper understanding of the problems of wall decoration than appeared on the surface.

National Possessions

It is Sargent's importance as summing up and closing a period which, apart from his individual powers, makes peculiarly appropriate the generous provision by Sir Joseph Duveen of a special room at the Tate Gallery to contain his works in the national possession. They will include, presumably, the nine "Wertheimer Portraits," bequeathed by the late Mr. Asher Wertheimer and at present housed in the National Gallery; "Lord Ribblesdale" and "Miss Ellen Terry as Lady Macbeth," in the costume designed for Irving's revival of the tragedy at the Lyceum and once in his possession, both presented to the nation by the late Sir Joseph Duveen; "Carnation, Lily, Lily, Rose," and a number of drawings.

No account of Sargent would be complete without some reference to his water-colours, appearing in the exhibition of the Royal Society of Painters in Water Colours – of which he became a member in 1908 – and elsewhere; broad and summary, producing the full illusion of Nature, but kept by the medium from undue insistence upon the facts. From the very nature of his powers Sargent was not at his best in black-and-white, and a collection of his portrait drawings shown some years ago at the Grafton Galleries left a feeling of disappointment. Masterly in some respects, they had too much the effect of means to an end, and lacked the finality, as of something existing only in that form, which is the mark of a supremely good drawing.

Sargent was honorary D.C.L. of Oxford and honorary LL.D. of Cambridge, and an officer of the Legion of Honour: he was also a member of numerous British, American, and foreign artistic societies. He is represented in all the principal galleries of the world – in the National Gallery of Ireland by a portrait of President Wilson, painted in 1917 at the request of the executors of the late Sir Hugh Lane, who, as the highest bidder, bought the blank canvas in Christie's Red Cross sale of 1915, but did not live to choose the sitter; in the National Gallery of Modern Art, Rome, by a portrait of "Antonio Mancini," presented by Sargent in 1924; and in the National Gallery of Victoria Melbourne, by "Hospital at Granada." His club was the Athenaeum, to which he was elected under Rule H. in 1898.

Sargent was born on January 12, 1856, and died on April 14, 1925.

Lord Sinha

The first Indian to sit in the House of Lords
March 6, 1928

Lord Sinha of Raipur, whose death is announced on another page, was the first Indian to enter the Executive Council of the Viceroy, and so far the only Indian to become a K.C., to be a member of the Home Ministry, to be raised to the British peerage, and to be appointed Governor of a province of British India. He was the second Indian to be appointed a member of the Judicial Committee. His career was thus one of high achievement, which is without parallel in the history of British and Indian relations.

Satyendra Prassano Sinha owed nothing to early advantages or family influence. The youngest son of a Kayastha pleader in the small village of Raipur, in the Birbhum district of Bengal, he was born in June, 1864. At the age of 14 he matriculated in the University of Calcutta, entering Presidency College. In 1880 he married the daughter of a land-owner. In the following year, with his elder brother Narendra, afterwards Major Sinha, I.M.S., he came to England. His preparation for the journey had to be in secret, owing to the strong prejudice of his people against foreign travel. He joined Lincoln's Inn, where he won many of the prizes offered by the Inns of Court, and was called to the Bar in July, 1886. A few months later he was enrolled at the Calcutta High Court. Industry and ability, hard study and regular attendance in Court soon made up for lack of family or social influence. Mr. Sinha rose by degrees to be the leading junior, and by the beginning of the present century was one of the foremost figures at the Calcutta Bar, where up to that time the European element had had an almost unchallenged supremacy.

At the end of 1903 Sinha was appointed Standing Counsel to the Government of India, a position only once before held by an Indian. Refusing a High Court Judgeship, he was appointed in 1907 Advocate-General of Bengal, having previously acted as such for six months, and he was the first Indian to receive the permanent post. Such advancement might have been unwelcome to his English brethren at the Bar if the selection had fallen on one less Europeanized in his habits and outlook on life. The next step forward, however, did occasion misgiving to the supporters of Anglo-Indian administrative orthodoxy, including two ex-Viceroys, Lord Lansdowne and Lord Curzon. King Edward was strongly opposed, on general grounds, to the proposal of Lord Morley early in 1909 that the Council of the Governor-General should be made accessible to Indians. It was obvious that the Secretary of State had Mr. Sinha in mind when he told the House of Lords in February, 1909, that there was no valid reason why the impending vacancy in the Law Membership should not be filled by an Indian lawyer of large practice and great experience in his profession – a man of unstained professional and personal repute, in close touch with European society, and much respected, and the actual holder of important legal office. The Secretary of State, strongly backed by the Viceroy, and with a unanimous Cabinet, gained his point, and he was able to report in a letter to Lord Minto, with whom King Edward had been in correspondence on the subject, that the announcement of Sinha's appointment had produced no shock: "*The Times*, which in Indian matters is almost the only journal that really counts, shakes its head a little solemnly, but without scare".

The tenure of the first Indian successor to Macaulay and FitzJames Stephen did not extend beyond 18 months. He had never coveted a post which involved for him heavy pecuniary loss and the necessity, painful to a man of his quiet domesticity, of spending a large part of the year at Simla away from his home and all his friends and connexions in Bengal, and he resigned when Lord Minto's Viceregal term came to an end. Lord Minto publicly testified afterwards that no one could have served him more loyally or more ably.

Sinha had been on the point of leaving the Council some months earlier because he could not support certain clauses of the Press Bill; but he withdrew his tender of resignation the same day in consequence of a political assassination in Calcutta, writing to his chief that in such circumstances he would not desert his post. Returning to the Bar, Sinha was knighted in 1914, and at the close of the following year yielded to the pressure of his "old friend", the late Mr. B. N. Basu, to accept the presidency of the Indian National

Congress session at Bombay by way of countering the efforts of the Left Wing. In a closely reasoned presidential address, he made the first authoritative claim for a declaration of the ultimate goal of British policy in India – a claim met by the historic declaration of August, 1917.

In June, 1917, Sinha, after serving again for a short time as Advocate-General, became a member of the Bengal Executive Council. Very soon afterwards he came to this country with the Maharaja of Bikaner as the first Indians to participate in Empire deliberations. They were associated with the Secretary of State at the meetings of the Imperial War Cabinet, and were members of the Imperial War Conference. Both received the Freedom of the City of London at Guildhall. In the following year "Sir S. P.," as he was called, was in London again as a member of the Imperial War Cabinet and the War Conference. He had barely reached Calcutta on his return when he was recalled to represent India, in association with the Secretary of State and the Maharaja of Bikaner, at the Peace Conference in Paris. He was thus the only Indian commoner to share in Imperial and inter-Allied deliberations on the War and on the Peace terms.

In the middle of 1918 Sir Satyendra was appointed a King's Counsel, a distinction not previously or since conferred on a barrister of Indian birth, or indeed of Indian practice. But greater honours awaited him. He had given Mr. Montagu more whole-hearted and unequivocal support in the details of the reform policy envisaged in the Montagu-Chelmsford Report than any other prominent Indian. The Secretary of State naturally felt it desirable to associate this acceptable and eloquent Indian directly with himself in piloting the Reform Bill of 1919 through Parliament. Mr. Lloyd George welcomed the picturesque touch the proposal gave to the reconstruction of his Ministry after the "Khaki" Election, and accordingly Sinha was selected to succeed Lord Islington as Under-Secretary for India. The story goes that he was given only ten minutes to make up his mind as to whether he would forgo for this purpose the return to Bengal, to which he was looking forward, for in later years he never took kindly to prolonged sojourns in our uncertain climate. In order that he might conduct the Bill in the Lords he was created Baron Sinha of Raipur, and was so far the only Indian to be raised to the peerage, while he was the second Indian to be called to the Privy Council, the first having been Mr. Ameer Ali. He conducted the Bill through the Upper House, where he was confronted with the opposition of several ex-Indian Governors, with modesty, skill, and judgment.

His Under-Secretaryship was of brief duration, for in the autumn of 1920 he left this country to establish another "record," that of the first Indian headship of a province. At the end of the year 1926 he assumed charge as Governor of Bihar and Orissa, being also made K.C.S.I.. At Patna and Ranchi, as at Simla and Darjeeling, he was most careful to fulfil the duties of social hospitality appertaining to his position. He was not spared the unwelcome attentions of the Indian-Cooperationists; but many of those who would ordinarily have sympathised with them deprecated efforts to thwart the administration of the first Indian Governor. Bihari and Orissa is something of a backwater in the currents of Indian life, and Lord Sinha's tenure was the less eventful since, with the caution of the lawyer, he was always slow to accept responsibility when it could be avoided. There was no real opportunity to test the new departure, for the Governor, highly conscientious, and inclined to hypochondria, had a serious nervous breakdown in the late autumn of 1921, and consequently resigned after 11 months' tenure, and less than three weeks before the arrival of the Prince of Wales at Patria. Within five years he had established no fewer than six remarkable "records" in Indian achievement, and in all of them he was simple and unspoilt.

For four years Lord Sinha nursed his health, chiefly in India, before taking any further part in public affairs. Towards the close of 1925 he interested himself in the editorial conduct of the Bengalee as a Liberal journal. He wrote a series of articles on his political faith, urging patience and restraint in building up the machinery of a democratic country. The event was treated as of first-rate importance by the Indian Press, but for the most part he was subjected to attack for his refusal to depart from those principles of moderation and fairness he had always upheld. His written and spoken utterances were the more unpalatable to extremist writers since even they could not suggest doubts of his firm patriotism. He deplored the emergence of Hindu-Moslem animosities in the last two or three years, and pleaded earnestly for mutual good will. In view of the divided state of the country and the many evidences of political immaturity, he was opposed to the setting up of the Statutory Commission at an earlier date than was contemplated in the Act of 1919, which he guided through the Upper House; but when the decision was once taken, he gave the most hearty support to the Simon Commission and the arrangements made for Indian influence to be brought to bear through Committees of the Legislatures. When Sir John Simon and his colleagues were approaching the shores of India and widespread boycott and hartal were threatened, Lord Sinha, who had gone out to India a few weeks earlier, sent a wireless message of most cordial welcome, and later was one of their hosts at Calcutta.

There was no truer or more outspoken Indian friend of British and Indian partnership than this gifted, unassuming man. Lord Sinha loved his profession and was happy to return to it in a judicial capacity when his medical advisers offered no objection to his appointment, in August, 1926, to the Judicial Committee of the Privy Council. His pleasure was enhanced from his holding the appointment under the statute of 1883, which empowers the Sovereign to appoint, in addition to those qualified by high judicial office, "any two other persons being Privy Councillors." The "other person" at the time was Lord Oxford and Asquith, so that both seats have been vacated by death within a month. It is understood, however, that if the Bill providing for two paid appointments – the salary of £4,000 being divided between British and Indian revenues of lawyers of Indian experience – had been carried, Lord Sinha would have welcomed selection to one of them.

Though without previous judicial experience, Lord Sinha was learned, patient, and courteous, and showed himself from the first to be possessed of an exact judicial temperament and method. He spoke but little (a virtue not as a rule associated with Indian experience), and always to the point. It fell to him to preside over the Board on several occasions, and a dozen or so of his judgments have appeared in the Law Reports. The tributes paid to his memory yesterday at the Judicial Committee will find an echo in the thoughts of all who practised before him. Soon after he became a Judge he was elected an honorary Bencher of Lincoln's Inn, which gave him great satisfaction, and at the invitation of the Committee of the Athenaeum he became a member of the club, where he used to say he felt more at home than at any other, and where he was becoming a familiar figure. A by no means inconsiderable element in his life of achievement was the freedom from hampering caste limitations which membership of the small but highly intellectual Brahma Samar confers. He was eclectic in acquiring the culture of East and West in harmonious combination. But he had his full share of the manifold anxieties of the headship of a family, with all its ramifications, which is a persistent tradition of Indian life. His wife had indifferent health and poor eyesight.

His four sons and three daughters were all partly educated in this country. The eldest son, Aroon, who is now in Switzerland, was born in 1887, and is a barrister practising in Calcutta. He has been twice married, and has an heir, Sudhindro Prossanno, who is still a child. Lord Sinha's second son, Shisher, is also a barrister, while the third son, Sushil, I.C.S., is Judge at Berhampore. The youngest son was in the first batch of Indian cadets at Sandhurst, but had not the physique for a military career, and afterwards went to Hertford College, Oxford. The three daughters are all married, the eldest to Mr. A. C. Gupta, of the Finance Department, the second to Mr. N. N. Gupta, a Judge of the Calcutta Small Cause Court, and the third to Mr. R. L. Dutt.

Lord Sinha was born in 1864.

Sir Henry Wellcome

Founder of the modern pharmaceutical industry and patron of science

July 27, 1936

Sir Henry Wellcome, D.Sc., F.R.S., who died in London on Saturday at the age of 82 after an operation, was known in name to every one who has had occasion to take his drugs in the tabloid form which has ousted the bottle of physic and the pill prescribed by former generations of doctors.

Born in Wisconsin, United States, the son of the Rev. S. P. Wellcome, he spent his early childhood in the midst of the Dakota Indian tribes. He attended the schools of the frontier, including one which was held in a typical Western log school house. As a youth he was in the midst of the great Sioux Indian War in Minnesota, when more than a thousand whites were massacred. He was made captain of the boys whose appointed duty was to cast rifle bullets for the defence of the settlement and actively assisted his uncle – a famous surgeon – in treating the wounded. Having at an early age chosen chemistry and pharmacy as his career, he studied these and cognate subjects in Chicago and Philadelphia, and shortly after taking his diploma at the latter city went to New York, where his strong bent towards literary activity was shown by various articles contributed to the scientific journals. He visited most parts of the North American Continent, and finally South America, where he studied the native cinchona (quinine) forests. On his return from South America he contributed to scientific publications the result of his observations.

Attracted by the idea of London as an ideal manufacturing and distributing centre for chemical industries, he decided to make England, the land of his ancestors, his future home, and, in conjunction with the late Mr. S. M. Burroughs, established the firm of Burroughs Wellcome and Co., manufacturers of fine chemicals, alkaloids, and pharmaceutical products. A man of great business ability, the business he founded in London in 1880 increased with extraordinary rapidity, and now has works, offices, and warehouses in most of the great centres of commercial activity throughout the world. The firm was among the first to take advantage of the improvements made possible by the advance of pharmaceutical chemistry and by the improvements in machinery. It was thus able to supply pure drugs in a solid and compressed form. These drugs were sold under the registered name of "Tabloids," a term so convenient that it soon came into common use as a part of the English language to denote anything compressed and consolidated. It had, however, a stormy passage, for it began to be used by other manufacturers, and it was not until March 14, 1884, that the Court of Appeal decided that it could only be used by Messrs. Burroughs and Wellcome. Mr. Burroughs after some time ceased to take part in the business, and Mr. Wellcome became the sole partner until in 1913 it became the Wellcome foundation with Wellcome as the governing director.

Wellcome employed his large income to further the many projects which interested him for he was a man of great versatility and of wide outlook. He contributed much to the advance of tropical medicine; he was an anthropologist, a field archaeologist, a buyer of books, and a collector on a large scale. Being practical, he preferred experiment to theory. He was not content to supply pure drugs in his business, but he wished to know why they acted and how they could be put to the best use. For this purpose he founded in 1894 a physiological research laboratory at Beckenham, a chemical research laboratory in 1896, a medical research museum to include tropical medicine and hygiene with anthropology in 1913, an entomological field research centre at Claremont in 1915. These laboratories were placed in charge of men highly skilled in their own departments and much experimental work of great scientific value emanated from them. He soon found that the different institutions were too widely scattered, and in 1930 he built the Wellcome Research Institution, a fine building at the corner of the Euston Road and Gordon Street. It was opened with befitting ceremony on November 25, 1931, and there they are all housed under one roof.

One of the first civilians to enter the Sùdan after it had been recaptured by General Gordon, Wellcome then saw for himself and studied for some time the unhealthy climatic conditions of the country. In 1900 he founded the Wellcome Tropical Research Laboratories in connexion with the Gordon Memorial College at

Khartoum. He placed the laboratories in charge of Sir Andrew Balfour, and attached a floating research laboratory which cruised through the waterways of the Nile and its tributaries in the Sudan. Some years later he gave great help in securing the foundation of the Gorgas Tropical Research Laboratories on the Panama Canal, which were maintained as a memorial to Surgeon-General Gorgas, of the United States Medical Service, a great pioneer in tropical hygiene.

Wellcome also founded at different times the Lady Stanley Maternity Hospital, a medical hospital and dispensary at Uganda, and a fund which he placed under the control of the Medical Missionary Association to translate into Chinese the various medical, surgical and chemical text-books required by native students who were being educated on the lines of European medicine. During the War he constructed, equipped, and supplied to the British Army Medical Service a chemical and bacteriological motor field research laboratory, which was put to good use in Palestine and Egypt. As an archaeologist he personally conducted explorations in the Upper Nile in 1901 and in 1910. They revealed some Ethiopian sites which had not been previously known.

Personally Wellcome was a quiet, reticent, and almost shy man, slightly above middle height, clean shaven, alert, and quickly brightening up when he became interested in some topic of conversation. He married a daughter of Dr. Barnardo, the founder of Barnardo's Homes, and had one son. Generous and often lavish in supporting projects which appealed to him, Wellcome was always insistent that his light should not be hidden and that the name of Wellcome should always be prominent. The Wellcome Medical Museum was perhaps nearest to his heart after his business. It is a wonderful collection of anthropology, medical appliances, coins, pictures, statuary, and books. Too little known to Londoners because until lately it was housed in Wigmore Street, it will be more visited now that it is suitably placed in the Euston Road building.

Many honours came to him from many different sources. He was knighted in 1932, and he received the Legion of Honour. In addition to being D.Sc. and F.R.S., he was an LL.D. of the University of Edinburgh, a Fellow of the Royal Society, an honorary Fellow of the Royal College of Surgeons of England, and a Fellow of the Society of Antiquaries. In 1885 he was awarded the medal of the Royal Humane Society for life-saving.

Born on August 21, 1853, Sir Henry Wellcome died on July 25, 1936.

Lord Rutherford

Leading theoretician of radioactivity and nuclear energy
October 20, 1937

Lord Rutherford, O.M., F.R.S., the famous experimental physicist, died last night at Cambridge at the age of 66. He was a great man who did fine work himself and had a marvellous influence on the work of others. Born in New Zealand on August 30, 1871, he was the son of parents who at that time were farming at Brightwater, near Nelson; shortly afterwards they moved to Pungarehu, in the Taranaki Province, where they cultivated the New Zealand flax. The boy attended a State primary school near Brightwater, and won a scholarship taking him to the secondary school at Nelson. Again he won a scholarship which enabled him to enter at Canterbury College, Christchurch. In his university career he showed such outstanding ability and energy that he was awarded, in 1894, an 1851 Exhibition scholarship, and came home to work at Cambridge under J. J. Thomson. He had already given evidence of his powers by constructing a novel and ingenious detector of electric waves, based on the effect of oscillating currents upon a highly magnetised needle. He continued the development of his detector at Cambridge, and received signals over a greater distance than had at that time been attained. His work was published in the "Transactions" of the Royal Society in 1897.

Radioactivity

The famous researches of J. J. Thomson on the passage of electricity through gases were at that time in full swing. Rutherford was naturally drawn into the work, and gave material assistance, especially in respect of the behaviour of the charged particles or "ions" by which gaseous conduction is accomplished. In many of these investigations the ionisation of the gas was produced by Rontgen rays: it was an obvious step to experiment with the rays which Becquerel had just shown to be emitted from certain substances, afterwards to be called "radioactive". Thus began the series of researches on radioactivity, in which Rutherford displayed marvellous ingenuity, judgment, and, it is right to say, courage. They stand high among the great researches of the world, not only for their own merits but also for their revolutionary effect on scientific thought. The greater part of this work was done at McGill University, Montreal, where he was appointed to the Macdonald Chair of Physics in 1898. Two years later he married Miss Mary Newton, of Christchurch.

In 1907 Rutherford accepted the offer of the Langworthy Chair of Physics in the University of Manchester. Here he carried on his radioactivity researches, and extended their scope by the inclusion of further brilliant generalizations, to which reference is made below. In 1919 he was transferred to Cambridge, to fill the Cavendish Professorship, previously held in succession by Maxwell, Rayleigh, and Thomson. His activities were still in full tide, and were mainly devoted to the study of the atomic nucleus, whose existence he had established when he was at Manchester. Rutherford's splendid contribution to physical science consisted mainly in the suggestion of two hypotheses of the first rank with their corollaries, and in the experimental work by which he established the truth of his conceptions.

The New Physics

The first of these hypotheses presumed a natural transmutation of the elements. For many centuries men had supposed that the earth consisted of certain ultimate constituents. The number and nature of these ultimates were variously and erroneously conceived until the work of Dalton and his fellow-chemists introduced the modern conception of the atom and explained the laws of atomic combination. The older knowledge had some truth in it, nevertheless; for it presumed a permanent distinction between such "elements" as gold, silver, copper, lead, mercury, and so on. It also imagined that one element might be "transmuted" into another if the proper means were found. In particular, men were ever employed in the fascinating and elusive search for the method by which the base metal lead could be converted into the precious metal gold. When, however, the accurate work of the modern chemist began a new day, the dream of the alchemist faded. In the nineteenth century the astonishing progress of chemical science rested on the immutable character of the elements. When, therefore, the young Professor of Physics in Montreal proposed that, after all, transmutation was not only possible but was actually in continuous progress, he was clearly in need of plenty of evidence to support his most unorthodox hypothesis. The brilliant experiments by which he established his position are classical examples of research.

Transmutation

It will be remembered that in the early nineties the work of Becquerel, the Curies, Crookes, and others had demonstrated the existence of substances emitting continuous radiation capable of action upon a photographic plate, of causing a fluorescent screen to emit light, and of ionising (rendering conductive of electricity) gases through which the rays passed. When Rutherford began his work in Montreal something was known of the nature of the radiations and of the state of the "ionised gas." In fact, as already said, Rutherford himself had contributed to that knowledge. It was also known that the radioactive property could be "induced" in various ways; transferred, that is to say, from one substance to another. Thus air which had been standing for some time in a vessel containing radium became itself radioactive, in the sense that if withdrawn from the vessel it could pass any one of the three above-mentioned tests for radioactivity. And again, if this active gas were left in contact for a time with a solid surface, the latter became independently active. But all these induced activities decayed with time, while the original material, which seemed to have lost some of its power to the benefit of the substances which had been made active, gradually regained it. Finally, it was shown by Rutherford that all the observed effects could be explained on one hypothesis and one only: of which the transmutation of the elements was the principal feature. Radioactivity was simply a consequence of the bursting of the atom. In its most violent form this implied the separation of the radioactive atom into two parts, of which one was an atom of the gas helium, and the remainder a new atom requiring in general a new name. The new atom was also radioactive, usually: for instance, the section of the radium atom produced a helium atom and an atom of a rare gas, which in his first doubt as to its nature Rutherford cautiously called "the emanation." The emanation atom exploded in its turn after an average life of three to four days. The induced activities which had aroused his interest were simply due to the transference of the radioactive descendants, the emanation and the rest to new surfaces to which they could often adhere. The details of this wonderful and fruitful conception were worked out by Rutherford and his pupils, and in time by many others. The average lives of the radioactive substances, their genealogies, the nature of the radiations, their physical effects, and other similar matters were studied systematically with great skill and patience; and as the pages of the new book were turned over one by one the fascinated students of science, all the world over, read therein a story which opened up new views on all branches of knowledge.

Nature Of The Atom Analogy Of The Solar System

The second great hypothesis due to Rutherford was put forward by him during his tenure of the Manchester chair. It had been shown that when the radioactive action exploded the two new atoms were hurled apart through their surroundings, solid liquid or gas, in lines that were very nearly straight. This was easily observed in the case of the helium atom, which was far lighter than the other and therefore took the lion's share of the energy of the explosion. It had been proved that the helium atom pursued its rectilinear motion, not by pushing to one side the hundreds of thousands of atoms it met on its path, nor by pursuing a path which was straight on the whole, and in detail consisted of the deviations necessary to pass by those atoms, but by going through all that it met. Thus one atom could pass through another; two atoms could be, so to speak, in the same place at the same instant. They could not therefore be mutually impenetrable if they were of the size usually assigned to them. They must resemble miniature solar systems in their emptiness, and not solid spheres.

Taking up the inquiry at this point and using his own methods, Rutherford showed that the helium atom was occasionally deflected from its straight line path, and that the change in the direction of motion could be most violent. One solar system sweeping through another could not suffer such a deflection unless it might be supposed that the two central suns, coming sufficiently close to each other, and being thus turned aside from their original paths, carried their trains of planets with them. Rutherford therefore argued that the analogy of the solar system must also be complete to the provision of a central sun; that this must be a positive nucleus in the atom, containing practically all the mass, but occupying a relatively minute volume at the centre; and that the electrons revolved about the nucleus in orbits, as the planets moved about the sun. This hypothesis was backed up, like the former, by a volume of beautiful experimental work. It has been extraordinarily fruitful, leading through the fundamental development by Bohr, which the latter expressed in terms of the quantum theory, to the wonders of modern mathematical physics, with all their strange thought and many-sided suggestiveness.

Rutherford himself pushed on a stage further to show that the atoms could even in some cases be broken at will by bombarding them with the helium atoms of the radioactive process. In recent years the artificial disintegration of the elements through the agency of various forms of radiation has become a common experiment in the Cavendish Laboratory and in other places where Rutherford's lead has been followed. Wide new fields of knowledge have thus been opened up and exploration proceeds rapidly. The very terms that are now in familiar use among scientific workers – wave mechanics, photon, positron, neutron, cosmic rays, and so forth – are an indication of the breadth and the variety of the advances that are being made, advances to which Rutherford's work has been an introductory, fundamental, and essential contribution.

Personal Qualities

Rutherford's personal qualities were remarkable and interesting. In some respect he was like Faraday, in that by sheer force of will and innate ability he rose from small beginnings to the highest positions in the scientific world. Like Faraday, Rutherford was first and last an experimenter who made very little use of mathematical machinery either in his work or in his explanations; success was due to shrewd insight, to the capacity of drawing broad, simple, comprehensive deductions from most careful, effective, and yet often complicated and tedious work in the laboratory. Again like Faraday, Rutherford lived to be a centre of universal affection as well as esteem. He was devoted to his work, because he was enthusiastic in the cause of science, not because he thought of his own advancement; for which reason he was a great colleague, always ready to give others their due credit, and careful that all who helped him should receive full recognition. In one remarkable side of his character Rutherford differed much from Faraday. The latter preferred to be without assistants or students; his experimental work, matchless in its amount and variety, was conducted in the solitary quiet of his laboratory. His extraordinary powers of exposition were the principal means by which his results were so readily apprehended and absorbed.

On the other hand, Rutherford could, and did, work surrounded by a body of assistants and students who were devoted to him and were inspired by his strong, breezy enthusiasm. Through them his work was enlarged and enriched and spread through the world. In particular, there were those whose mathematical abilities were able to draw most important conclusions from his experimental generalizations. Clerk Maxwell did a similar service for Faraday. Not only in his own universities did his strength of character, thorough honesty, shrewdness, and genial nature make him an acknowledged leader, but also in all the scientific circles of the world he was given a principal place. It was curious to observe how, in an international council where lack of mutual understanding, want of initiative, possibly even jealousies, seemed to hinder all progress, Rutherford would march in with a laugh, draw all together, and carry a smiling meeting to a useful conclusion. Outside his laboratory he delighted in the society of his friends and loved to play. There were quite famous golf matches within a small circle where sometimes the unevenness in skill was balanced by permission given to the weaker party to say "Boo" loudly and suddenly on a stated number of occasions when the expert was about to make a stroke. His cheeriness was no small factor in the width and strength of his influence.

Rutherford, who was knighted in 1914, was created Baron Rutherford of Nelson, of Cambridge, in 1931. His coat of arms bears the figure of Hermes Trismegistus and a Maori as supporters, and a kiwi as the crest. He was loaded with honours by scientific societies all over the world. The Royal Society gave him the Rumford medal in 1905 and the Copley in 1922, and he received the Franklin medal of the Franklin Institute in 1924 and the Faraday medal of the Institution of Electrical Engineers in 1930. The Nobel prize for chemistry was awarded him in 1908, and his services to science and the State were recognized when the Order of Merit was conferred on him in 1925. He was president of the British Association at the Liverpool meeting of 1923 and of the Royal Society from 1925 to 1930, and in 1927 he succeeded Sir J. J. Thomson as Professor of Natural Philosophy at the Royal

Institution. Taking a full share in public work he served on many
Government Committees and in 1930 became chairman of the
Advisory Council of the Department of Scientific and Industrial
Research. Besides many papers in the '"Transactions" of the
Royal Society, the Philosophical Magazine, and other scientific
journals he published books on "Radioactivity" (1904), "Radio-
active Transformations" (1906), "Radioactive Substances and their
Radiations" (1912), and (with James Chadwick and C. D. Ellis)
"Radioactive Substances and their Radiations" (1930). "Newer
Alchemy," which he published a few months ago, was an expanded
version of the Henry Sidgwick memorial lecture he delivered at
Cambridge last year.

Lord Rutherford was born on August 30, 1871 and died on
October 19, 1937.

Walter Richard Sickert

Artist and lover of life's curiosities
January 24, 1942

Mr Richard Sickert, the painter and etcher, died at St George's Hill, Bathampton, Bath, on January 22, at the age of 81.

Considering his rank and kind as an artist, not the least remarkable thing about Walter Richard Sickert – or Richard Sickert, as he preferred to call himself in later life – was the range and variety of his other interests. A person who knew him only by hearsay and never saw his work, who read his frequent letters in *The Times* and other newspapers on all kinds of subjects, from wearing his kilt to the decline in the quality of fresh herrings, and was told of his witticisms in several languages, bewildering variations of Christian names, and changes of appearance and address, might be pardoned for supposing that his was a case of "Paints a little, too, I believe" – to quote the famous remark of his early friend and master, Whistler, on Leighton. But, to anybody competent to judge, a single glance at any work by Sickert, whether painting, drawing or etching, would be enough to dispel the illusion. Whatever else it might be the work was clearly the result of intense concentration and infinity of pains, if not at the moment at any rate beforehand.

This combination in Sickert of the serious artist and the roving mind, chameleon-like in its changes of personal expression, appears to need some explanation, but the explanation is probably in the facts themselves. Sickert could cut loose and range afar because he was very definitely the professional artist, in a sense in which other artists comparable to him in rank have not been professional. He was an intensely methodical and systematic worker, and there was nothing about him of Stevenson's "excited amateur". He had neither the desire to cut a figure, artistic or otherwise, nor the consciousness of a weakness to conceal. As nearly as may be Sickert seems to have been free from what is called the "inferiority complex" and his public appearances may be put down to excess of vitality, the professional task well and truly fulfilled.

For practical purposes it may be said that Sickert never painted direct from Nature. His method, like that of the old masters, was to prepare a series of the most careful drawings, so that the subject was learnt by heart, and then to paint from them in a systematic scale of tones in a given colour scheme.

From his earliest to his latest works the development of Sickert was perfectly logical and consistent. Its nature may be described as that of an increasing inclusiveness; a more inclusive style of drawing; and a more inclusive character, with wider intervals between them as a result, in the selected scale of tones, together with a lightening of key and a brightening of colour. It was, at bottom, a progress in generalisation, with lightness and brilliancy – an increased economy of statement – as a result. His earlier paintings at Dieppe and Venice were low in pitch, though full of colour, and the tones in them were both small in area and closely related in value. As he advanced Sickert was able to make "fewer bites at his cherry" until, in works like "Lazarus Breaks his Fast", a self-portrait from a snap-shot photograph, and "Bath" it is dispatched with a "one, two, three"; each broad area of tone representing the mean value of many smaller tones. This logical progress was somewhat obscured by Sickert's habit throughout his life of painting from drawings made at a much earlier date, so that the characteristics of one phase are found in the subject matter of another; but his development was essentially as described.

Like George Moore, in his general attitude to life Sickert seems to have been moved by an insatiable curiosity, particularly about certain aspects of London life – as instanced in his back-bedroom subjects and his preoccupation with the associations of the Crippen case. It is a nice question how far this curiosity was purely artistic, and how far human.

That Sickert, for a short time an actor, was susceptible to the glamour as well as the decorative opportunities of theatre can hardly be questioned, and in his later paintings of the stage the glamour takes the lead. In his dealings with "ordinary" life, too, though never at the expense of the picture, there was tenderness as well as irony, as may be seen in such paintings as "Mamma Mia Poareta" the head of an old Venetian woman, and "The Area Steps" and "The Evening Primrose" two sympathetic interpretations of the little maidservants craving for romance.

Finally, Sickert himself defended illustration in art. He had a high opinion of Frith and John Collier, and in his later improvisations upon themes from Sir John Gilbert and others he revelled in the illustrative opportunity.

Sickert, who came of an artistic family of Danish descent, was born at Munich in 1860. His grandfather, Johann Jürgen Sickert, was a painter and head of a firm of decorators, and his father, Oswald Adalbert Sickert, was born at Altona, where the family business was carried on. Oswald Sickert came to England in 1859 and married an Englishwoman at Harrow, becoming a naturalised British subject nine years later. He was an excellent painter, particularly of coast scenery, contributing regularly to the Royal Academy and the other exhibitions, and he also drew for *Fliegende Blätter*. His musical abilities were inherited by his son, Leonard, and, as represented in a memorable drawing by Mrs Helen Bedford, his wife was a woman of great beauty and distinction. At an exhibition at the Goupil Gallery in 1922 all three generations of the Sickert family were represented.

Richard Sickert, who was the eldest of a family of five sons and a daughter – his brother, Bernard, who died in 1932, was a talented artist, hindered by ill health, and another brother, Oswald, obtained distinction as a writer and editor – was educated at Bayswater Collegiate School and King's College London. In 1881, after a short period on the stage, he went to the Slade School under Legros and also worked with Otto Scholderer at Putney and for a short time at Heatherley's, Newman Street. But, though well prepared, as he said, by his father and Scholderer, his true masters were Whistler and Degas. To the former he acted as assistant, and of the latter he was one of the few intimates, the warm friendship between them ending only with the death of Degas in 1917.

In 1884 Sickert appears to have exhibited for the first time at the Royal Society of British Artists, Suffolk Street, the subject being "A Portrait Sketch". As a pupil of Whistler, who was then President, he continued to exhibit until 1888, when Whistler "took away the Artists and left the British," and Sickert accompanied him; his next appearance at the RBA being in 1928, as President, though he very soon resigned. He was, in fact, in and out of a good many societies, including the New English Art Club, the Royal Society of Painters, Etchers and Engravers, and the London Group, at the inaugural meeting of which, in 1913, he presided. Sickert was elected an Associate of the Royal Academy in 1924, becoming an RA 10 years later. In May, 1935, he resigned, as a protest against the "inaction" of the Academy in regard to the proposal to remove the Epstein statues from the former headquarters of the British Medical Association in the Strand. In 1932 Sickert gave his "Raising of Lazarus" to be sold for the benefit of the Sadlers' Wells Fund.

In both young and old age Sickert was a strikingly handsome man, and he was a most entertaining, if somewhat disconcerting, companion, his witty remarks gaining point from the touch of "old world courtesy" in his manners. His changes of appearance were bewildering. For a time it would please him to grow a full beard, and dress like a Norfolk farmer in pepper-and-salt tailed coat and flat-crowned bowler, and the next time you saw him he was clean-shaven and garbed in a good imitation of a Regency buck. A few months ago a notable book, "The Life and Opinions of Walter Richard Sickert" by Mr Robert Emmons, was published. In it the life of the artist, intensely interesting and often very amusing, and his opinions were presented with sympathy and skill.

Sickert was three times married. His first wife, whom he married in 1885, was a daughter of Richard Cobden, who brought him enough money to free him from anxieties and also added a political contingent to the circle of his literary and theatrical friends and acquaintances. Christine, the daughter of John H. Angus, died in 1926, when he returned to London after a happy sojourn at Dieppe. Thirdly, in 1926, he married Thérèse Lessore, a painter of rare talent – he spoke of her as a genius – member of a well-known family of artists, whose father, Jules Lessore, was an accomplished water-colourist, and whose grandfather was a designer at Wedgewood's. Sickert had no children.

Sickert was born on May 31, 1860 and died on January 22, 1942.

Ludwig Wittgenstein

A founding father of logical positivism
May 2, 1951

Dr. Ludwig Wittgenstein, who died in his sixty-second year on Sunday at Cambridge, was a philosopher with a reputation as an intellectual innovator on the highest level. His earlier and later work formed the points of origin of two schools of philosophy, both of which he himself disowned. He came of a well known Austrian family (his ancestors included the Prince Wittgenstein who fought against Napoleon), and he was brought up in Vienna. After studying engineering at Manchester he went to Cambridge in 1912 as an "advanced student" to study under Bertrand (now Lord) Russell.

At the outbreak of war in 1914 he returned to Austria to serve with the Austrian Army until he was taken prisoner in 1918 in the Italian campaign. While thus serving he completed a manuscript, the Tractatus Logico-Philosophicus which, appearing in 1921 in German in the last number of Ostwald's Annalen der Naturphilosophie and in English in book form in 1922, at once made for its author an international reputation.

Throughout his life Wittgenstein showed the characteristics of a religious contemplative of the hermit type. Thus he alternated between periods of great prominence in academic life and periods of extreme abnegation and retirement, and in 1922 he renounced his fortune and took a post as a schoolmaster in a mountain village near Wiener Neustadt. Here he stayed until 1928. He maintained, however, contacts with Vienna, where he went in the school holidays and where, through his acquaintance with the Professor of Philosophy, Moritz Schlick, he originated a school of philosophy – the famous Vienna Circle, later known as the logical positivists.

Quite apart from the intrinsic merit of his ideas, Wittgenstein's historical importance in this period consists in the fact that through him the work of a long series of formal logicians, culminating in Russell, became known to the inheritors of an equally long tradition of philosophy of science, culminating in Mach (Schlick's predecessor in his chair). The intellectual results of this fusion were such that, a decade later, they spread all over the philosophic world.

By this time, however, Wittgenstein was reinstalled in Cambridge, having arrived there for a short visit in 1929. Trinity College elected him to a five-year research fellowship in 1930, and he also started lecturing. Apart from one paper in 1929, he published nothing in this period but two sets of notes. Dictated to groups of pupils and known respectively as The Blue Book and The Brown Book, they were widely circulated, contrary to Wittgenstein's wishes. Again, it is not too much to say that he inaugurated a new "school," or perhaps rather a new method in philosophy – namely, that of which John Wisdom and Gilbert Ryle are the best known exponents, and which is often referred to as "the philosophy of ordinary language." The point of view put forward in these notes diverges widely from that of the Tractatus Logico-Philosophicus, though it is not difficult to see how the second grew out of the first. The way had been prepared for this new philosophical departure by the emphasis placed by G. E. Moore, who was at Cambridge, on "the language of common sense."

In 1936 Wittgenstein left Cambridge and went to Norway, where it is said that he lived in a mountain hut, and from which he returned in 1938, after the fall of Vienna. In 1939 he succeeded G. E. Moore in the Cambridge Chair of Philosophy, and was also naturalized as a British citizen. He continued lecturing for a time, but in 1943 he went to work, first as a porter in a London hospital and afterwards as a research assistant. In 1945 he returned, but found that his teaching duties prevented him from doing creative writing, and in 1947 he resigned from his chair. The second book, however, which he had sacrificed so much to complete and publish (in order, as he said, to show how very wrong the Tractatus was), was not destined to appear.

In 1949 he became seriously ill, of a disease from which he knew there could be no great hope of recovery, and retired from active life. He formed round him a small group of philosophers who were also his friends, with whom he worked and discussed to the last. We are still too close to Wittgenstein to form a just estimate of his work. His Tractatus is a logical poem, consisting as it does of the development of a gigantic metaphor, constructed round two senses of "language." It is thus an exceptionally difficult book to interpret with any reliability. His sets of notes, and his incomplete manuscript, also show, in the opinion of all who have read them, signs of indubitable genius; but Wittgenstein himself took all the steps in his power to prevent their being circulated on the ground that, if they were, they would be bound to be misunderstood.

What is beyond doubt is that, like Descartes in one way, like Locke in another, he started a world-wide philosophical trend. In so far as this can be described in one sentence, it consists in following up the idea that thinking consists in using a language. Thus thought, which it had been easy to conceive of as a private, indefinable, amorphous entity, becomes the manipulation of some symbolism; something public, something which can be "nailed down" and to which the techniques of formal logic can be applied.

Dr Wittgenstein was born on 26 April, 1889 and died on 29 April, 1951.

Lord Cherwell

Winston Churchill's eminence grise

July 4, 1957

Viscount Cherwell, the distinguished scientist and formerly Professor
of Experimental Philosophy at Oxford, died there yesterday. He
was 71. The Rt. Hon. Frederick Alexander Lindemann, P.C.C.H.
F.R.S., Viscount Cherwell, of Oxford, Baron Cherwell, of Oxford
in the peerage of the United Kingdom, was the younger son of
Adolph Frederick Lindemann and Olga Noble and was born at
Baden-Baden on April 5. 1886. The paternal grandfather was an
Alsatian who decided to retain French citizenship after 1871 and
make his home in Paris. The father was a wealthy engineer, with
varied business interests who had married an Englishwoman and
settled as a naturalized Englishman at Sidmouth, in Devon.

Lindemann and his elder brother grew up there in a happy
wealthy and cultured home where family affection was strong. He
was sent for a short time to Blairlodge School at Polmont and then
to a gymnasium at Darmstadt where the curriculum was of the
thorough, Continental type. The family were great travellers, with
friends all over Europe. In consequence, Lindemann early became
a good linguist with a wide knowledge of the Continent. He was a
devoted son, and it was largely his father's love of astronomy and
skill as an instrument maker that inclined the son to mathematics
and physics. He entered the University of Berlin late, studied under
Rubens, Planck and Nernst, and took his Ph.D. degree there in
1910.

Atomic heats, low temperatures, the quantum theory and the
special theory of relativity were then the great subjects of study.
Lindemann's doctoral dissertation on the atomic heat of metals
at low temperatures marked him out as a man with a future in a
laboratory where many brilliant young men were working. After
Berlin Lindemann continued his work, both experimental and
theoretical, in Paris. By 1914 he had published much in physics and

his reputation there was so high that he was given the directorship of the R.F.C. experimental physics station at Farnborough. Both in the laboratory and as experimental pilot he showed his metal. His courage, his flair for the essential point of a problem, his quickness in argument, his wide knowledge, and his complete independence of opinion on everyone and everything, stood him in good stead. His best known exploit at Farnborough was his demonstration of the safest way of pulling an aircraft out of a spin. Lindemann first evolved a mathematical theory of how an aircraft got into a spin, deduced from theory the simplest way of getting it out of it, then learnt to fly, next, in due course, put his machine into a spin, applied his principles, found they did what he had predicted they would do, landed it and then quietly and modestly reported the incident. This demonstration was not a fluke. He showed courage in repeating it at other times, and he underwent similar trials in testing later theories. When flying ordinarily, it should be said, he was not a very good pilot.

In 1919 he was offered and accepted a chair of physics at Oxford. This was the professorship of Experimental Philosophy attached to the then moribund Clarendon Laboratory. It carried with it a fellowship of Wadham College, which became an honorary fellowship in 1956, and, after 1921, a Studentship of Christ Church, which he retained after retirement. Oxford was glad to welcome this tall, fine-looking, well-dressed, rich, athletic, Continentally educated stranger with a low voice and an informing and critical tongue, who in his fastidious way was a "card." At Wadham, where he lived for a few years before going to a stately set of rooms in Christ Church, he met Lord Birkenhead, and, through him, his friend Mr. Churchill. Through them Lindemann formed a wide acquaintanceship among those who lived in country houses and combined rank and wealth with interest in politics. He was himself a good host, putting his rooms and his cars at the disposal of his friends. In the midst of luxury he preserved an attractive simplicity. He was an abstainer, a non-smoker, and a life-long vegetarian.

In 1920 Lindemann was elected a Fellow of the Royal Society. His success in the following 20 years as a professor was partial only. A fair stream of published work came from his laboratory, after he had refurnished it and partly endowed it, but he never went hard and continuously at one important thing. He preferred to busy himself and his young men with a succession of smaller researches in various branches of physics. He was temperamentally averse from the hard drudgery of experimental work and more content to be director, adviser, and stimulator of young research men than their co-worker and leader. As a lecturer he was adequate. He lectured late in the fore-noon in a low voice, with few of the arts of an expositor, but his matter was good and read well. Everything, indeed, that he published was a model of clear expression.

He was devoted to Oxford and to the advancement of science as a subject of study and research there and worked harder for this end in private than in committees or on boards of faculties. Largely through his influence and efforts the new Clarendon Laboratory in the Parks, then by far the best of its kind in the country, was built and equipped by the University in 1939. He resigned his Chair on reaching the age of 70 in 1956 but retained his home in Christ Church. A measure of the change which had been effected during the years that he had been in charge of the Clarendon can be gained by the fact that when he took over there was no research of any kind going on in physics and fewer than 10 undergraduates were reading the subject. Today there are over 40 senior research workers, 120 advanced students reading for higher degrees, and some 250 undergraduates reading physics.

In 1937, Lindemann, who felt very strongly the necessity of an immediate large increase in our air power and the great need for State endowment of research for all scientific problems involved in the mastery of the air, stood for Parliament at a by-election as Independent Conservative candidate for Oxford University. He was unsuccessful but the defeat only made him more pertinacious in bringing before those in power the gravity of the situation as it seemed to him. Mr. Churchill, a friend of long standing, then out of office, held the same views, and it was not surprising after the outbreak of war when Mr. Churchill took office that Lindemann was given the post of his personal assistant, which he retained to the end of the war. His main task in that post was to advise the Prime Minister generally. He was there not as a specialist primarily concerned with difficult scientific problems but as a man of completely independent judgment with a wide experience of French and German mentality, whose views on problems involving numbers and quantities of any kind were found to be unbiased and useful. At first he was a target for criticism. Those who disliked him – and they were many – saw him largely as a thwarter of designs he personally did not care for. Some Ministers and Civil servants thought it irregular that one of no higher status than a private secretary should have the powers of a cabinet minister. Criticism on this point was partly allayed when Lindemann was created Baron Cherwell in 1941.

The position was further regularized in the following year by his being given ministerial rank and sworn of the Privy Council as Paymaster-General. This office he held from 1942 to 1945. Throughout the war he toiled hard at the many problems the Prime Minister referred to him. Highly confidential work of this kind cannot at this stage be easily assessed, but it is believed on good authority that at times it was of the highest value. When Mr. Churchill formed his Government in 1951 he again called on Cherwell to assist him and once more appointed him Paymaster-General. Between 1951 and 1953 Cherwell was the Prime Minister's adviser on atomic energy research and development and on scientific and statistical matters generally. He resigned his Cabinet post in October, 1953, to resume his academic duties but it was made clear that his personal advice would continue to be available to the Prime Minister and the Government on atomic energy questions and other scientific matters.

He was made C.H. in the same year. In 1954 he was appointed a member of the United Kingdom Atomic Energy Authority set up under the Atomic Energy Act and with his wide experience made a powerful contribution to the progress of atomic energy in Great Britain. He was advanced to a viscounty in 1956. He had downright views on the testing of hydrogen bombs and speaking in a defence debate in the House of Lords in May he said that he could not understand how anyone with a logical mind could argue that Britain ought to have thermo-nuclear weapons, but ought not to test them. The argument that the tests constituted a danger to the health of humanity was "unmitigated nonsense." He was unmarried and by his death the peerage becomes extinct.

Lord Cherwell was born in 1886. He died on July 3, 1957.

Melanie Klein

A pioneer of child psychoanalysis
September 23, 1960

Mrs. Melanie Klein died in a London hospital yesterday in her 79th year. Her name may not be widely known to the general public and is only gradually gaining recognition in psychiatric and psychological circles. Yet her work revolutionized Psychoanalysis and has directly or indirectly exerted a profound influence on psychiatry, Psychology, child upbringing and infant care and more remotely on such disciplines as sociology, anthropology, and art criticism.

Melanie Klein was born in 1882 in Vienna of Jewish parents, trained in psychoanalysis by Ferenczi and Abraham and she started practising in the Berlin Psychoanalytical Society. Soon her interest centred on the then hardly explored possibilities of child analysis and in 1921 she published her first paper. She gradually evolved a technique in child analysis which gave her access to the deepest layers of the conscious mind. She provided the child with small toys and used his free play and spontaneous communications in the same way in which associations are used in psychoanalysis of adults. Both her technique and her findings provoked strong criticism, even from her psychoanalytical colleagues.

First of all her technique aroused opposition since she used Freud's interpretative technique without any concession; she would give neither advice nor reassurance nor any educational guidance. She used this technique in her work with children, however small, and the youngest was under three years old. Her aim was to analyse the child's unconscious and by rendering it conscious to help the child to integrate various aspects of his personality.

Secondly, her findings were found shocking and therefore unbelievable; even to those who had come to accept Freud's views about child sexuality Melanie Klein's discoveries came as a shock. Freud, in analysing adults, had established that many of their feelings, anxieties, and phantasies had their roots in childhood.

Analysing children Melanie Klein discovered that many of the processes described by Freud had their roots already in earliest infancy, for instance, in a patient aged two and a half she found evidence of a superego and an Oedipus complex which had already a long and complex history. She also recognized that aggression and sadism play in a child's mind a role still greater than had been assumed by Freud.

The discoveries she made in child analysis enriched her understanding of adults. In 1926 Ernest Jones, one of the first to recognize the potential greatness of her work, had invited her to come to England and work within the British Psychoanalytical Society, and it is in London that she spent most of her working life and did her greatest work – for instance, her study of the depressive and paranoid-schizoid illness and their origins in infancy.

In other psychoanalytical societies her work is often referred to as "the English school", not quite correctly, since only some of the analysts of the British Psychoanalytical Society were trained and taught by her and used her technique, though there is no doubt that the whole of the British society is deeply influenced by her work. To work with Melanie Klein and to come into contact with her was an experience leaving a deep impact. The power and acuity of her intellect had strength and integrity, her originality and abundant creativeness left one in no doubt that one was in touch with an outstanding personality. Those who worked with her were inspired by her attitude as well as by her achievements.

Melanie Klein was born in 1882 and died on September 22, 1960.

Lady Nancy Astor

Socialite, wit and political pioneer

May 4, 1964

Nancy Viscountess Astor. C.H., the first woman to take her seat as a member of the House of Commons, died on Saturday at Grimsthorpe Castle, Lincolnshire. She was 84.

In any age or country, Nancy Astor would have been remarkable for outstanding vitality, personality, charm and will power. She was always a delight to the eye, small, compact, a finely drawn profile, a classic head, growing more and more exquisite with the years. She was made all of one piece, a perfect working model, always well-dressed. From the first day she entered the House of Commons in neat black with touches of white at collar, in appearance she struck the exact note and set the style for her feminine colleagues in years to come.

Nancy Witcher Langhorne was born of an old Virginian family on May 19, 1879, on the same day as her future husband William Waldorf Astor, was born in New York. In 1897 she married Robert Gerald Shaw of Boston, from whom she obtained a divorce in 1903, and in 1906 she married Waldorf Astor. When he succeeded to the viscountcy and resigned from the representation in Parliament of the Sutton Division of Plymouth Lady Astor was elected as Unionist member on November 28, 1919.

She was the first woman to sit in the House of Commons, being introduced by Balfour and Lloyd George. Countess Markieviecz, who did not take her seat, had been elected by an Irish constituency in the Sinn Fein interest at a slightly earlier date. From 1919 to 1945 Lady Astor continued to represent Plymouth and most of her life and work were closely identified with the city, of which during the Second World War she was Lady Mayoress.

In Parliament she naturally devoted herself mainly to the claims of women and children, speaking with gaiety or gravity according to her mood, but never dully and always briefly and sometimes brilliantly. Her worst fault was a habit of interruption which, however tempered with wit, was apt to cause annoyance. Temperance, education, nursery schools, women police were subjects which deeply interested her.

Like Zenobia, and also in St. James's Square, Lady Astor was a famous political hostess and her house was the meeting place of distinguished visitors to the metropolis, especially Americans. One day it might be Gandhi, the next Grandi and the following day a batch of social workers or Cabinet Ministers or Charlie Chaplin or Ruth Draper or G.B.S. And there were from time to time the huge party gatherings comparable with those of Londonderry House or of the Devonshire House of an earlier day. On the top of the staircase, sparkling with jewels, she welcomed each guest with a bantering quip or jest and was the central figure throughout the evening.

Her energy was extraordinary. After a long day in London and in the House she would return to Cliveden about seven, change into tennis clothes and play two or even three sets of singles with one of her nieces; then down to the river (before the war) in her cream-coloured car, driven at speed; she would swim across the Thames, talking all the time about God, or advising someone on the bank about the way to live his, or usually her, life, touch the bottom on the far bank, tell the swans to go away, and swim back still talking. In earlier years she was a dashing rider and a sure shot; later golf was her favourite game. She played it well and conversationally and distinguished herself in parliamentary matches.

She had a sharp sense of the ridiculous and could have made a fortune on the variety stage. No one who saw her Christmastide impersonations in the old days at Cliveden, egged on by her sisters Phyllis and Nora, will ever forget her clever performances. Dressed in a hunting coat of her husband's and her hair hidden under a large black velvet huntsman's cap she became the little foreign visitor, here for the hunting season; or with a row of celluloid teeth worn crookedly, an upper-class Englishwoman who thought Americans peculiar.

Someone once said she was a cross between Joan of Arc and Gracie Fields. She wasn't courageous, if by courage is meant mastery of fear, for she did not know about fear. She was fearless of physical dangers, of criticism of people. No one could be kinder, more tender, generous, comforting and swift to help in time of trouble. She loved being needed and was at her best in a crisis. She would have denied it but she had an innate sense of drama and had a flair for dealing with people en masse. American politicians and journalists of the old school were bewitched by her. The later, war-time journalists were scared by her outspokenness and refused to be charmed. It is recorded that Gladstone asked his wife whether she would prefer to know nothing and say anything she pleased, or to know everything and say next to nothing on matters of foreign and domestic policy. Lady Astor got the best of worlds, knowing everything and saying anything she pleased.

Her matriarchal feelings were strong and she liked to feel in touch with the whole circle at all times. She held the family together, including nieces and nephews. Within this circle she loved to recall Virginia days, her father, Colonel Langhorne, her sisters and their beaux. During a visit to the States in 1922 she made 40 speeches, mainly in Virginia, "without a single faux pas" reported an American correspondent. Her deep religious sense found its formal setting in the Christian Science Church and she was a diligent student of the Scriptures, with a strong horror of sin and a crusading spirit which spurred her to pursue reforms regardless of party divisions. There were four persons whose influence and friendship and characters she was never tired of acknowledging with gratitude and affection: Rachel Macmillan, Henry Jones, Arthur Balfour, and Philip Lothian.

After her withdrawal from Parliament in June, 1945, when she did not stand for reelection, Lady Astor continued her interest in the city she had represented so long and made regular visits while her health permitted On July 16 1959, she was made an honorary Freeman of the City of Plymouth. In the same year Lady Astor performed the launching ceremony for H.M.S. Plymouth, first ship for 250 years to bear the name, presented a diamond and sapphire necklace to be worn by Lady Mayoresses of Plymouth, and gave her home at 3 Elliot Terrace, overlooking the Hoe, to the city for use as a Lord Mayor's residence. Its use was later modified to a place for the accommodation of official visitors. She was made C.H. in 1937.

Her husband died in 1952 and she is survived by her four sons, Viscount Astor; David Astor, editor of the Observer; Michael Astor; Major J. J. Astor; and by her daughter, the Countess of Ancaster.

Nancy Astor was born on May 19, 1879.

Marina Duchess of Kent

A beauty who was born a Greek princess and married into the House of Windsor

August 28, 1968

Her Royal Highness Princess Marina, Duchess of Kent, C.I., G.C.V.O., C.B.E., who died yesterday at the age of 61, was greatly admired for her remarkable personal beauty and respected and loved for her high sense of duty, her modest charm, her dignity in sorrow, and her devotion to her family.

Princess Marina was the most recent of a long line of foreign princesses to marry into the British Royal house, and none of her predecessors were more successful in winning the affection of the British public. She was the youngest of the three daughters of Prince Nicholas of Greece and a granddaughter of the Danish prince who became King George I of Greece in 1863. She was thus a great-niece of Queen Alexandra, of whom she reminded many older folk when first she came to England as a bride. Her mother was the Grand Duchess Helen Vladimirovna of Russia.

She was born at Athens on December 13, 1906. The Greek royal family was neither wealthy nor pretentious; and though as a child Princess Marina had glimpses of the splendour of the Imperial Russian Court, her own upbringing was simple and strict. Her parents approved of well-disciplined children, and entrusted their daughters to an English governess of the old school, Miss Fox, to whom, for all her sternness, they remained devoted. The family usually spoke English together; and English was Princess Marina's first language, though she always spoke it with an attractive foreign intonation. But the children were taught to be good linguists, and they never forgot that they were Greek princesses. To the last Princess Marina was a sincere member of the Orthodox Church; and her intense love for her native country survived all political upheavals.

The first of these upheavals occurred in 1917, when Prince Nicholas and his family went into exile for four years, spent mainly in Switzerland. They returned to Greece in 1921, but soon had to leave again and in 1924 settled in Paris, where Princess Marina was already at finishing school. Their financial circumstances were not easy. Prince Nicholas, who would have much preferred to be a painter rather than a prince, devoted himself to his favourite but unprofitable pastime, while Princess Nicholas spent all the money that could be spared in helping Russian refugees in worse circumstances. Princess Marina shared in both her parents' ploys. She assisted her mother in her good works, and she worked seriously to develop her own natural talent for painting. At the same time she acquired a practical knowledge of dressmaking, which, with her instinctive good taste, enabled her to be all her life one of the best dressed women of the time. She was a real trend-setter; "Marina green" became all the rage.

The family was closely knit; and it was with mixed feelings that she welcomed the marriages of her sisters. Princess Olga had married Prince Paul in Yugoslavia in 1923; and early in 1934 Princess Elizabeth married the Bavarian Count Toerring, a nephew of Queen Elizabeth of the Belgians.

Her summers were spent mostly in Yugoslavia with Princess Paul. It was there, in August 1934, that she became engaged to her distant British cousin, Prince George. The engagement was warmly welcomed by King George V, and by Queen Mary; and the British public, to whom she had been unknown, was at once enchanted by her radiant beauty and her obvious happiness. Her wedding to the Duke of Kent, as Prince George was created in October, 1934, took place at Westminster Abbey on November 29 that year.

The new Duchess of Kent was at once plunged into a series of public engagements, which she performed with great grace and growing confidence. They were interrupted only by the birth of her elder son, the present Duke of Kent, in October, 1935, and her daughter, Princess Alexandra, on Christmas Day, 1936. She and the Duke were a striking and popular couple, with their good looks, their wide interests and their zest for living. Both had artistic tastes, and together they transformed Coppins, the somewhat ugly Victorian house near Iver which the Duke had inherited from his aunt, Princess Victoria, into a charming home; and their house in Belgrave Square was a meeting place for men and women in public life, for distinguished and interesting foreigners and for representatives of the arts and the stage. The only untoward incident during these years was in June, 1939, when a welder's assistant, a

New Zealander, with a history of mental illness, fired a gun in the direction of a car in which she was a passenger as it left Belgrave Square.

The outbreak of war in 1939 was the cause of her many sorrows. Her father had died early in 1938, and her mother had retired to Athens, where she was caught by the Nazi invasion of Greece. Of her sisters, Countess Toerring was living in Germany and Princess Paul was in exile in South Africa after the collapse of Prince Paul's regency of Yugoslavia in 1941. In spite of her private worries, the Duchess was entirely devoted to the cause of her husband's country. She trained herself as a V.A.D. under the name of "Sister Kay"; but her services were chiefly given to the W.R.N.S. of which she became Commandant in 1940. Her taste and influence were rumoured to be responsible for the W.R.N.S. being allotted a more attractive uniform than any of the other Women's Services. Her activities were interrupted early in 1942, when she prepared for the birth of her younger son, Prince Michael, which occurred in July, 1942. One of the child's godfathers was President Roosevelt.

The following month, on August 25, the Duke of Kent was killed in a flying accident in northern Scotland, when on his way to inspect R.A.F. units in Iceland. It was a terrible blow to the Duchess, only slightly mitigated by the kindness of King George VI, who insisted that her sister, Princess Paul, should be allowed to come from South Africa to visit her. As soon as was possible, she returned to her public duties, helped by the genuine sympathy of the public. The end of the war increased their number, and many of them were of the highest importance. In 1952, she made an extensive tour of the Far East, visiting Ceylon, Malaya, Borneo and Hong Kong, visiting the Royal West Kent Regiment, of which she was Colonel-in-Chief, during its operations against the rebels in the Malayan jungle. In 1957 she represented the Queen at the Independence celebrations in Ghana. Other journeys took her to Mexico and South America, and to Australia. On all these tours she proved a highly successful ambassadress.

Her life was not altogether easy. After the death of her husband, neither she nor her children received a penny from the civil list; and it was not always easy for her to perform her duties in a suitable style, as well as to educate her children. The end of the war enabled her to see her mother and sister freely. But in 1955 Countess Toerring suddenly died, and Princess Nicholas died in 1957. Her children were, however, a continual pleasure to her. She was delighted by the marriage of the Duke of Kent and of Princess Alexandra to British spouses; and she was immensely proud of Princess Alexandra's popularity. After her son's marriage she made her home at Kensington Palace, in an apartment which she furnished beautifully, and where she loved to entertain her friends.

Of her public duties Princess Marina was particularly interested in the Royal National Life-Boat Institution, of which she was for many years President. In that capacity she visited many small harbours round the British coasts to launch lifeboats. She took enormous pleasure in being President of the Lawn Tennis Association and was present almost daily at Wimbledon during the championship matches. She was very proud of being the first Chancellor of the University of Kent, and greatly valued the honorary degrees given her by a number of universities. Her interest in painting and music was genuine and eager. She was warm-hearted and generous, always a little diffident and to the last nervous before she had to make a public speech or even a public appearance, but perfectly controlled. She was a fiercely loyal friend and a delightful companion, full of interest and of humour, with natural dignity but no self-consciousness of her rank.

Princess Marina was born in 1906 and died on August 27, 1968.

Learie Constantine

Brilliant West Indian cricketer who campaigned for racial equality in Britain

July 2, 1971

Lord Constantine, the spectacular and popular West Indian all-round cricketer, the greatest of all fieldsmen and an effective campaigner against colour prejudice, died in London yesterday. He was 69. To a wide public in the nineteen-twenties and thirties he was the personification of emergent West Indian cricket and he used his standing as a games-player with judicious dignity to further the causes of political independence and social equality for his people.

He was born in Diego Martin, near Port of Spain, Trinidad, on September 21, 1901, the son of Lebrun Constantine – "Old Cons" – a sugar plantation foreman who was a member of the West Indian teams which toured England in 1900 and 1906, and the first West Indian to score a century in England. Family practice with his father, his uncle, Victor Pascall, a slow left arm bowler for Trinidad, and his mother keeping wicket, early instilled cricket into the younger Constantine. But obvious natural aptitude and keen fielding, rather than any outstanding figures, won him a place in the Trinidad team in 1921.

He had played in only three first class matches when he was told to be ready to join the 1923 West Indian side for England. On that tour, apart from a brave innings of 60 not out in a total of 97 against Derbyshire, he made an impression only by brilliant fielding at cover point. During the next five years in the West Indies, however, unremitting practice made him a genuinely fast bowler and a sure slip fieldsman while, through his fine eye, natural timing and speed of reaction, he became an explosive, if inconsistent, attacking batsman. Those years of application bore fruit in England in 1928. In the three Tests of that summer – the first ever played by West Indies – he achieved no more than five wickets and

79

89 runs: but on the tour he became the first West Indian to perform the "double" of 1,000 runs and 100 wickets in a season.

Above all, a single match established him and his country's cricket in English public imagination. At Lords in June, Middlesex batting first, declared at 352 for six wickets and put out the West Indians for 230 runs, in which only Constantine, with 86, scored more than 30. In the Middlesex second innings Constantine took seven wickets for 57. West Indies, needing 259 to win, were 121 for five, and apparently losing, when Constantine went in. He hit with such force that one straight drive broke the finger of the bowler, Hearne, and went on to strike the pavilion rails and fly up into the seating. Constantine scored 103 out of 133 in an hour and won the match for the West Indians by three wickets.

From that day, until he retired from all play some 30 years later, Constantine attracted crowds as few other cricketers have ever done. In 1929 he was engaged by the Nelson club and except in 1939, when he joined the West Indies team in England, he continued as a League professional with considerable success for Nelson, Rochdale, Bootle, Crompton and Windhill until 1948. For some years he bowled at such pace that he was menacing to the best batsmen even on good wickets. Of little more than average height, wide-shouldered and long-armed, he took a short, lively run and bowled off a fine leap with a high action and a full follow-through. He developed many variations, including a well disguised and controlled slower ball, which was often a leg break or googly and, as he grew older, took many wickets by guile and accuracy. In the deep field he made catches that seemed far beyond his reach, swooped to pick up at full speed with an apparently boneless ease, and his throwing, on or off balance, was strong and accurate: while close to the wicket his catching was bewilderingly quick and certain. As a batsman he was prepared to attack any bowler; he cut, pulled, hooked and drove exuberantly, produced some remarkable, spontaneous strokes to counter the unexpected and struck some blows of phenomenal length.

The essence of his cricket was that by batting, bowling or fielding he might win any match from almost any situation. Before he left the West Indies Constantine had, in the words of his fellow Trinidadian. C. L. R. James, "revolted against the revolting contrast between his first-class status as a cricketer, and his third-class status as a man". Professionalism enabled him to settle in England to study law and to argue the causes of West Trinidadian self-government and racial tolerance. In many Lancashire towns where he played cricket, there were children who had never before seen a coloured man: and, by speeches and lectures and the publication of pamphlets he did much to foster understanding of his people's problems. He and his wife fitted happily into Lancashire life and in 1963 the freedom of the Borough of Nelson was bestowed on him.

In 18 Test matches for West Indies between 1928 and 1939 he scored 641 runs at an average of 19.42 and took 58 wickets at 30.10. These are unimpressive figures but at Georgetown in 1930 his nine wickets for 122 linked with Headley's two centuries to give West Indies their first win in a Test match: and in his last Test, at The Oval in 1939, he took five English first innings wickets for 75 and then scored 78 out of 103 in less than an hour. Because he spent so much of his career in the leagues, he played only 194 innings in first-class cricket; scored 4.451 runs and took 424 wickets. Figures, however, cannot reflect his aggressive approach, tactical acumen or his quality as an athlete, entertainer and match-winner, nor prove the fact, which his contemporaries never doubted, that he was the finest all-round fieldsman the game of cricket has ever known.

He remained in England during the Second World War. From 1942 to 1947 he was a Welfare Officer, with particular responsibility for West Indian workers in the Ministry of Labour and National Service, and received the MBE for his services. In 1944 be took action against The Imperial Hotel London for "failing to receive and lodge him and won the nominal damages he sought. In 1954, after a long struggle, he passed his Bar Finals and was called by the Middle Temple in 1954; he became an honorary Master of the Bench in 1963. He published his book Colour Bar in 1954. When he returned to Trinidad in 1954 he was called to the Bar there and elected as a People's Nationalist Movement member for Tunapuna to the first Trinidad Legislature, in which he became Minister of Works and Transport.

Disillusioned by politics, he did not stand for re-election in 1961 and in the following year was appointed High Commissioner for Trinidad and Tobago in London, a post he held until his resignation in 1964, after trying to help to solve difficulties in Bristol when busmen were said to be operating a colour bar. He subsequently practised in the English courts, wrote and broadcast on cricket, and in 1966 became a member of the Race Relations Board. He was knighted in 1962. In 1967 he became Rector of St Andrews

University; in 1969 be became a life peer. He was also a governor of the BBC.

A man of quiet manner, religious conviction and high principles, Constantine was popular on all the many levels at which he lived and worked. He married, in 1927, Norma Agatha Cox: they had one daughter.

Learie Constantine was born on September 21, 1901 and died on July 1, 1971.

Air Chief Marshal Sir Keith Park

Defender of London and Malta in the Second World War
February 7, 1975

Air Chief Marshal Sir Keith Park, GCB, KBE, MC, DFC, who died yesterday in hospital in Auckland, New Zealand, at the age of 82, had a distinguished career of nearly 36 years with the New Zealand and British armed forces, and was in command of forces which greatly contributed to the defeat of the Axis countries in two principal war theatres. In 1940 he became AOC No 11 Group, Fighter Command, which bore the brunt of the fighting in the Battle of Britain; later he successfully used his wide knowledge of air defence in Malta.

Keith Rodney Park was born at Thames, New Zealand, on June 15, 1892, the son of Professor J. Park, and was educated at King's College, Auckland, and Selwyn Collegiate School, Dunedin, Otago Boys School and Otago University of Mines. In 1911-13 he served as a private in the New Zealand Field Artillery (Territorial Force) and in December, 1914, joined the NZ Expeditionary Force. He was commissioned in the Royal Field Artillery in 1915, and transferred to the RA (Regular Army) in 1916, seeing service in Gallipoli and France.

A year later he was seconded to the Royal Flying Corps and on the formation of the Royal Air Force in 1918 was promoted captain. Between 1917 and 1919 he served with Nos 8 and 38 (Reserve) Squadrons and No 48 Squadron, becoming commanding officer of the last-named on April 10, 1918. He gained the MC and bar in 1917, the Croix de Guerre in 1918, and the DFC in 1919.

In between the wars he commanded RAF Northolt, and was chief instructor of the Oxford University Air Squadron. He took the Imperial Defence College course in 1937, became officer commanding RAF Tangmere in January, 1938, and later that year, as air commodore, and became senior air staff officer at HQ, RAF Fighter Command.

In April, 1940, he was appointed Air Officer Commanding, No 11 Group, being confirmed in the rank of air vice-marshal the following July. No 11 Group was responsible for the greater part of protective fighter patrols, and after the German invasion of the Low Countries in May, 1940, Park on more than one occasion flew his own Hurricane over Dunkirk to gain first-hand intelligence of the progress of the evacuation. When the Battle of Britain began Park instructed his Hurricane and Spitfire pilots to split their attacks, half going for the bombers and the others attacking the escort, tactics which resulted in the German formations flying tighter and thus presenting better targets.

Towards the end of the Battle, after heavy attacks on No 11 Group's stations, Park's handling of his fighters, and Dowding's overall strategy, were the subject of an informal inquiry, instigated primarily by the AOC, No 12 Group (which covered the Midlands), Air Vice-Marshal T. Leigh-Mallory. Park – with the greatest area to protect, stretching from Southampton to Norwich – had intelligently used his squadrons, with the help of radar, to place them where the enemy raids were expected, and successfully broke up the formations, even though he had very little warning of their approach. Leigh-Mallory, on the other hand, employed his fighters in larger "'wing" formations, concentrating as many as five or even seven squadrons against the raiding bombers, having had time to amass them and in any case having by that time a better idea of the enemy's targets. The differences between the two commanders became so pronounced that eventually the Air Council had to intervene. As it happened, the "wing" tactics were officially more favoured, and Park, along with Dowding, was moved to another post. But the fact remains that the Battle of Britain was won while Park commanded the largest of the fighter groups.

While the battle was on he flew 100 hours, mainly in his own fighter. He had, at the end of July, 1940, in cooperation with the Vice-Admiral, Dover, acquired some Lysander aircraft to work in conjunction with launches to retrieve aircrew who had come down in the sea, which may be regarded as the beginning of a comprehensive air/sea rescue organization.

In December, 1940, Park became AOC, No 23 Group, Training Command, where his hard-won experience could be passed on to the next generation of pilots. He was appointed AOC, Egypt, in January, 1942 and in July, 1942, became AOC Malta, where his first-hand experience of air defence was immediately put to

Prince Albert of Saxe-Coburg-Gotha

Karl Marx

Jenny Lind

Lady Randolph Churchill

Lady Nancy Astor

Marina, Duchess of Kent on her wedding day

Learie Constantine (left)

Air Chief Marshal Sir Keith Park

good use. He introduced new tactics, instructing his pilots (then beginning to receive Spitfires in place of Hurricanes) to intercept enemy raids well out to sea and, besides attaining greater victories, reduced the possibility of bombs falling on the island itself.

By the skilful use of his still-limited fighters and bombers he was able to restrict movements of enemy convoys to North Africa. His aircraft supported Tedder's forces at El Alamein, the advance to Tunisia, and the invasion of Sicily. When supplies began to flow more readily into the Mediterranean, Park, with typical energy, began intensive modernization of the Malta bases. He became AOC-in-C, RAF Middle East, in January, 1944 and – when the emphasis of the war switched from Europe to the Far East – Allied Air Commander, South-East Asia, in February, 1945. Here he assumed the immense responsibility of providing a colossal airlift by RAF and American aircraft of materials to support the Allied troops in Burma, besides the overall control of bombers and fighters, which contributed to the successful conclusion of the war in the Far East.

Park retired from the Service in December, 1946. In 1947 Oxford University conferred an honorary DCL on him. He married Dorothy Marguerite, daughter of Lieutenant Colonel Woodbine Parish, CMG, CBE, in 1918. He had two sons one of whom was killed on active service in 1951. His wife died in 1971.

Sir Keith Park was born on June 15, 1892, and died on February 6, 1975.

Lydia Lopokova

Russian ballerina, and widow of John Maynard Keynes
June 9, 1981

Lydia Lopokova (Lady Keynes), the celebrated Russian ballerina, died yesterday at the age of 88.

To those who never saw Lydia Lopokova (properly Lopukhova) in her heyday, it is difficult to convey her extraordinary appeal. She was not a classical dancer in the strict sense of the term. She was short and even rather dumpy. Her features were anything but regular. Her arms and legs had none of the long flowing lines admired in most prima ballerinas; nor did she ever give much thought to her make-up, her costumes, or indeed her appearance in general. Nevertheless, she was past question one of the greatest dancers of our time.

The secret lay in her character: her unconventionality, her vitality and exuberance, and her ability so to convey the joy of life to audiences that when she appeared everyone else on the stage ceased to matter. Indeed, as Mr Cyril Beaumont remarks in his Diaghilev Ballet, she was a born comedienne – and few dancers indeed are that. Hence her incomparable performance as Mariuccia in The Good-humoured Ladies, an interpretation of Goldoni surely unsurpassed for delicious gaiety and wit. Although Lopokova lacked classical features, she was technically strong and intensely musical. She possessed the mysterious gift of holding audiences in the hollow of her small hand; and they adored her because she made them smile and feel happy. Ovations such as greeted her at the end of the can-can in the Boutique Fantasque can surely seldom have been equalled.

Lydia Vasilievna Lopukhova was born in St Petersburg on October 21, 1892, where her father was a commissionaire at the Mariinsky Theatre, her mother, whose surname was Douglas, being of Scottish descent. She was the third of four children, having an elder sister and two brothers, all of whom were admitted as pupils to the Imperial School of Ballet and later became well-known dancers.

Lydia remained at the Imperial School until she was 16, appearing at the same time in small ballet parts. From the first she was singled out for her histrionic talent as well as her technical aptitude and attracted attention enough among the cognoscenti to be invited in 1910 by Diaghilev to dance the exacting role of the Firebird in Paris. This, her debut, with the Diaghilev company, was highly successful, but she almost immediately left it, though not to return to the Mariinsky.

She went to the United States, where she remained several years, even appearing at times in musical comedy. It was not until 1915 that she rejoined Diaghilev, and not until the autumn of 1918 that she was first seen in London, where she immediately won an overwhelming success. Personal reasons, however, again caused her to leave the company – and the stage – after less than a year with it; and her next roles were those of the Lilac Fairy and Princess Aurora in Diaghilev's superb production of Tchaikovsky's Sleeping Princess at the Alhambra in 1921. As the princess she alternated with Trefilova, Spesivtseva and Yegorova. Strictly speaking this classical part par excellence was not exactly "her line", but thanks to her enchanting personality she triumphed in it too.

Lydia Lopokova was first married to R. Barrocchi, at one time business manager to the Diaghilev company. But the marriage was dissolved after some years and in 1925 she married the celebrated economist John Maynard, later Lord, Keynes. After her marriage she appeared only now and again in ballet, but on several occasions she tried her hand at acting: as Olivia in a season at the Old Vic, as Nora and Hilda in A Doll's House and in the Master Builder at the Criterion, and as Celimene in a translation of Le Misanthrope at the Arts Theatre Club. Her strong Russian accent stood in the way of her achieving real success in these parts, however. She soon abandoned the stage for good and thenceforward, until his death in 1945, devoted her entire attention to her husband, who was for some years in precarious health, accompanying him on all his economic missions abroad. After his death, although at first taking an intimate interest in the ballet enterprises fostered by the Arts Council, she adopted a more and more retired mode of life, spending most of the time at her country house on the Sussex Downs.

Lydia Lopokova was born on October 21, 1892, and died on June 8, 1981

Nikolaus Pevsner

Chronicler of the buildings of England
August 19, 1983

Sir Nikolaus Pevsner, CBE, distinguished art historian, writer, and lecturer, and an outstanding interpreter and recorder of English architecture and design, died yesterday at his home in Hampstead after a long illness. He was 81. He won the admiration of scholars all over the world and of all shades of opinion through the breadth of his knowledge on these subjects and the quality of his writing. In all this he combined deep learning, sound judgment and quiet humour. One of his most valuable characteristics at a time of conflicting theories was his good humoured refusal to be either bluffed or stampeded by extremists on either side, academic, preservationist or modernist, or to be shocked at the progress of events. He had a great capacity for getting down to essentials in any phase of art and for distinguishing between what was inevitable in the circumstances and what was likely to blow over as a passing fashion. His judgments were often refreshingly unconventional for the simple reason that they were consistent. He could study mediaeval, baroque, Georgian or Victorian design with the same acuteness and impartiality. Because he was deeply founded in the history of the past he was able to follow contemporary developments with equanimity.

Son of the late Hugo Pevsner, Nikolaus Bernhard Leon Pevsner was born on January 30, 1902 and educated at St Thomas's School, Leipzig, and the universities of Leipzig, Munich, Berlin and Frankfurt, taking his degree of PhD in the history of art in 1924. From that year until 1928 he was assistant keeper of the Dresden Gallery and from 1929 to 1933 he was lecturer in the history of art and architecture at Göttingen.

In 1934 Pevsner came to England, a refugee from Nazi Germany. He had specialized in English art and architecture and already knew more about its history than many in this country. He held a research fellowship at Birmingham University for one year, where he first met Sir Gordon Russell and became his adviser on modern furniture; Pevsner was thus partly responsible for some of the better trends in furniture in the 1930s. During the Second World War, after a short period of internment as an enemy alien, Pevsner assisted in clearing from the London streets the rubble of buildings which he might otherwise have later recorded, until he was offered the task of keeping The Architectural Review in being. He edited it almost single handed from 1942 to 1945, when the regular editor was on war service.

Pevsner lectured well and often, and in several languages. His first public talk in England was on "English Art: How it strikes a foreigner". What struck a foreigner in the best English painting, he said, was English harmony; the portraits of Gainsborough were all quiet and harmonious like the English countryside. He later returned to and elaborated on the theme in his Reith Lectures on "The Englishness of English Art", given in 1955. In a lecture on Continental Art delivered at the Royal Society of Arts in 1935 he broached a subject in which he showed especial interest, the influence of William Morris, not only in England but on the Continent, together with that of architects like Mackintosh and Voysey.

This was a theme of his book Pioneers of the Modern Movement from Morris to Gropius, first published in 1936, which arrived at the conclusion, novel perhaps to many people in this country, that the modern idea of architecture and industrial design had an origin in English thought and effort at the end of the last century and the beginning of the present one. In 1942 he became a lecturer at Birkbeck College, and the titles of some lectures that he gave during one week there show how wide ranging were his interests. They included "Iconography in French Cathedrals", "William Blake", "Baudelaire and Dramatic Criticism" and "The Bauhaus". In 1959 he became Professor of the History of Art at Birkbeck, and he remained there until his retirement in 1969, when he became Emeritus Professor.

But Birkbeck was not the only scene of his academic activities. From 1949 to 1955 he was Slade Professor of Fine Art at Cambridge, as well as a Fellow of St John's; and in 1968-69 he was Slade Professor at Oxford. As editor and author Pevsner was no less active than in his academic role. Before he left Germany he had published in 1928 a study of Baroque Architecture in

Leipzig and (1927-1930) Italian Painting from the end of the Rococo. In England, following his Pioneers, he wrote An Enquiry into Industrial Art in England, (1937), which showed that he was capable of pointed criticism as well as appreciation. It gave a far from glowing picture of the artistic quality of British manufactures (excepting for such things as tweeds and sporting equipment). Of more general and practical importance were his account of "man shaping space", in An Outline of European Architecture, first published as a Pelican book in 1942; and his series of super guide-books The Buildings of England which appeared from 1951 onwards.

In these with omnivorous appetite and discriminating taste, he aimed to record every notable product of architecture from the distant past to the present day, county by county, the two volumes on London alone being remarkable in the ground they covered. The thorough-going manner in which Pevsner set about the realisation of this aroused an equal amount of astonishment and praise. The task, which involved visits to some 30,000 buildings, was begun in 1949 and ended 21 years later with the inspection of a building in Staffordshire.

Pevsner became a founder-member of the William Morris Society in the 1950s and in 1963 he became chairman of the Victorian Society, which he had earlier helped to found. The Victorian Society had on the whole a young membership, and Pevsner often found himself confronted by vigorous supporters of some extravagant product of 19th-century capitalism, who suspected that he would have preferred it replaced by something more like the Bauhaus. They were often wrong, for Pevsner was the first to admit that time could modify some of his views on modern architecture. He also revised certain earlier judgments on 19th-century buildings gleefully quoted by would-be demolishers.

Pevsner had a wide acquaintanceship among young people. They soon found, like his other friends, that the image of a desiccated Middle European professor who analysed the beauty out of art and architecture was completely false. Pevsner loved a joke, not least at his own expense, and though normally precise in diction occasionally startled his friends with a sudden lapse into cockney or toffee-nosed English. He would show equal interest in hearing about a building unfamiliar to him whether in Kensington or Katmandu; the somewhat owl-like features would assume a look of concentration and out would come the little notebook. His stamina was phenomenal; walks of 12 miles or more in search of a building were nothing to this non car-driver. There were stories of guided tours of medieval cathedrals lasting nine hours.

Among the positions Pevsner held were membership of the Royal Fine Art Commission, the Historic Buildings Council, the National Council of Art and Design, the Advisory Board on Redundant Churches and the Advisory Board to the Ministry of Housing and Local Government. He was honoured by many societies, and was one of the very few non-architects to be awarded the Royal Gold Medal of the Royal Institute of British Architects. He was appointed CBE in 1953, and received a knighthood in 1969 for services to art and architecture. An indefatigable worker, he was greatly helped, both at home and on his travels, by his wife Lola, whom he married in 1923. She entertained scholar and students with equal hospitality in their small Victorian house, hidden away in a corner of Hampstead Heath, and motored him about the English counties. Her early death occurred in 1963.

Nikolaus Pevsner was born on January 30, 1902, and died on August 18, 1983.

Professor Peter Medawar

Nobel Prize winner renowned for his work on skin grafting and immunology

October 5, 1987

Sir Peter Medawar, OM, CH, CBE, FRS, died on October 2, at the age of 72. Although his career was cruelly disrupted by illness when he was only 54, he was one of the outstanding scientists of his generation. He won the Nobel Prize in 1960, for his research on tissue grafting, which is basic to organ transplants.

Peter Brian Medawar was born in Rio de Janeiro on February 28, 1915, to an English mother married to a Lebanese businessman. He was sent to England for his education, which included Marlborough and Magdalen College, Oxford. He was unhappy at Marlborough and he later spoke disparagingly of its sexual and intellectual climate in those days.

He took a first in zoology at Oxford, where he was much influenced by Professor Howard Florey. In Florey's department he met Jean Taylor, a fellow student. They married in 1937.

Medawar's early work was on the regeneration of nerves, but the studies that proved to have the most profound influence were in the field of tissue grafting. It was largely thanks to his experiments with rabbit skin grafts that the immunological basis of graft rejection became accepted.

The impetus for this work stemmed directly from the war, for the Medical Research Council had recognized that more effective means than those available at the time were needed for the treatment of severe burns. Among his earliest publications was a study carried out with a Scottish surgeon, Thomas Gibson, on the rejection patterns of human skin grafts.

In 1947 Medawar accepted the Chair of Zoology at Birmingham University. In 1951, he was invited to become Jodrell Professor of Zoology at University College, London, where he stayed until 1962, when he became Director of the National Institute for Medical Research.

His close collaborators were Rupert Billingham and Leslie Brent. This team produced a series of incisive and elegant scientific publications that ushered in the era of cellular immunology – the main preoccupation of immunologists having been, up to then, with the blood-borne antibodies that are frequently the end-product of immunological responses. Now attention was focused on cells, in particular lymphocytes, that Medawar and his collaborators showed to be closely associated with graft rejection and other immunological phenomena.

The most significant contribution by Medawar's group – for which he won his Nobel Prize, jointly with the Australian immunologist, Sir MacFarlane Burnet – was the demonstration that graft rejection can be entirely prevented in mice and chickens if foreign cells from the future graft donor are introduced into the recipient during foetal or neonatal life (that is, at a time when the animals are still immunologically immature).

The theoretical framework that led to this study had several sources: the long known observation that cattle fraternal twins have a common intra-uterine blood circulation; Dr R. D. Owen's demonstration in the United States that such twins exchanged red blood cells and their precursors in utero and possess each other's red blood cells in adult life; the finding by Medawar's own group in Birmingham that skin grafts exchanged between fraternal non-identical twin calves are not rejected; and the brilliant speculations by MacFarlane Burnet and Frank Fenner on the concept of 'self' and 'non-self'.

Medawar's group set about showing that immunological unresponsiveness can be established experimentally and that it is highly specific for the donor's tissue antigens. Although it was later shown that the mechanism underlying this phenomenon is not quite as straightforward as their experiments had led them to believe, the impact of the discovery was dramatic.

First, it was a clear demonstration that the immunological barriers to the transplantation of foreign tissue and organ grafts – thought to be insurmountable – could be overcome by subtle immunological interference, rather than by the blunderbuss approach of whole body X-irradiation or antimitotic drugs, and it opened up a vast new field of scientific endeavour. Second, it provided an insight into why the body does not normally respond to its own cellular substances and what happens when it does, as for example in patients suffering from auto-immune disease. And third, it directly led to the discovery by Billingham and Brent of graft-versus-host disease, a condition caused by the presence of mature lymphocytes in certain kinds of graft. Even now this poses considerable clinical problems in the transplantation of bone marrow.

On his move to the National Institute for Medical Research Medawar combined the duties of Director with his research interests. He had a succession of bright young colleagues, and the flow of innovative scientific publications continued unabated.

Then, in 1969, came the grievous blow. He was at the time President of the British Association, which was meeting in Exeter, and whilst reading the lesson during the Sunday service in the cathedral he suffered a brain haemorrhage that left him seriously handicapped for the remainder of his life.

A few years later he gave up his directorship and moved to the Clinical Research Centre in Northwick Park, where he maintained a small research group and turned his attention away from tissue transplantation to the problem of cancer. It was his hope that he might be able to devise a cancer vaccine – another typically audacious objective he set himself. In this instance his hopes may, however, have been less realistic and they have yet to be realized.

Medawar was the international leader in his field and he inspired his research teams with his infectious enthusiasm, and by example. He loved nothing better than to work with his own hands in the laboratory. He was also an inspiring lecturer and writer.

His earlier critical essays were published as monographs (The Uniqueness of the Individual, The Art of the Soluble, A Hope of Progress, for example) and are classics of their kind. Although his later books tended to be more eclectic (The Life Science, and From Aristotle to Zoos, both with Lady Medawar; Advice to a Young Scientist, and most recently Pluto's Republic) they continue to have a wide readership.

His last book was the widely acclaimed Memoirs of a Thinking Radish (1986), an account of some aspects of his life and scientific endeavours. In it he described with great detachment and humour what it is like to be physically handicapped, avoiding self-pity and being careful not to reveal too much of himself.

Like many other great men Medawar brought his vast talents to bear on subjects peripheral to his main endeavours. For example, he had a deep and lasting interest in philosophy and he was much influenced by Sir Karl Popper, who became a close friend. In his writings, as in his lectures, he discussed the methods and limitations of science and the place of science in society. He disdained all manifestations of 'Naturphilosophie' and his devastating critique of Pierre Teilhard de Chardin's book, The Phenomenon of Man, displays all his analytical powers.

Medawar was much in demand on public bodies. He was the first President of The (International) Transplantation Society in 1966 and he became President of the British Association in 1969, as well as a member of the Governing Body of the BBC. He delivered the Reith lectures in 1959 on 'The Future of Man'.

Virtually every honour that the academic world can bestow came his way. He was an FRS at 34, and was awarded honorary degrees by a score of universities all over the world. He was knighted in 1965, made a Companion of Honour in 1972 and made a Member of the Order of Merit in 1981.

Medawar was a man without a trace of pomposity and with a mischievous sense of humour, even in his darkest days. He delighted in conversation (whether accompanied by ale in a pub or claret in his home) and relished village cricket. He was a keen squash player until his paralysis put a stop to his sporting activities.

Almost to the end he indulged in his other hobbies of chess and music. He was an ardent lover of opera, with a particular passion for Wagner and Verdi.

One of the most extraordinary aspects of his life was the way he coped with his severe afflictions. New setbacks were met with an unflagging determination that life must go on.

Medawar is survived by two daughters and two sons, and by his wife, Jean, whose devoted support and encouragement was such a crucially important feature of his life, particularly during the last exacting years.

Peter Brian Medawar was born on February 28, 1915, and died on October 2, 1987.

Alec Issigonis

The father of the Mini
October 4, 1988

With the death at the age of 81 of Sir Alec Issigonis, CBE, FRS, on October 2, Britain has lost its most famous car designer, a man whose name will forever be linked with the Mini, the revolutionary car he introduced in 1959 and which remains in production in fundamentally unchanged form to this day. Earlier, as chief engineer of Morris Motors, he had been responsible for another outstandingly successful car, the Morris Minor, over 1.3 million examples of which were produced between 1948 and 1971, and which has subsequently become a collector's item for classic car enthusiasts.

Alexander Arnold Constantine Issigonis was born on November 18, 1906, in Smyrna, Asia Minor, the son of a Bavarian-born mother and British-naturalized father of Greek extraction. In 1922 the family found themselves amongst the many evacuees fleeing the conflict between the Turks and Greeks.

They planned to rebuild their life in England, but Alec's father, by then in poor health, died in Malta, leaving Mrs Issigonis to complete the journey with her 16-year-old son. These were difficult times, but she managed to integrate her son, already fascinated by cars and engines, into an educational background suited to his developing technical abilities.

His skill on the drawing board pointed towards an art school course but he insisted that he should join the Battersea Polytechnic where, although he failed to matriculate, he quickly revealed his potential as a practical engineer. His studies over, he spent several months touring the Continent by car with his mother, then he returned to England to face the task of becoming the family breadwinner.

His first job was as a draughtsman with Edward Gillett, with whom he became involved in the design of an ingenious form of semi-automatic clutch in which Chrysler in the United States and both Rover and Humber showed interest. In 1934 he was persuaded to leave London and join the Humber staff at Coventry. For the next two years he found himself increasingly involved in investigating independent front wheel suspension systems, then in their infancy. In 1936, when he joined Morris Motors, he continued this work.

Meanwhile, a love of fast cars and driving had steered him inevitably towards motor sport, his first sports car being an Austin Seven Ulster, which he had acquired in 1931. Specializing in sprints and hill-climbs, he had become well aware of the limitations placed on car performance by inferior suspension systems, so he decided to design a purpose-built competition car which would overcome these deficiencies.

The result was his famous Lightweight Special, a single-seater which was built for him in 1937 by his long-time friend George Dowson. Like the Mini of more than 20 years later, this outstanding hill-climb car featured independent suspension incorporating rubber spring units. During the Second World War Issigonis was assigned to a variety of special projects and experimental work for the Services, including a motorized wheelbarrow for Combined Operations use, an armoured car and an amphibious tank, but in his spare time his Morris Minor, to be codenamed Mosquito, was already taking shape.

It became one of the stars of the 1948 Earls Court Show and quickly established itself as a car of impressive simplicity, rugged reliability and, for its time, outstanding steering and roadholding qualities. All it lacked was sufficient power, a defect remedied in 1952 when Morris joined with Austin to form the British Motor Corporation and the Minor inherited a more powerful Austin-designed BMC engine. The BMC merger put a temporary stop on new design projects, so Alec Issigonis moved to Alvis, where he designed a luxury car with a V8 engine, which would have gone into production but for the company's military contract work. By 1956 Issigonis was back with BMC, where he became deputy engineering co-ordinator. By 1961 he was technical director, and in 1963 he joined the BMC main board.

The Mini was all that he wanted it to be, a 'box on wheels'. It was just 10ft long, yet with room for four people as a result of brilliant packaging aided by mounting the engine transversely across the frame and driving the front wheels through an integral transmission. Utterly functional in shape (he refused to have the car 'styled' as this would have added unwanted inches), its uncompromising appearance ironically soon made it a cult car. He had not anticipated this, and although he pretended to be annoyed by it, in truth he was delighted. Its huge success in competitions, whether winning racing championships or the Monte Carlo Rally (equally unexpected) caused him further joy.

This brilliant engineer showed the car world how to get a quart into a pint pot. He was something of a showman, sometimes outrageous, occasionally irascible, but invariably good company. He remained a bachelor all his life.

With the Mini he showed designers throughout the world the way to lay out small cars, but his lessons of space conservation and utilisation did not remain there. They were demonstrated again with his 1100 and 1300 saloons, which carried all six BMC marque badges, then again with the Maxi, 1800/2200 and 3-litre saloons. Officially he retired from what had become the British Leyland Motor Corporation in 1971, but though increasingly confined to his home in Edgbaston, Birmingham through the progression of Parkinson's Disease he remained an advanced engineering consultant to the company. His considerable contribution to society was rewarded officially three times: he became a CBE in the 1964 Birthday Honours List, he was made a Fellow of the Royal Society in 1967, and in 1969 he was knighted "for services to automotive engineering" . The sale of more than 5 million Minis and nearly 3 million of their larger cousins bears him rich testimony.

Alec Issigonis was born on November 18, 1906, and died on October 2, 1988.

C. L. R. James

Trotskyite politician and author, who wrote about cricket on the side

June 1, 1989

C. L. R. James, who died yesterday at his home in south London, was an author and political activist who became something of a legend in his native Trinidad and throughout the Caribbean.

He was best known for The Black Jacobins, an account of the Haitian revolt against the French at the time of the French Revolution, and was active for many years on colonial and related issues.

Cyril Lionel Robert James was born near Port of Spain in 1901. From his school days, history absorbed him. His other enthusiasm was playing and writing about cricket. James's father was a schoolmaster and, after attending Queen's Royal College, the island's leading boys' school, to which he won a scholarship, he, too, became a teacher.

He left Trinidad in 1932, at the instigation of Learie Constantine (later Lord Constantine), then a professional cricketer, and went to stay with him in Nelson, Lancashire. James published his first book soon after he arrived in Britain: this was his Life of Captain Cipriani, a Trinidadian politician agitating on behalf of the working class of the island. The book was financed by Constantine.

With the support of Neville Cardus, James began to write about cricket for the Manchester Guardian: he was to make a significant contribution to the literature of the game, with books such as Beyond a Boundary.

Moving to London, James involved himself in the political causes of the time, becoming a Marxist. He was close to his fellow Trinidadian, George Padmore, who, in 1935, having been head of the Comintern department responsible for "Negro propaganda", broke with Stalin and came to London, producing a journal of African emancipation which was edited by James.

From the time of his arrival in Britain, James had been gathering material on the black revolution in Haiti, led by Toussaint L'Ouverture, against the slave-owning French. With the rise of fascism, and Mussolini's invasion of Ethiopia, James wrote with African freedom very much in mind. Published in 1938, the book was an epic of revolutionary struggle and achievement. It is undoubtedly the best account in English of the Haitian revolution, even though it makes no pretence of objectivity.

While writing Black Jacobins, James steeped himself in French radical historians; he concurrently read Marx, Lenin, and other Communist texts, and came to reject the Stalinist position, preferring Trotsky's (he was to meet him in 1939). Soon after the publication of Black Jacobins, he went to the United States; he had established a close relationship with Paul Robeson in London, where they had worked together on African and Negro issues.

He spent the next 15 years in America, addressing his frequent books and articles on dialectical questions to small black, Marxist and labour groups.

Expelled from the USA in 1953, he again involved himself in the African independence movement. Then, in 1958, he returned to Trinidad at the invitation of Dr Eric Williams, the Chief Minister, to edit his party's newspaper. Rather curiously, James also became the secretary of that most unideological and moderate of coalitions, the West Indies Federal Labour Party, making unavailing efforts, in common with others alongside Sir Grantley Adams, to prevent the break-up of the Federation. James soon quarrelled with Williams, left Trinidad, and in the 1960s and 1970s lectured much in colleges in the USA.

Though it can hardly be said that in practical politics James was greatly successful, his writing was to be part of the broad inspiration of many young intellectuals in the Caribbean, particularly his Black Jacobins. Ideologically, his Trotskyite stance did not attract them, however, and no "C.L.R. James tendency" was to establish itself there.

Back in Britain, to which he finally came, he was, however, the subject of much admiration, a Trotskyite sage with a group gathered around him, mostly young and black. In his eighties, he remained as industrious as ever.

C.L.R. James was born at Port of Spain on January 4, 1901, and died on May 31, 1989.

Berthold Lubetkin

Modernist architect who housed the
penguins at the London Zoo

October 24, 1990

During the 1930s Berthold Lubetkin was one of the most influential personalities among the avant garde of British architecture. For the generations that followed, however, he was little more than a figure of legend. He retired altogether from the profession, for reasons even his close friends never fully understood, at the age of 52 and thereafter became something of a recluse.

Lubetkin's position in the history of modern English architecture is nevertheless unique. He studied architecture in Moscow and then in Paris under Auguste Perret. From the latter no doubt he acquired the rigorous sense of architectural form that was notable in all his work. After practising briefly in Russia (and gaining first prize in the 1925 competition for the Urals Polytechnic), he returned to Paris and became for a time a partner with Jean Ginsberg.

In 1930 he moved to England, and a couple of years later he formed, with half-a-dozen young architects who had just qualified from the Architectural Association in London, a group which called itself Tecton. Under Lubetkin's leadership the group soon made its mark, and during the early 1930s was responsible for most of the buildings, other than private houses, erected in England in the revolutionary style of architecture then flourishing on the Continent. They included the Highpoint flats at Highgate (first block, 1935; second block added in 1938), the Gorilla House (1934) and the Penguin Pool (1935) at the London Zoo and a health centre (1938) for the London borough of Finsbury.

The two zoo buildings evoked an immediate response from the public and did much to show that modern functional design was capable also of gaiety. Tecton went on to design other zoo buildings at Whipsnade and Dudley. The group was at the same time a training-ground for many of the more forward-looking architects of the next generation. Sir Denys Lasdun, for example, worked for Tecton and from 1938 became for a time one of the partners.

The group was dispersed during the second world war and Lubetkin became a farmer in Gloucestershire, a genuine working farmer who spent long hours on the driving-seat of a tractor. He managed a largish farm, in a spirit of constant inquiry into the validity of accepted methods, with little help but that of his wife Margaret (née Church, whom he had married in 1936 when she was a young architect working in the Tecton office). By her he had a son and a daughter.

The Lubetkin farm had one remarkable feature in the early days of the war. Through his connection with Sir Peter Chalmers Mitchell, secretary of the London Zoological Society, for whom just before the war Tecton had built a house on the downs near Whipsnade, Lubetkin and his wife were asked to give a temporary home to a number of rare animals and birds that the zoo was anxious to evacuate from London. No-one who visited the farm at that time will forget the surprising sight of exotic animals peering over the stable-doors of traditional Cotswold farm buildings and of strangely-plumed birds pecking about in the farmyard among the English ducks and poultry.

After the war Lubetkin resumed architectural practice in London in partnership with Skinner (one of the original Tecton group) and Bailey. They designed a quantity of housing for Finsbury, which showed a strong sense of social as well as architectural responsibility, but more of the formalism and less of the aesthetic vitality of Tecton's pre-war work. In 1948 Lubetkin was appointed architect-planner of one of the post-war new towns: Peterlee in the coal-mining area of County Durham. He produced an ambitious master-plan, very different from the suburban-type plans of the other new towns, with high buildings dominating a compactly-planned centre; but it was in advance of its time and after the whole project had been the subject of a succession of political and economic disputes, the plan was finally rejected. Lubetkin thereupon resigned.

It was soon after this that he decided to give up architectural practice. He retired to his farm in the Cotswolds where he led a secluded life. In 1968, because of his wife's health, he moved to a flat at Clifton, near the Avon gorge, and only emerged briefly from his self-sought obscurity to play a leading part in the successful campaign to save the gorge from disfigurement by a monster hotel in 1971.

Tolek Lubetkin, who was always known as Lubetkin by his friends, was a man of complex character. Those who could not get on with him thought him difficult and devious. Even those closest to him did not always fathom his motivations. Yet he was a friend who inspired affection, and a fascinating companion with a distinguished analytical intellect that ranged widely over political and historical as well as architectural subjects. He was always seeking the theory behind the practice and the philosophy behind the theory. His talk was lightened by humour and he had a way of leaving his listeners with a rare and exciting sense of illumination.

In 1978 Lubetkin's wife died after a long illness. They had been very close and since his retirement had enjoyed little company but each other's. The problems this loss created were aggravated by a motor accident which left him severely crippled. Nevertheless when he was awarded the RIBA's Royal Gold Medal in 1982 he travelled to London and at the presentation ceremony gave a memorable address. In 1985 he defended some of the buildings attacked by the Prince of Wales. Two years later he managed the journey to London to attend a ceremony at London Zoo to mark the restoration of his Penguin Pool but his public appearances after that were very few.

The little Lubetkin built revealed an architect of unusual sensibility. During his years of retirement he was said to have spent much time writing, but he published nothing. If what he wrote ever emerges it will almost certainly prove to have been worth waiting for.

Berthold Lubetkin was born in Tiflis, Georgia, on December 14, 1901, and died on October 23, 1990.

Freddie Mercury

Rock star extraordinaire
November 26, 1991

Freddie Mercury, rock star and lead singer of Queen, died of Aids on November 24 aged 45. He was born Frederick Bulsara in Zanzibar on September 5, 1946.

To mark the occasion of his 41st birthday in 1987, Freddie Mercury hired a DC9 and flew 80 of his friends to Ibiza. There he took over Pikes, one of the island's most exclusive hotels, and threw an outrageously lavish party complete with flamenco dancers, a fireworks display flashing his name in lights across the sky and a 20-foot long birthday cake carried in by six Spaniards dressed in white and gold.

The affair was typical of a life lived, until the last two or three reclusive years, to the hilt in an unashamedly extrovert, over-the-top fashion. "I always knew I was a star," he declared after the first flush of success, "and now the rest of the world seems to agree with me."

Be that as it may, Mercury was also a remarkably private man when out of the limelight, granting few interviews and giving little away about his family background. The son of Bomi and Jer Bulsara, he was born in Africa; his father was of Persian descent. Part of his childhood was spent in comfortable surroundings in India, where he went to boarding school, before his family moved to Feltham, Middlesex, in 1959.

There Mercury's early interest in music took him into the ranks of a local blues-based band called Wreckage. For a while he studied design and ran a clothes stall in Kensington market. He was helped by a friend, Roger Taylor, who was a student at London University and the drummer in a group called Smile. Mercury would go along to see Smile perform on the local college circuit. "Why are you wasting your time doing this?" he would exclaim to Taylor and the group's guitarist, Brian May, also a London University student. "You should be more demonstrative."

When Smile split up in 1970, Mercury invited Taylor and May to start a new group featuring himself as lead vocalist. He also suggested the name Queen, a deliberately camp, attention-grabbing title which he was well equipped to embody. They recruited bassist John Deacon from the small ads, and played their debut performance at the London College of Estate Management in February 1971.

In the years that followed the group forged a unique combination of heavy metal thunder, complex vocal harmonies and a preposterous glamrock image, woven into a package of dramatic excess. Mercury made a pivotal contribution not only as singer, pianist and one of the group's principal songwriters, but also in defining the group's image thanks to his flamboyant persona and ambiguous sexual appeal.

It was Mercury who wrote the group's best known hit, "Bohemian Rhapsody", a long, elaborate piece which incorporated a cod-operatic sequence followed by a bludgeoning heavy metal finale. The single stayed at No 1 in Britain for nine weeks in 1975 and its host album, A Night at the Opera, also sailed to the top of the chart. Such was the group's popularity at the start of 1976 that all four of their albums released to that date appeared simultaneously in the Top 30.

In keeping with the grandiose splendour of their music, Queen's live shows became ever more spectacular events, employing vast sets and lighting rigs. Deacon and May were both naturally retiring types and Taylor was stuck behind his drums, so the group depended heavily on Mercury's commanding stage presence. Prancing down multi-layered catwalks in a sequinned, skin-tight jump suit and ballet slippers, preening his way through a myriad of costume changes, and singing in his majestic, slightly frayed tenor voice, Mercury always matched up to the demands of projecting the group's music and image to the four corners of the world's biggest stadiums.

The group's popularity continued unabated into the Eighties. The Game (1980), Greatest Hits (1981), A Kind of Magic (1986) and The Miracle (1989) all topped the UK chart. At the Live Aid concert in 1985 they turned in arguably the most resounding performance of that remarkable event, and their Greatest Hits album was rarely out of the UK chart for the following two years.

Mercury embarked on a sporadic solo career, which he slotted into breaks in Queen's schedule. His debut album, Mr Bad Guy, reached No 6 in 1985, while his greatest success with a single was his cover version of the Platters' 1956 hit "The Great Pretender", a typically overwrought performance which he took to No 4 in 1987.

Also in 1987 he teamed up with Montserrat Caballe to record "Barcelona", a mock-operatic folly composed by Mercury which was then mooted as the official anthem of the 1992 Olympics. It is still in contention for that accolade. In 1986 he contributed three songs, including the title track, to the cast recording of Dave Clark's stage musical Time, but despite his various outside activities his first commitment was always to Queen whose personnel remained unchanged to the end.

The group's last tour, which included two shows at Wembley Stadium and a pioneering appearance in front of 80,000 Hungarian fans at Budapest's Nepstadion, ended with a date at the Knebworth Festival on August 9, 1986.

Mercury's renowned bisexual proclivities made him the target of sustained speculation when the Aids epidemic began to take its toll. "Yes, I did have an Aids test and I'm fine," he told Woman's Own magazine in November 1987, but rumours persisted that he had tested HIV positive.

In February 1990, after Queen pulled out at the last minute from an appearance at the BRITS Awards, photographs of a very sick-looking Mercury were circulated. But by the autumn of 1990 he was back in the studio with Queen, recording what was to be the group's last new album. Entitled Innuendo, it entered the UK chart at No 1 earlier this year and was followed more recently by a compilation, Greatest Hits II, which also topped the UK chart.

The current single "The Show Must Go On", which has been in the chart for the last six weeks, has a decidedly valedictory flavour and is accompanied by a video stitched together from old footage of Queen. In a nostalgic sequence of vignettes, Mercury's enduring generosity of spirit and his arch sense of humour continue to shine through.

"I don't expect to make old bones," Mercury once said. "What's more I really don't care. I certainly don't have any aspirations to live to 70. It would be boring."

Friedrich Von Hayek

Monetarist who challenged both Maynard Keynes and socialism

March 25, 1992

Friedrich Hayek, CH, the economist who was known as the "father of monetarism" died at his home in Freiburg in Breisgau, Germany, on March 23 aged 92. He was born in Vienna on May 8, 1899.

Friedrich Hayek was the last, and among the most distinguished, of the Austrian school of economists. During a long and fertile intellectual life, his wide interests enabled him to organise his ideas into one of the most original and impressive of all systems of political thought. From a single fundamental principle, which he called "spontaneous order", Hayek sought to deduce the evolution not only of markets, but of law and knowledge itself. All the greatest human achievements, he believed, arose from unintentional activity, to which human design was nearly always inimical. His work embraced psychology and the history of ideas as well as economics and political theory. Though based firmly on empirical research, in the end Hayek's philosophy amounted to a vast systematic elucidation of man and society.

Hayek never held office; nor, with the exception of his best-seller The Road to Serfdom, did he engage in political debate. But he exercised a profound influence upon the climate of thought in Britain, his adopted homeland, in America and ultimately throughout Eastern Europe. His systematic defence of individual liberty, private property and the rule of law attracted countless victims of socialism. Hayek was loathed by those who advocated state intervention into social and economic activity in order to produce a certain outcome. His last book called this vain desire "the fatal conceit" .

Hayek grew up in a recently ennobled Viennese family of Czech origin. His father was a professor of botany, and the Hayeks moved in a cosmopolitan milieu which Friedrich later described as

philosemitic. As a young man he served in the Austrian army on the
Italian front, where he met his distant cousin Ludwig Wittgenstein;
the two had little in common.

At this stage Hayek was a moderate social democrat, much influenced by the leading economist and minister Friedrich von Wieser.
Only when, in his mid twenties, he met Ludwig von Mises, an
uncompromising believer in the free market and the ideas of Adam
Smith, did he abandon socialism. Having gained doctorates in both
economics and law at Vienna University, Hayek worked as a civil
servant. In 1927 he became director of the Institute of Economic
Research, at which he wrote important papers on monetary theory
and the trade cycle, published in book form in 1929.

By the time of the collapse of the Austrian banking system
in 1931, Hayek was already sufficiently well-known for Lionel
Robbins to invite him to the London School of Economics, where
he became Tooke Professor of Economic Science and Statistics.
But his fame as an economist dates from the lectures he gave at the
LSE, published as Prices and Production in 1931. It was a brilliant,
original, brief analysis which was highly relevant to a nation
suffering from a severe deflationary slump. At the age of 32, Hayek
was instantly established as a serious rival to Keynes, whose star
rose as the helplessness of politicians became more evident with
the formation of the National Government.

By 1932 Hayek was the champion of those who maintained,
against Keynes, that state intervention in general, and demand
management in particular, would be more likely to prolong the
depression than to curtail it. Having published a detailed critique
of Keynes's Treatise on Money, Hayek was dismayed to find that
the Cambridge economist had already abandoned some of his
main positions in that book before the review appeared. When
Keynes published his General Theory in 1934, therefore, Hayek
refused to attack it: a grave error, as he later acknowledged, for
Keynesian economics thereafter speedily became dominant in
Britain. The two men remained on good personal terms, however,
and it was Keynes who ensured that Hayek was given rooms at
King's when the LSE was evacuated to Cambridge during the war.

Meanwhile Hayek had not been idle. He published a steady series
of books and articles: Monetary Nationalism and International
Stability (1937), in which he broke a lance for free trade and a
substitute for the gold standard; Prices, Profits and Investment,
which continued the argument of Prices and Production; and in

1941 there appeared what he hoped would be his magnum opus, The Pure Theory of Capital. This book, almost unnoticed amid the tumult of war, was the high watermark of Hayek's concern with technical economic theory. But the ascendancy of Keynes had given economics an empirical thrust, and Hayek was interested neither in macroeconomic policy nor in econometrics. Unlike Keynes, he did not welcome the opportunities to put his theories into practice offered by the quasi-socialist war economy.

Even before 1939, however, Hayek's work had taken a new turn, with his interest in the theory of centrally planned economies. Having demonstrated in debate with the left-wing economist Oskar Lange the impracticability of substituting a central authority for the decentralised decision-making of the market, Hayek began to develop his distinctive theory of spontaneous order. He also wrote a celebrated paper not published till 1948 in the first of several important volumes of essays, Individualism and Economic Order on the two traditions of rationalism, one (beneficent) deriving from the Scottish enlightenment, the other (malevolent) from the French Revolution. In The Counter-Revolution of Science (1952) Hayek later developed this rich theme even further, into a critique of the "constructivist" rationalism popular among intellectuals, of which modern socialism was only one consequence.

During the 1939-45 war, however, Hayek had produced his one popular book, and the one for which he will always be remembered: The Road to Serfdom. It was not intended to be a prophecy, but to warn against the potential for creeping totalitarianism which Hayek saw hidden in the burgeoning welfarism of the Labour party after Beveridge. The Road to Serfdom has sold millions of copies, though Hayek, like many economists a poor businessman, never made a penny from royalties. But from the first it made him enemies. When Churchill picked up its attack on state intervention and planning in the 1945 election campaign, Attlee made a withering reference to "the Austrian Professor Friedrich August von Hayek" (Hayek had long since become a naturalised British subject). He was hurt more by Orwell's strictures: free competition would impose a tyranny "probably worse, because more irresponsible, than that of the State" . Keynes called it a "grand" book, but stuck to his advocacy of "moderate" planning. For Hayek, the Labour landslide of 1945 presaged years in the wilderness.

In 1950 he therefore moved to Chicago, where his break with formal economics was signalled by his acceptance of a chair

in social and moral science. It was a fruitful time, after his last
unhappy years at the LSE. He published his theory of mind
and the senses, The Sensory Order, in 1952; though ignored by
most psychologists, it influenced the aesthetic ideas of his fellow-
Viennese E.H.Gombrich.

In 1960 came his magisterial political treatise, The Constitution
of Liberty, which took many years to establish itself as a modern
classic. Together with Law, Legislation and Liberty, which appeared
in three volumes between 1973 and 1979, The Constitution of
Liberty represents Hayek's mature political thought. Hayek is
no longer primarily concerned to refute socialism, whether in its
democratic or undemocratic forms, but turns his attention to the
characteristic corruptions of liberal society.

Hayek was uncompromising in his readiness to limit the meddling
of politicians. His ideal was indeed mid-19th century England; he
was suspicious even of J. S. Mill's egalitarian tendencies, though
he edited Mill's correspondence with Harriet Taylor. He abhorred
what he called "weasel words", widely used by conservatives as
well as social democrats, such as "social justice" . All attempts to
redistribute wealth were not merely inimical to the market, but to
civil society itself.

In 1962 Hayek returned to Europe, this time to Freiburg in
Germany, where he held a chair of economics until his semi-
retirement in 1969. By this time his following around the world
had grown. In Germany he had enjoyed considerable respect since
Ludwig Erhard rose to power in 1948; he was close to the Ordo
circle of liberal economists and jurists who influenced the Federal
Republic's Basic Law. But Hayek always treated the "social market"
as a propaganda tool for free competition.

When in 1974 Hayek was awarded the Nobel Prize for Economics,
jointly with his old opponent Gunnar Myrdal, it was clear that
the enfant terrible of the profession had become one of its grand
old men. Another triumph was the election of Mrs Thatcher's
government, which was strongly influenced by think tanks in which
Hayek had played an important role, above all the Institute of
Economic Affairs and later also the Adam Smith Institute. Hayek
played no part in the British government, but he was treated with
great respect and his books were once again quoted with respect.
His bold ideas on the denationalisation of money were not taken
up, but his strong views on inflation undoubtedly strengthened
the government's resolve not to reflate the economy during the

recession of the early 1980s. In 1984, at Mrs Thatcher's instigation, Hayek was made a Companion of Honour.

Hayek's last years were marred by illness, but he was able to finish The Fatal Conceit, his last book. He lived to see the collapse of communism in Eastern Europe, and only in his final year or two did he lose touch with events.

Hayek was twice married: to Hella von Fritsch (died 1960), by whom he had a son and a daughter, and to Helene Bitterlich. His second wife and his children survive him.

Sam Wanamaker

**Actor and director who built
London's new Globe Theatre**

December 20, 1993

Sam Wanamaker was the leading force, for over 20 years, behind the crusade to build an authentic working replica of the Globe Theatre on its original site in South London.

When, as a bright-eyed young American actor, he first visited England in 1949, he made straight for a certain spot in Southwark to see what was left of the old theatre. He was astonished to find that the world's most famous playhouse had been reduced to a blackened plaque, the gift of the Shakespeare Reading Society's subscribers in Britain and India, which had been placed substantially off-target on the walls of a nearby brewery.

It was not until 1971 that Wanamaker founded what became known as the Shakespeare Globe Trust and began actively fundraising to rebuild the 1599 auditorium near to its original site. In his time, he had to fight the Shakespeare scholars who dismissed the project as a Shakespearian Disneyland; the hard-line left wing Southwark Council, who saw it as an elitist conspiracy; and supporters of the Royal Shakespeare Company and the National Theatre, who feared losing out on audiences. But Wanamaker had the satisfaction of seeing construction well underway by the time of his death, and plans to open the theatre in spring next year on target.

Wanamaker was already an established name to British and American theatre audiences when he took up the Globe project. He had settled with his family in England in 1952, and proceeded to galvanise British theatre, films and even opera with something of his own abrasive but likable American vivacity. Wanamaker was the man impresarios sent for whenever they felt a show needed that thrusting, spacious and hugely theatrical dynamism which is peculiar to Broadway at its best. As both actor and director he lent authenticity to plays imported from America, and was later responsible for mounting productions of modern operas at Covent Garden and Sydney Opera House.

He made an immediate impact with his London stage debut in Clifford Odets's Winter Journey (1952), in which Michael Redgrave and Googie Withers also appeared under his direction, in what was then a new departure for classically-trained British actors into the realms of method acting.

Tense, intelligent, chain-smoking and spitting out his lines, Wanamaker played a restless egomaniac who rescues a drink-soaked actor from his destructive wife. "Lady," he shouted at her, "you ride him like a broom!" He had London queuing for months to hear him. His tactful production concealed the play's artificiality, for Wanamaker was a master at wringing all the thrills out of a melodrama while so controlling the atmosphere that it never went over the top. He brought high tension again to Odets's anti-Hollywood diatribe The Big Knife (1954).

Wanamaker was also the right director to bring out, at the Royal Court in 1956, everything harsh, gritty and pungent in an adaptation of Brecht's The Threepenny Opera. Here again he demonstrated his command of humour, as he did in the most endearing of his performances, in N. Richard Nash's sentimental comedy The Rainmaker (1956). Wanamaker played a starry-eyed rogue whose romantic vocalising brought rain in a drought and who persuaded a neglected spinster that she was really a beauty. For years London was indebted to Wanamaker for bringing over other highly-flavoured slices of raw New York theatre. So too was Liverpool where, in 1957, he became artistic director of the New Shakespeare and staged productions of Tennessee Williams, Arthur Miller and William Inge.

Born in a Chicago ghetto, the second son of Russian-Jewish immigrants, Samuel Watenmaker (the name was later smoothed down to Wanamaker) was forced as a child to fight his way out of school past Jew-baiters. He went to Drake University in Iowa, joined the city's Civic Repertory and rapidly established himself as an actor, appearing on Broadway with Ingrid Bergman. During the war he served in the Pacific with the US Marine Corps units who captured Iwo Jima in the Spring of 1945.

Afterwards he returned to Broadway, then a place of increasing self-censorship as Joseph McCarthy began to investigate allegedly un-American activities among entertainers. Wanamaker, whose politics had always been well left of centre though he had never joined the Communist Party, left for London in 1952 to film Give Us This Day, a film considered too radical to be made in America. While there he found he had been subpoenaed by the House Un-American Activities Committee in his absence and decided to stay in Britain. But he never severed his connection with American theatre and television, and even appeared as Macbeth in Chicago in 1964.

Although he was primarily a stage actor, he was seen in many popular films, including Those Magnificent Men in Their Flying Machines (1965), The Spy Who Came in From the Cold (1966) and Private Benjamin (1980). Subsequently he turned to directing films and television series, including such hits of the 1970s as Hawaii Five-0 and Columbo.

But he maintained his presence in the high arts and particularly enjoyed directing opera. His Covent Garden production of Michael Tippett's King Priam (1962) was both dramatic and impressive and, in 1973, his interpretation of Prokofiev's War and Peace (1973) opened the new Sydney Opera House to warm reviews.

Wanamaker's devotion to Shakespeare began with a boyhood visit to a mock-up of the poet's Globe Theatre at the Chicago World Fair. As a drama student he worked in another replica at the Great Lakes festival in Cleveland, Ohio. Though he had neither the training nor the voice for verse-speaking (his Iago to Paul Robeson's masterful 1959 Othello at Stratford was disconcertingly naïve, a slick gangster devoid of any plausible air of honesty), his enthusiasm for Shakespeare's work was always genuine and infectious.

This was all to the good considering the determination he needed to push through with the building of the new Globe, a 24-sided polygon using Elizabethan materials and techniques, to be built opposite St Paul's Cathedral. The 20,000 sq ft site was also to include a modern 250-seat playhouse, the Inigo Jones, based on drawings by the Renaissance architect. The project entailed a long legal battle with Southwark Council which cost Wanamaker all his considerable charm and entailed the curbing of a quick temper never easy.

Even with the Duke of Edinburgh as patron, Sir John Gielgud as president, and directors of the trust who included Dame Judi Dench, Sir Anthony Hopkins, Diana Rigg and Derek Jacobi, the plans took years to bear fruit. Work finally began in 1989, although at the time Wanamaker had collected only £3 million of the £20 million required. In June this year, Prince Edward unveiled the building's first two bays.

While aware of his reputation as a cranky American eccentric, Wanamaker's extraordinary vision and optimism could yet endow the nation with a unique tool for the understanding and appreciation of its greatest playwright. His reputation as the creator of the new Globe will almost certainly endure far longer than his fame as a performer. In 1993 he was appointed an honorary CBE for his work on the project.

He is survived by his wife Charlotte, whom he married in 1940, and three daughters, one of whom is the actress Zoe Wanamaker.

Sam Wanamaker was born in Chicago on June 14, 1919, and died in London on December 18, 1993.

Ralph Miliband

**Political theorist, whose two sons competed
to lead the Labour Party**

June 10, 1994

Ralph Miliband, political scientist, died on May 21 aged 70. He
was born on January 7, 1924.

Ralph Miliband, who served for 23 years as a lecturer at the
London School of Economics and after that for six years held
the chair of politics at Leeds, consistently stuck to a coherent,
left-wing view of the world. In the Marxist tradition he saw class
conflict as inevitably flowing from an industrial system based on
the private ownership of capital. This led him into a highly influential discussion of the role of the State and its institutions which,
he tirelessly argued, were deliberately used by the dominant ruling
class to contain political pressures which might otherwise pose a
threat to its own hegemony.

Yet he was in no sense a rigid Marxist, never a member of
the Communist Party and a strong anti-authoritarian, hence his
support for the student protest at LSE in the late 1960s. But no one
could have been a less natural advocate of Dave Spart. An engaging
and humorous companion, he was also an extremely good writer,
something which even his critics on the orthodox Left, such as Dick
Crossman, always conceded, and he had little patience with the
more convoluted versions of left-wing (or any other) theory.

The book which made his name, Parliamentary Socialism (1961),
is a model of cogency and clarity. Its thesis, the betrayal of the
Labour movement by its elected leaders at Westminster, may have
been a familiar one but it had seldom been deployed with quite
such wit and contempt. His most considerable work is probably,
however, The State in Capitalist Society (1972), which became a
classic text for politics and sociology students of the 1970s. His last
book, Socialism for a Sceptical Age, of which he saw the proofs just
before he died, is due out later this year.

Born in Belgium, the son of a Jewish leather worker from Warsaw, Miliband made his way with his father from Brussels to Britain in 1940 (his mother and younger sister, with whom he was reunited after the war, were left behind). Initially attending Ealing Technical College, he won a place at the London School of Economics the attraction there being Harold Laski in 1941. But he spent only two years at LSE, in its wartime exile at Cambridge, before volunteering for the Royal Navy: it was thanks to Laski, who characteristically wrote a letter to his friend, the First Lord of the Admiralty, that despite still being a Belgian subject he was enlisted. In 1946 he returned to LSE, then back in Houghton Street, where he took his expected first and wrote a doctoral thesis on French socialist ideas in the 1790s (a subject always close to Laski's own heart).

But Miliband himself never had any illusions about the imminence of socialist change. As late as 1988 he wrote that conditions would not exist for the coming to power of a government that would seek to bring about the radical transformation of the existing social order for several decades. He had, of course, long since become disillusioned with the Labour Party as an instrument for that purpose. Although he had flirted with the outer fringe of the Bevanites in the 1950s, his outright attack on the party's leaders from which former Bevanites, like Harold Wilson, were not excluded ensured that from 1961 onwards he would operate with nothing but a sectarian base.

None of this, however, affected his ability to attempt by argument to influence the political process whether in his writing or his teaching. Besides his books, he wrote important articles in the New Left Review and in the New Reasoner (the academic, outside LSE, to whom he felt closest was E.P.Thompson). In his teaching he always told the truth directly as he saw it, while never seeking to abuse his authority over his pupils. He was a powerful lecturer, adopting a style of deliberate instancy which commanded attention. As a tutor he had gifts of patience and understanding and never condescended. Academically, he was almost equally well known in North America as he was in Britain, having spent particularly after his retirement from Leeds in 1978 a number of semesters lecturing there as a visiting professor.

He is survived by his wife Marion, whom he married in 1961, and by two sons, the older of whom is secretary to the Labour Party's Commission on Social Justice and the younger of whom is research assistant to the Opposition's shadow Chief Secretary, Harriet Harman.

Karl Popper

Analyst of logic, society and thought
September 19, 1994

Sir Karl Popper, FRS, CH, Professor of Logic and Scientific Method at the London School of Economics, 1949-69, died on September 17 aged 92. He was born on July 28, 1902.

Karl Popper was a philosopher of uncommon originality, clarity and depth, and his range was exceptional. Besides the large problems and issues dealt with in his first two major works, The Logic of Scientific Discovery (originally Logik der Forschung, 1934) and The Open Society and its Enemies (1945), the subjects he worked on included pre-Socratic philosophy, foundations of mathematical logic, the probability calculus, the direction of time, Kant, and the rise of polyphonic music.

As well as rigorously technical work in the philosophy of natural science, he could arrest the attention of ordinary people, for instance on educational or political issues. He had a knack of hitting on memorable labels (or "right-to-left definitions", to use one of them): for instance, "the bucket theory of the mind", "horizon of expectations", "moral futurism", "the theory of manifest truth", and of course "the open society" . He developed a liking, in everyday speech, for homely Anglicisms like "Not my cup of tea" and "I may have to eat humble pie" (though this last phrase was not constantly on his lips).

He called the writing of The Open Society his "war work" . The book made him something of a hero to many intellectuals who had experienced oppressive regimes, for instance in Germany and also in Poland, the Soviet Union and China. He had devoted followers in developing countries, such as India. And he came to be honoured in Japan. His work was translated (often clandestinely, in Eastern Europe) into more than twenty languages.

Apart from music, he had virtually no relaxations. He was physically small, with an expressive face. He read with intense concentration, his eyes seeming to suck the meaning from the page. Though often pessimistic about the future of the West, he was, at bottom, a great optimist.

Karl Raimund Popper was born into a cultured home, full of books and music, in the centre of Vienna close by the cathedral. His parents had abandoned the Jewish faith. His father was a lawyer, writer, and social reformer. This comfortable world was shattered by the First World War and the inflation, hunger-riots and shooting that accompanied its closing stages and aftermath.

At 16, Popper left home and school in a mood of private revolt. He did manual work, and also enrolled at the University of Vienna. In Unended Quest (1976) he tells how he flirted briefly with communism, but turned sharply against it in 1919 after seeing unarmed young socialists shot outside a police station during a demonstration engineered by communists, who saw revolutionary violence as necessary for progress towards the dictatorship of the proletariat.

Popper now became deeply suspicious of the scientific pretensions of Marxism to foretell the future course of history, pretensions which he would expose later in three articles, "The Poverty of Historicism" (published in Economica in 1944-45). He now became a democratic socialist, identifying himself wholeheartedly with the Vienna workers' movement, with its ideal of emancipation through education, its pacifism, its concern for better housing, and the pleasure that many of its members took in mountaineering, classical music and literature.

The year 1919 was also a turning-point for him in other ways. It was the one in which the eclipse expeditions confirmed Einstein's theory of gravitation. The young Popper was deeply impressed by the contrast between this hard-won success for that great scientific theory and the mass of easy "verifications" which their respective supporters were claiming for the theories of Marx, Freud, and Adler (with whom Popper was working in 1919). Popper now began to grapple with what he called "the demarcation problem", namely: what differentiates genuinely scientific theories from pseudo-scientific ones? Not empirical verification; no theory had seemed better verified, more secure, than Newton's, but it was now displaced by Einstein's. Popper's answer was: their falsifiability or openness to falsification by experiment. He first published this idea in 1933.

In the meanwhile, he had to live, however frugally. He earned a little money coaching American students. During 1922-24 he learnt his trade of cabinet-making (but the long hours of planing bored him). Then he did social work with neglected children. In 1925 he enrolled in the newly formed Pedagogic Institute, where he met Josefine Henninger, his future wife. They became schoolteachers in Vienna. He was now studying psychology, physics and mathematics; and he had started to grapple with Hume's problem of induction. He came to believe that his solution for the demarcation problem in terms of falsifiability also provided a solution for this other fundamental problem: a scientific theory, no matter how good, always remains a conjecture; it should have withstood rigorous and ingenious tests, but these provide no inductive support for it; the problem of induction falls away. (This claim has been much questioned.)

By 1932 he had completed (under encouragement from Herbert Feigl) the first volume of a big work on "The Two Fundamental Problems in the Theory of Knowledge" . This work (which has been published only in German, in 1979) was much read and discussed by members of the Vienna Circle, including Carnap, Neurath, Schlick and Waismann.

Parts of it were incorporated in his Logik der Forschung (1934). This book, though read only by a rather small circle (until translated into English in 1959), raised this secondary schoolteacher to the rank of a foremost philosopher. It was brought to Einstein's attention by Frieda Busch, wife of the founder of the Busch quartet. Einstein told Popper that, purified of certain errors, the book "will be really splendid" . At Susan Stebbing's invitation, Popper spent a considerable time in England during 1935-36, meeting Ayer, Berlin, Russell, Ryle, Schrodinger, Woodger and, at LSE, Hayek and Robbins. He lectured on Tarski's theory of truth and, at LSE, on "The Poverty of Historicism" .

His book appeared at a difficult time. The Vienna Circle, with which he had close contacts without being an official member, was beginning to break up, the Nazi menace was looming, and the political situation in Austria was close to civil war. Although he still supported the Social Democratic Party, Popper had become disillusioned with it: it had undermined working people's faith in democracy without really being prepared to fight the anti-democrats of the Right; he was against the idea that the social democrats should arm themselves against fascism: it would provoke militarism on the Right, and few social democrats would know how to handle their new weapons.

A senior lectureship in Philosophy at the then Canterbury University College in New Zealand was advertised; foreseeing a Nazi takeover of Austria, he applied, and got it, arriving there in 1937. He now forced himself to think and write in English. He worked on the "Poverty" (published as a book in 1957, with the dedication: "In memory of the countless men and women...who fell victims to the Fascist and Communist belief in Inexorable Laws of Historical Destiny"). A section on Plato developed runaway tendencies and eventually grew into the first volume of The Open Society and its Enemies, a brilliantly written defence of rationality and democracy against Utopianism and historicism. (Police suspicions were aroused when in 1943 he cabled "Consider Enemies Better" in reply to a suggestion from London that the title should be ...and its Opponents.)

These two works contained important ideas about the methods of the social sciences; and in 1945 he was invited to a readership at LSE. (He became a professor there in 1949.) His large lecture audiences (which often included a sprinkling of distinguished visitors) listened absorbed to his low-voiced thinking aloud (he had no notes), at once clear, serious and deep, and often enlivened by puckish jokes. He became an active member of a Philosophy of Sciences Group which met at UCL; it founded The British Journal for the Philosophy of Science, and his important paper on Indeterminism was published in two early issues.

His weekly LSE seminar was often stormy; the speaker was expected to explain his problem, announce his thesis, and then, often under a running fire of criticism, argue for it without any surreptitious shift of position, and there could be trouble if these exacting demands were not met.

In the early 1950s he developed an allergy to tobacco smoke, and took to avoiding public places and working, with his wife Hennie's devoted assistance, mostly at their charming home in Penn. He was visited regularly by a small circle of devoted friends. He usually drew them into whatever problem was absorbing him, but occasionally unburdened his bitterness about some alleged plagiarism or the misdeeds of a renegade pupil. His reputation as a "difficult man" was not entirely baseless.

In the mid-1950s he was working on an English edition of his first book, with important new appendices on probability, simplicity, and corroboration, and also a long postscript which grew into a work of 800 pages, and was published in three volumes, with the help of Bill Bartley, only in 1982. It argues for, among other things, indeterminism and a propensity interpretation of physical probabilities.

His Conjectures and Refutations (1963), as well as reproducing some classic papers, had a long new chapter elucidating the idea that a sequence of false theories may be converging with the truth, or have ever increasing verisimilitude, verisimilitude being sharply separated from probability. (When a serious logical defect in his definition of this idea was pointed out to him, he responded angelically: several philosophers have since been trying to repair the damage.) His Objective Knowledge (1972) is notable for an evolutionist approach to language, knowledge, and the mind-body problem, and for the thesis (foreshadowed by Plato, Hegel and Frege) that in addition to the world of physical things (World One) and the world of mental experiences (World Two) there is a World Three of abstract but objective products of human thinking.

His last major work, The Self and its Brain (1977), written in collaboration with Sir John Eccles, revives an interactionist, neo-Cartesian view of the mind-brain relation. It had a mixed reception.

He was knighted in 1965. In 1974 came the philosophical accolade of two thick volumes in Schilpp's Library of Living Philosophers. In 1976 he was elected a Fellow of the Royal Society, and in 1982 he was made a Companion of Honour. He was awarded many honorary degrees, and received several rare prizes.

He and his wife were devoted to each other, and his life was darkened by her long and painful illness. She died in 1985, which was a terrible year for him. But he still felt that, despite all the pain and suffering, it is a wonderful privilege to be in this great world and to participate in our amazingly successful understanding of it. Even death, he said, adds value to our lives. He worked on indefatigably until almost the end, bringing out A World of Propensities, a slim but elegant volume, in 1990, and In Search of a Better World, a collection of essays and addresses, in 1992.

There were no children.

Hugo Gryn

Auschwitz survivor, rabbi, broadcaster and activist for Jewish causes

August 20, 1996

Hugo Gryn, CBE, rabbi and broadcaster, died from cancer on August 18 aged 66. He was born on June 30, 1930. A pillar of one of the BBC's most enterprising and successful radio programmes, The Moral Maze, the name and reputation of Hugo Gryn became known to many outside his own faith. More perhaps than anyone else, he symbolised the responsible voice of Reform Judaism in Britain

Hugo Gabriel Gryn was born in the Czechoslovak town of Berehovo. He was named after his great-grandfather, a renowned Talmudic scholar, who had just died. In May 1944, shortly before his fourteenth birthday, he was deported to Auschwitz, together with his family, the Jews of Berehovo, and all the Jews of Carpathia.

His younger brother and his grandparents were murdered on arrival in the camp. He and his father survived for a year in a succession of slave labour camps. They also survived the notorious death marches. They were liberated together at Gunskirchen (a sub-camp of Mauthausen) on May 5, 1945. His father died of starvation and typhoid a few days after liberation. His mother survived.

In August 1945, aged 15, Hugo Gryn was brought to Britain with several hundred other young survivors of the concentration camps. Within a year he was awarded a scholarship to study mathematics and biochemistry at King's College, Cambridge. He completed the special two-year course in the summer of 1948, and, together with his best friend, Jonathan Balter, volunteered to fight in Israel's war of independence. Balter was killed in action.

Returning to London (he had contracted jaundice while in Israel), Gryn worked briefly as a biochemist for Glaxo, and then as a teacher in a boarding school. It was at this time that he met Leo Baeck, the distinguished Reform rabbi from Berlin who had survived long incarceration in the Theresienstadt camp. He studied Talmud with Baeck, and then accepted a teaching post at the Hebrew Union College in Cincinnati, the one seminary for Reform rabbis that had survived the war.

While a student rabbi at Cincinnati he officiated for several years at the Jewish High Holy Day services at Jasper, Alabama. There he befriended Martin Luther King, marched with him, and spent a night in jail with him. In 1956 he became an American citizen, and in the following year was married to Jacqueline Selby and ordained as a rabbi. His first congregation after ordination was the Jewish Religious Union in Bombay.

While in India, Hugo Gryn befriended Jawaharlal Nehru and learnt Sanskrit. After nearly three years in India he returned to the United States, where he served as executive director of the World Union of Progressive Judaism. From 1962 to 1964 he was senior executive for the American Jewish Joint Distribution Committee ("the Joint") helping distressed Jewish communities all over the world. Morocco and Romania were two countries in which he was particularly active. He was instrumental in bringing many Jews from those regions to Israel.

In 1964, in search of a new pulpit, he considered becoming the rabbi of Waco, Texas, but accepted instead the position of junior rabbi at the West London Synagogue for British Jews at Marble Arch (also known as the Upper Berkeley Street Synagogue). He gave his first sermon the title, "What is sin?" Soon afterwards he was made senior rabbi. His pastoral work was of the highest quality, his sermons were profound homilies, suffused with a positive optimism and fighting spirit – which was all the more extraordinary, and all the more inspiring, given his terrible experiences during the Holocaust.

In 1990 Gryn became president of the Reform Synagogues of Great Britain. He was also vice-president and lecturer at the Leo Baeck College, where Reform and Liberal rabbis are trained and ordained. For 11 years (1980-91) he was chairman of the European Board of the World Union for Progressive Judaism. He was indefatigable in his work on behalf of Jews who had been forbidden to leave the Soviet Union (refuseniks) and those imprisoned for teaching Hebrew. A high point of his life was when those for whose liberation he and his wife had worked so hard, were allowed to leave the Soviet Union, and were affectionately welcomed in his synagogue hall in London.

A man of deep humanitarian conscience, keenly aware of the evils that arise from division and hatred, Gryn took a leading part in interfaith initiatives. From 1972 he was on the standing committee for Interfaith Dialogue in Education, and of the Central Religious Advisory Committee of the BBC and the IBA. He was a co-founder, with Bishop Jim Thompson, of the Interfaith Network (UK). Together with Edward Carpenter, then Dean of Westminster, he was active from 1975 in the London Rainbow Group. As a governor of Atlantic College, he organised an annual interfaith conference for students from all over the world, and was proud that from great diversity could come reconciliation and understanding.

He made particular efforts to open dialogues with Muslim religious leaders. He was a vice-chairman of the Spitalfields Trust, through which Christian, Jewish and Muslim leaders restored an old London synagogue (and former Huguenot place of worship) to be a centre for the study of minorities. He was a member of the executive committee of the recently formed Maimonides Foundation, established to create links of understanding and co-operation between Jews and Arabs in the fields of science, medicine and philosophy. He was a mediating and imaginative member of every committee on which he sat. He never despaired of setbacks in the work of reconciliation, and was a doughty fighter against all forms of religious, racial and social intolerance.

In 1992 Gryn was appointed CBE for his services to interfaith relations. In the following year he took out British nationality. In addition to his BA and MA from Cambridge University, he held an MA at Cincinnati, was a Doctor of Divinity at the Hebrew College, London, and was awarded an honorary Doctorate of Divinity by London University in 1995 (reputedly the first Jew to be thus honoured). At the ceremony conferring his DD, which was conducted by the Princess Royal, another of the honorands was the former President of Germany, Richard von Weizsacker, whose earlier denunciation of German participation in the Holocaust had moved him greatly.

Having survived the Holocaust, Hugo Gryn became an important spokesman for the historical record, and for the feelings and concerns of other survivors. He was a vice-president of the 45-Aid Society, the group of survivors who had come to Britain in 1945-46, and at whose gatherings he was a focus of hope and (where needed) comfort. He recently became an adviser to the new Holocaust Museum at the Imperial War Museum.

Hugo Gryn gave of his time unsparingly. As a frequent speaker to Jewish and non-Jewish audiences throughout the country, he combined wisdom with a tremendous sense of fun. His synagogue community of 2,500 families represented only a fraction of those who turned to him for guidance. Even before The Moral Maze, more than two decades of radio and television work saw to it that his homilies and his humour became familiar to millions.

He is survived by his wife Jackie, a son and three daughters.

Georg Solti

Masterful opera and concert conductor

September 8, 1997

Sir Georg Solti, KBE, former music director of Covent Garden and of the Chicago Symphony Orchestra, died on holiday in the South of France on September 5 aged 84. He was born in Budapest on October 21, 1912.

Any Solti appearance, whether in the opera house or the concert hall, was an event. When he was present there was electricity in the air. He had the power to excite audiences and the even rarer power to inspire other musicians. Instrumental players knew that there could be no coasting when Solti was in charge, even during a rehearsal. Singers of greater and lesser stature paid tribute to his ability to squeeze from them performances of which they had not known themselves capable.

From a distance, Georg Solti hardly cut an impressive figure. He was already balding in his forties, with protruding bat-like ears, plump in middle age. He could have been taken for a Central European businessman, although the muscular shoulders were those of a conductor. A little closer up, the Solti magnetism became evident. He exuded energy. He spoke at high speed in an English which even after many years of residence in Britain was heavily fractured, and his speech was supplemented by dramatic gestures with hands and arms. Most impressive of all were the eyes, which fixed the listener with a searing intensity. Solti conveyed everything con tutta forza: his enthusiasms, his dislikes, his passions of the moment.

During his early days at the London Philharmonic Orchestra he was dubbed "the screaming skull", and he was often charged, especially by the London critics, against whom he conducted a lengthy warfare, with over-excitability. Gradually he grew calmer but without ever losing that vital performance energy, which stayed with him right through to old age. At a time when other conductors would have been withdrawing to a not too demanding repertoire, Solti deliberately launched himself into large-scale works.

He had just turned 70 and was recovering from some heart problems when he tackled a new Ring at Bayreuth. He was nearly 80 when he conducted and recorded Strauss's Die Frau ohne Schatten at Salzburg. His 80th birthday itself was celebrated back at Covent Garden with a performance of Otello, with a cast led by Domingo and Te Kanawa, after which he was appointed music director laureate of the Royal Opera.

By this time, Karajan and Bernstein were dead. Giulini, Solti's junior by two years, was making fewer and fewer concert appearances and had given up for good the opera, which he had never much cared for. Solti was the undisputed Grand Old Man of music.

Born Gyuri Stern to a closely knit Jewish Hungarian family in Budapest, he used to relate how as a child he played the piano in a local pub to help to pay off the gambling debts of a black sheep uncle. His father was a none too successful small businessman, but the young Solti managed to reach the Liszt Academy in Budapest and to study under the composers Bartok, Dohnanyi and Kodaly. He was an accomplished pianist and remained so, prepared late in life to join in duets with the likes of Murray Perahia.

But conducting was an early aim. He became a repetiteur at the Hungarian State Opera in 1937. In that same crucial year he was given a similar job by Toscanini at the Salzburg Festival, rehearsing Die Zauberflote. The revered conductor was impressed, and that was to stand Solti in good stead in the war. A few months later Budapest gave him his first chance, when he was offered a Figaro to conduct. The evening was ill-fated. Solti was fond of telling how at the end of the first act the baritone, a fellow Jew, singing the title role, whispered that the Nazis had marched into Austria. By the end of the evening the rest of the house knew, too. Georg Solti saw there would be no more work in Budapest. He left abruptly for Switzerland, where he spent the duration of the war. He made half-hearted attempts to return to Hungary, but his mother warned him against it, and she was to die in a concentration camp.

Solti the refugee scraped a living, teaching piano and coaching singers. He was helped by winning the Geneva Piano Competition in 1942. Immediately the war ended, he used his Hungarian connections, not for the last time. He was engaged to conduct Fidelio at the Bavarian State Opera through the offices of Edward Kilenyi, a fellow Hungarian with the American Occupation Forces.

In a Europe short of conductors – and unwilling to employ those with Nazi sympathies – Solti swiftly won the post of music director of the Munich company.

Now began his long connection with Richard Strauss, the city's favourite son, and Solti was to conduct Der Rosenkavalier in the composer's presence. He was also to conduct at Strauss's funeral in 1949. Circumstances had forced Solti to start late, but he made up for this by forcing himself and all those around him to work very hard. He learnt his opera at Munich and forged his connections with Decca, first as an accompanist to the violinist Kuhlenkampf, and then as conductor proper. He returned to Salzburg to conduct Idomeneo in 1951, and in 1956 was in charge of the Zauberflöte that marked the anniversary of Mozart's birth.

By this time Solti had made his American debut with the San Francisco Opera as well as conducting his only Glyndebourne opera, Don Giovanni in 1954. Frankfurt had snatched him away from Munich, and he was being recognised as a man with a gift for lifting repertory performances well above the routine level. He stood no nonsense from stars with inflated egos.

In 1958, Decca, the recording company to which he always remained loyal, decided to place the entire Ring in his hands. This massive project, for which both Solti and Decca demanded the best, was to take seven years to complete in Vienna. It set new standards in performance and recorded sound, and is now being remastered for reissue.

Georg Solti made his Covent Garden debut in 1959 with Der Rosenkavalier. The cast was glossy, but the performance which caught the ear was Solti's own. The board of the Royal Opera began to see him as the man to follow Rafael Kubelik as music director. In particular, Solti was championed by the board's chairman, Lord Drogheda. Once again the Hungarian mafia worked: Drogheda's wife Joan was a pianist of some accomplishment, and her teacher was Hungarian.

There was only one problem. Solti had had a long stint in opera houses and was anxious for more concert work. He had all but accepted the post of music director of the Los Angeles Philharmonic. However, he discovered to his fury that the LA board had already appointed his deputy, Zubin Mehta. Solti thought again and was told by Bruno Walter that he should continue the great European opera tradition and take the Covent Garden job. Eventually, he agreed.

The first years at Covent Garden were turbulent, the meeting of two alien forces. Solti was a Middle European by upbringing and nature, who had spent most of his career in German theatres. He had little idea of British customs, and the Opera House, for its part, was not prepared for a martinet with a well developed ego, who was much more concerned with the excellence of his own performances than with the general welfare of the company. Early on Solti caused consternation when, dissatisfied with the performance of the chorus in a new production, he demanded an extra Saturday afternoon rehearsal. He had to be taken aside and told gently that the chorus was three quarters Welsh and that the Saturday in question was the day of the England v Wales international at Twickenham.

Solti was even more upset by the London critics. In Germany, the music director at that time was a tsar and those who took issue with him were generally brought to heel. Not so in London. Solti could not understand why some of the London reviewers found his Mozart hard and unrelenting. On a number of occasions in those early years Solti came close to resigning, and was prevented from doing so only by the diplomatic skills of Lord Drogheda.

Eventually he and London came to terms. He introduced Schoenberg's Moses und Aron, in a daring production by Peter Hall, to ensure that Covent Garden was not an operatic museum, although he tended to leave the conducting of new British works to his assistant, Edward Downes. The Strauss evenings became famous, with Arabella and Die Frau ohne Schatten coming into the repertoire, the latter being especially impressive. Above all, there were the Ring cycles of the mid-1960s. Solti was proving himself a great Wagnerian, and it was no surprise that he ended his Covent Garden reign in 1971 with a Tristan centred on the Isolde of Birgit Nilsson, an artist with whom he always had a special affinity.

In the recording studios, there were some legendary rows. One concerned Jussi Bjorling, who was scheduled to sing in Verdi's Ballo in Maschera. Solti, as usual, called for more and more rehearsal until Bjorling turned round and said: "I know the role, I sang it with Toscanini. You go and study the score, maestro." Bjorling was replaced by Carlo Bergonzi.

But Solti was beginning to mellow, and one of the influences was his second wife, Valerie Pitts. The conductor had a well-known penchant for tall, blonde ladies. Miss Pitts was sent by the BBC to interview him at the Savoy, and Solti was entranced by what he saw. They married in 1967 and made their principal home in Hampstead. Four years later he took British citizenship and was soon appointed KBE (he had been an honorary CBE since 1968).

Georg Solti left Covent Garden in 1971 to do what he had promised himself ten years earlier: give more symphony concerts. The Chicago Symphony, of which he had become music director a couple of years earlier, was his main instrument. It became renowned for its discipline, and had no serious rival in America. Solti liked everything about it apart from having to live in the Windy City. In London his chief links were with the LPO, which made him principal conductor and artistic director in 1979, a post he held until he became conductor emeritus in 1983. He was always happiest in the Viennese repertory of Mahler and Bruckner, but he also championed the music of his adopted country, Elgar and Walton especially.

The break with Covent Garden was far from complete. Although in the early 1970s he conducted a certain amount of opera in Paris, leaning heavily on the expertise of his London casting director, Joan Ingpen, he made regular visits back to the Royal Opera and was generally treated as a returning hero. Solti used to remark, only half-jokingly, that he was far better appreciated after he had left than when he was there.

In 1983 he was persuaded by Bayreuth, despite a period of poor health, to stage a new Ring cycle with his old partner Peter Hall. The naturalistic production infuriated many and was unjustly vilified, but Solti proved that in his seventies his powers of interpretation were undimmed. He proved it again seven years later when on the death of Karajan he took over the opening production of the Salzburg Festival, Un Ballo in Maschera.

In this there was a certain irony. Karajan had already recorded the work with the same cast for Deutsche Grammophon. For years he had blocked any proposal that Solti should conduct opera there. But the festival authorities quickly acknowledged that Solti was now the last in the grand tradition, and talked him into the job. Other links were quickly forged. Solti returned with a Frau ohne Schatten based on a recording, one of his very best. He was given charge of the Easter Festival, Karajan's special baby.

In 1991 Solti said farewell as music director to Chicago with four performances of Verdi's Otello, with Pavarotti in the title role, which were recorded live. Back in Europe he embarked on a new cycle of Mozart opera recordings, also based around concert performances, which showed a new, lighter and sunnier Solti. The most recent, Don Giovanni, is released this month.

In his eighties Solti seemed indestructible. He was due to conduct Verdi's Requiem this week at the penultimate night of the Proms. Earlier this year, at a party to celebrate 50 years with Decca, he talked of his plans for the millennium and beyond. Negotiations were well advanced for a new production of Tchaikovsky's The Queen of Spades after the reopening of the Royal Opera House.

Appropriately, on July 14 it was Solti who conducted the last pieces of operatic music at Covent Garden before the house's closure. In a throwaway line in the programme book, he mentioned that he had been associated with the house for almost 60 years, but – Hungarian to the last – he did not say what or when the first occasion was. (In 1938 he had conducted a pick-up ballet company.)

Georg Solti was twice married. He leaves his second wife, Valerie, and two daughters.

Lydia Lopokova

Alec Issigonis

Berthold Lubetkin's Penguin Pool at London Zoo

Freddie Mercury

Sam Wanamaker

Georg Solti

Yehudi Menuhin

Lucian Freud, self-portrait

Isaiah Berlin

Philosopher, polymath and friend
November 7, 1997

Sir Isaiah Berlin, OM, CBE, FBA, philosopher and first President of Wolfson College, Oxford, died yesterday aged 88. He was born in Riga, Latvia, on June 6, 1909.

Sir Isaiah Berlin was for many years one of the most influential figures in the intellectual life of the country, and also one of the most original. The part he played in the social and intellectual worlds of London and Oxford is very difficult to describe, because it was unique. It owed very little to any achieved position and status, but was due rather to the richness of his mind, his brilliance in conversation, his personal charm, and to the generosity with which he put his famous abilities at the disposal of others, without stint or calculation. He had a very unusual number of close friends, as much outside as within the academic world, all of whom felt entirely at ease with him, and who sought his advice, and loved to talk to him. Also, it was characteristic that he had met, in a totally unplanned way, and as it were by chance, Freud, Einstein, Picasso, Stravinsky, and most of the outstanding writers, musicians, and thinkers of his time. He was an exceptionally warm and responsive person, certainly not formidable, in spite of the famous speed and allusiveness of his conversation. It was always evident that he responded immediately to the individual character of the people that he met and that he was genuinely interested in them. He was a benevolent mimic of personal styles. He was at all stages of his life consulted by many men and women on all kinds of professional and personal problems, and he was outstandingly shrewd and conscientious in trying to fit square pegs into square holes. Not only was he one of the best, and best known, lecturers on both sides of the Atlantic, but he was also one of the most successful teachers of graduate students. Wherever insight into the differences between individuals was required, Berlin showed a restless power to penetrate beneath the surface, whether among the distinguished dead or among the living, distinguished and undistinguished alike.

Isaiah Berlin was born in Riga, the only child of Mendel and Marie Berlin. His parents were Russian, and his father was a businessman who moved to London shortly after the revolution. In later life Berlin could still recall scenes from the Russian Revolution, which he had witnessed as a child. In London he had to learn English as his second language at the age of ten. From St Paul's School he went in 1928, with a scholarship, to Corpus Christi College, Oxford. He obtained first class honours in Greats (Lit Hum) and in Modern Greats (PPE).

Even as an undergraduate it was remarked of him that his rooms in college were "always a place of resort". He was elected to a fellowship by examination at All Souls College in 1932, and he remained closely connected with All Souls in different capacities for the rest of his life, with only a short interval before and immediately after the war. In 1938 he succeeded R. H. S. Crossman as a fellow and tutor in philosophy at New College, then under the wardenship of H. A. L. Fisher (who was one of the first to recognise how outstanding his gifts were). In addition to regular tutoring and lecturing on philosophy, he began the study of Karl Marx and of Marxism which was to issue in 1939 in his authoritative and original book Karl Marx: His Life and Environment, which was first published in the Home University Library but went through a number of editions (the most recent in 1978). He had a wide and deep knowledge of the history of European socialism and of the origins and continuing developments of Russian communism.

His own philosophical position was formed as a critical response to the new analytical philosophy which came to Oxford in the immediate prewar and postwar years, having as its forebears the logical positivism of the Vienna Circle and Wittgenstein's lectures in Cambridge. Berlin acknowledged and enjoyed the intellectual excitement which the new philosophy brought to Oxford, but he was not convinced by the more drastic anti-metaphysical polemics of the logical positivists, or by the claim that all the problems of philosophy are problems arising from linguistic confusion.

It was a characteristic tribute to him that a group of the younger analytical philosophers chose his rooms in which to meet regularly for discussions from 1936 until the outbreak of war, and that the two dominant philosophers in the group, J. L. Austin and A. J. Ayer, were both his friends, though certainly not friends of one another. Berlin's criticism of the more sweeping claims of logical positivism were published in three powerful and original articles in philosophical journals, and reprinted in his Concepts and Categories (1978).

In the second year of the war, Berlin's life underwent an abrupt change, which was ultimately to lead him away from Oxford philosophy. He was, first, appointed to the Ministry of Information in New York, and then, in 1942, joined the British Embassy in Washington as a first secretary under Lord Halifax, a fellow of All Souls who had a strong personal regard for him and a high opinion of his judgment. Berlin quickly became a widely known and greatly respected figure in the political society of Washington, his admirers ranging from Felix Frankfurter and Walter Lippmann to Katharine Graham and Joseph Alsop. His delight in observing personal idiosyncrasies and incompatibilities made him an excellent political observer in a country where personality counts much more than party.

His reports to the Foreign Office on the political scene in the United States became famous in Whitehall for their colourful and amusing descriptions of personalities and of their motives, which made them vastly more readable than official dispatches are supposed to be. They strongly appealed to Churchill, who insisted on seeing them unabridged and on meeting their author. There was a mistake, and the guest invited to lunch in Downing Street, and surprised to find himself placed next to a disgruntled Prime Minister, was the songwriter Irving Berlin.

For the rest of his life, Isaiah Berlin remained a familiar figure in Washington, in New York and at Harvard, returning often to lecture, and in later life to visit his many friends. He was appointed CBE in 1946 for his work at the embassy, and was elected to honorary fellowships by at least ten American universities, a testimony to his unique reputation in the academic community there.

From the early Thirties onwards, Zionism and, later, Israel were never far from his thoughts. He returned repeatedly to Israel as a visitor. He had a thorough knowledge of Jewish history and of Jewish institutions and personalities. He enjoyed the friendship and confidence of Chaim Weizmann and wrote a brilliant essay about him, as well as one about Moses Moses, an early Zionist, and another about Lewis Namier and his ties to Zionism. English friends who visited Israel with him found that he had a peculiar and quasi-official standing there, as the most respected of all free-thinking Jews of the Diaspora, and that, as earlier at Oxford, his hotel room in Jerusalem immediately became "a place of resort". He strongly disapproved of the aggressive nationalism of recent Likud governments and of the religious parties, and he supported the Peace Now movement in Israel which opposes territorial expansion.

Berlin was a 19th-century liberal in politics in the mould of John Stuart Mill, but he drew some of his inspiration from Russian sources, specifically from Belinksy and Herzen, about whom he wrote brilliant essays, published in Russian Thinkers (1978). He abhorred the Leninism of some fellow-travelling intellectuals in the West. In all his publications and lectures he defended the value which was for him overriding: the value of individuality and human diversity, and of any relaxed political and social conditions which allowed it to flourish. He was suspicious of all general schemes of human improvement that do not take account of the peculiarities of local history and of local social conditions, because he believed that they must lead to enforced conformity and therefore to tyranny. He wished eccentricities to be protected, when they were both authentic and harmless, and unforced national differences to be respected.

During a wartime conversation in a transatlantic aeroplane with the distinguished American logician Scheffer, Berlin came to realise that his real interest was in the history of political thought rather than in philosophical analysis in a narrow sense. Even before he was appointed Professor of Social and Political Theory at Oxford in 1957, he had developed a style of lecturing on political thought which attracted very large and enthusiastic audiences of under-graduates, and his talks on the history of thought broadcast by the BBC Third Programme brought an unparalleled response from listeners.

It was his distinctive achievement when lecturing to be extremely serious and extremely amusing at the same time. Reconstructing social theories of the past, he related them to the temperament of thinkers and to the details of their inheritance and upbringing. The sceptical attitude behind his lectures, published and unpublished, was close to that of David Hume, but he was less abstract than Hume in his criticism, because he was a master of the telling detail and the odd quirk in a person's history which reveals his true nature.

When he gave the Mellon Lectures in Washington on German Romanticism, a very large audience, much of it far from academic, remained to the end, undaunted by a torrent of unknown German names flashing past in Berlin's headlong manner. It is reported that when he gave a course of lectures at Columbia University in New York a phenomenon was observed that has not been seen there before or since: the audience at the end of the course was considerably larger than at the beginning.

In 1966-67, his life took a new direction for the second time when he became the first president of Wolfson College, Oxford, and resigned his professorship. He said at the time that he took this step into administration, away from his natural inclinations, as a kind of thank-offering to Britain. He was very much more than the first president of the new college: he was in effect its founder, like an archbishop of the Middle Ages, having found and put together the very large sum of money necessary for an endowment. The university had proposed a college without an endowment and without the power to select its own fellows. Having successfully approached the Ford Foundation and the Wolfson Foundation, Berlin negotiated with the university, step by step, to establish a real and self-governing college for graduate students, with a splendid modern building on the Cherwell. Given the rigidities of university planning, this was an extraordinary triumph of skill and energy, and the college – which makes uniquely generous provision for families and indulges in no college pomposities – is much loved and greatly aspired to by home and overseas students alike. Its customs, and particularly its common room arrangements, reflect something of the humanity, freedom from prejudice and openness to the world of its first president.

In 1974 Berlin became president of the British Academy, and in 1975 he resigned as president of Wolfson. But he continued to supervise and to advise graduate students interested in political thought or in Russian studies. "The place of resort" continued as always, and a stream of foreign scholars came to talk to him. His fame extended across Europe, and he received the Erasmus Prize in 1983 and the Agnelli International Prize for Ethics in 1987.

He was for many years a director of the Royal Opera House, Covent Garden, and he was also a trustee of the National Gallery. His scattered articles and printed lectures continued to appear in a collected edition edited by Henry Hardy, which included also a magnificent set of memorial addresses in praise of friends

– Maurice Bowra, Hubert Henderson, Chaim Weizmann, Richard Pares, Lewis Namier, Edmund Wilson among others. Perhaps the most romantic and moving of all his essays on persons is his account of his two visits (1945 and 1957) to the Soviet Union; the essay has the title Two Russian Poets, and concerns Boris Pasternak and Anna Akhmatova, with both of whom he established strong personal ties. Akhmatova addressed some of her later poems to him.

Outstanding among his publications are The Hedgehog and the Fox (1953); Historical Inevitability (1954), an essay on Tolstoy; Two Concepts of Liberty (1959), his inaugural lecture as professor at Oxford, which introduced a very influential distinction between positive and negative conceptions of freedom; Russian Thinkers (1978), on 19th-century thought and the intelligentsia, and Against the Current (1979), essays on Machiavelli, Vico, and on various critics of scientific optimism and the Enlightenment. There is a unity of point of view in all these essays – and, indeed, in subsequent works of collected pieces such as The Study of Reality: Studies in Ideas and their History (1996) and The Proper Study of Mankind (1997); the point of view is liberal and pluralistic in ethics throughout, but Berlin never shared Mill's belief in the possibility of some radical reform of society. He believed that human aspirations and ideals are incurably divergent and can not be made harmonious without violence and suffering.

Part of the charm of his writing, and part of its wide appeal, comes from the spontaneity of a speaking force. The tone is far from academic, being rather worldly and free, even free-wheeling. Berlin had no ambition to produce a great work, an impressive monument of prose. His nature required that his work should be scattered and various and not confined to a single discipline, and that it should be accidental, in the sense of being a response to some demand made upon him rather than planned on his own initiative. In respect of his public performances, he thought of himself as a taxi rather than as a hired car.

His hero was Alexander Herzen, to whose memoirs he wrote an introduction. Classical music of the classical age, together with Italian opera, were always at the centre of his life, and his bias towards Rossini and Verdi conveyed his sense of pleasure and his love of the uninhibited expression of feeling.

But, finally, it has to be said that his extraordinary hold upon the minds and affections of very different people in several generations probably owed more to the delight of his conversation and to the innate benevolence and humanity of his personality than to his books, which have only been fully appreciated at their true worth in his later years. There was never the slightest suggestion of pretence or of self-assertion, or of the desire to dominate which sometimes accompany great intellectual powers and a worldwide academic reputation.

He was genuinely surprised by his own apparent eminence and by the accolades he received and the admiration which he evoked in many different circles; as a young man he had not expected anything of the kind, and this surprise was always evident in his manner. He did not aspire to be learned in any one discipline, but he had a great range of accurate knowledge and this entered in fascinating detail into his conversation: knowledge of contemporary personalities in England, Europe and the United States, of Russian life and literature, of Jewish history, of the history of philosophy and the history of music, of the history of scholarship and political theory and of much of modern European history.

He had a wonderful memory, both capacious and exact, and, if asked, he might, for instance, recall the titles and plots of some fifty or more Jules Verne novels. His older friends used to complain that his immense range of knowledge was inexplicable, since he always seemed to be either talking or listening to music, and as a young man he was scarcely ever found just reading. Yet his memory for people, dead and alive, was prodigious in its long reach and in its detail. He was a constant source of gaiety and of lightness among friends, and he was always attracted to gaiety and to originality in others. It was readily seen that he was deeply serious and reflective, both in his moral and in his aesthetic concerns, but he was never solemn. He shared with David Hume that quality which caused Hume to be called in France le bon David: the power to spread the enjoyment of life around him.

Isaiah Berlin was knighted in 1957. His admission in 1971 to the Order of Merit, leading to his being its senior commoner member, was an appropriate recognition of his many-sided eminence, including public service alongside academic achievement.

In 1956 he married Aline (née de Gunzbourg), who survives him.

Yehudi Menuhin

Musical genius who befriended innumerable good causes
March 13, 1999

Lord Menuhin, OM, violinist, conductor and philanthropist, died yesterday aged 82. He was born in New York on April 22, 1916.

Few people have ever lived so long with such fame as Yehudi Menuhin. As a child prodigy he played the violin in public from the age of seven, and was soon acclaimed as a genius; 75 years later he was still in the public eye, as much for his work for noble causes as for his music. He believed in and argued for green issues long before that term was invented.

At times, the fervour with which he espoused good works, and the sympathetic range of his ear and eye, made it seem as though he were the guardian of the human conscience. He persuaded politicians to listen to his views and sometimes even to go along with them. He was a regular contributor to the letters page of The Times, most recently as one of the signatories to a denunciation of the film Hilary and Jackie, about the cellist Jacqueline du Pre. The list of organisations of which he was founder, patron or a committee member ran to some 15 pages. They ranged from Justice for Tibet International to groups opposed to the fluoridation of water. At one time he even ran an organic food shop in Baker Street.

He championed the young as founder of the Yehudi Menuhin School in Surrey, which numbered Nigel Kennedy among its prize pupils, and the Menuhin Music Academy in Gstaad. In 1977 he founded Live Music Now, an organisation which enables young people to purchase concert tickets cheaply. As president of the Musicians International Mutual Aid Fund he helped to support the not so young.

Those who talked to him usually came away uplifted by the encounter. He had, one observer remarked, "an astonishing capacity for reminding people of the more generous side of their nature".

George Steiner went further and said that Menuhin was "probably the best-loved personality in the history of the performing arts".

There was, though, a price to pay for the aura of saintliness which followed Yehudi Menuhin around the world from his house in Belgravia. He was mocked behind his back for his devotion to the three Ys: yoga, yoghurt and Yehudi. Music critics were apt, especially in later years, to complain that he simply did too much; they were fond of pointing out the technical imperfections of his playing while paying tribute to its emotional content. Even as just a commentator as Desmond Shawe-Taylor – reviewing the collection of five CDs issued in 1991 to celebrate Menuhin's 75th birthday – wrote: "Perhaps no violinist of the first order has been so continuously busy as conductor and organiser, or had quite so technically chequered a career."

Others saw deeper flaws, in the man as well as in his music. Another supposed celebration of his 75th birthday, Tony Palmer's documentary Menuhin: A Family Portrait for Channel 4, was considerably less welcome than the collection of CDs. Palmer's thesis was that Menuhin had spent his life in the grip of two domineering women, his mother, Marutha, and his second wife, Diana. (Menuhin's first marriage to the Australian heiress, Nora Nicholas, was, according to Palmer, a desperate and unsuccessful attempt to cut loose from Marutha's apron strings.) The film dredged up jealousy from Yehudi's sister Yaltah and suggested that he had been a poor father to his four children (two from each marriage). Interviews with all four children did little to dispel this view.

Yehudi Menuhin was deeply wounded by all this, and the scars took a long time to heal. He tried to prevent publication of the book that Palmer subsequently wrote, but succeeded only in forcing a change of publisher. Friends told the rather unworldly Menuhin that he had been foolish to trust Palmer.

On one point Tony Palmer could not be challenged: Yehudi Menuhin had a very strange upbringing. He and his two sisters were educated at home and allowed none of the usual contacts with other children and teachers. Possibly motivated by their own privations, their Russian parents were determined that the children, and especially Yehudi, should succeed at the highest level. The cost in terms of childhood pleasures was enormous: bicycles and horses were banned in case an accident could affect a finger needed to play an instrument. Yehudi's mother, who came from Tartar as well as

Jewish stock, was highly selective when choosing whom her son should meet.

Yehudi Menuhin was given a toy violin when very small, but smashed it when he found that it would not "sing". He took his first violin lessons shortly after turning four and went to study with Louis Persinger, to whom he regularly paid tribute. His first professional engagement was in San Francisco when he was eight, and there he played Lalo's Symphonie espagnole. His New York debut came in 1926, and by the time he had reached 13 he had appeared in London, Berlin and Paris. The Paris debut in 1927 with the Lamoureux Orchestra – the Lalo again and the Tchaikovsky Concerto – was particularly impressive. Menuhin stayed on to study there under the Romanian composer and violinist George Enescu, who duly became another major influence.

Enescu's earthiness and vigour provided the perfect antidote to the cerebral and isolated world of the adolescent Menuhin. It was the performance of the Beethoven Concerto, with which Menuhin became particularly associated, under Fritz Busch in New York in November 1927 that turned him into a serious player with an immediate following. Busch, at first sceptical, had declared that you don't hire Jackie Coogan to play Hamlet, but he was soon converted by Menuhin's amazing precociousness, declaring "You can play anything with me, any time, anywhere". The critic Olin Downes wrote: "Few violinists of years of experience, known to the public, have played Beethoven with as true a feeling for his form and content."

Berlin acclaimed him in 1928, when he played with the Philharmonic under Bruno Walter; London followed a year later. His debut at the Queen's Hall on November 4 was with the LSO under Busch. The Times critic, though not ecstatic, was admiring.

By then, Menuhin was making his first records. He continued to study with Enescu and also with Adolf Busch. Already the depth and musicality of his performances were those of a player of much more mature years. He was truly a phenomenon. Indeed, few violinists past or present have tackled the Bach Chaconne or the Mozart and Beethoven concertos at the age of 12 or 13 with so many insights. On his second visit to London in 1932 he was chosen to record the Elgar Concerto with the composer, a disc that has remained a classic, unsurpassed to this day.

That year he tackled Bach and Mozart under Beecham at the Albert Hall, followed by the Elgar Concerto in the second half, conducted by the composer. The performance of the 15-year-old boy with the 75-year-old composer was peculiarly moving: the reception was rapturous. The Times critic capitulated: "Throughout one was impressed by the sympathy of the phrasing and the general vitality of the playing."

Menuhin continued his international career until the war, except for a break in 1936 to study and enjoy his private life. During the war be played more than 500 concerts for the Allied troops. He also broadcast frequently, introducing the Bartok Concerto No 2, then considered unfathomable by most people. Bartok wrote a solo sonata for Menuhin in 1942.

A studio account of the Brahms Concerto with the BBC, recorded during the war and recently resurrected from the BBC archives, shows Menuhin at this period in his most glorious form, eloquent and expansive. After the war he was the first artist to play at the Paris Opera when it reopened after the Occupation. He was also the first Jewish artist to play after the war with the Berlin Philharmonic, under Wilhelm Furtwangler (a gesture that brought him much criticism from those who felt that Furtwangler should not have remained in Germany under the Nazis). He frequently gave recitals at this time with his sisters Hephzibah and Yaltah, both accomplished pianists, and with his brother-in-law, the pianist Louis Kentner.

An experience that marked Menuhin deeply came in 1945, when he set off for Germany in the company of Benjamin Britten. They took with them, in Menuhin's own recollection, "more or less the whole standard violin literature – concerti, sonatas, little pieces – and played it, without rehearsal, in the ruins of the Third Reich". At Belsen they played twice in one afternoon. The prison huts had been burnt down. The surviving inmates of the camp, liberated some weeks before, had been transferred to the SS barracks, and dressed in clothing fashioned from army blankets. It was to them that Britten and Menuhin played. "I shall not forget that afternoon as long as I live," the violinist later wrote. In the decades that followed, several members of that audience were to make themselves known backstage after one of his concerts.

In 1947 Yehudi Menuhin took as his second wife the ballet dancer Diana Gould, in a marriage that was to last for the rest of his life. She was handsome and tall, possibly too tall for an ideal ballerina. But that did not prevent both Diaghilev and Pavlova engaging her for their companies. "A pity," Diana Menuhin remarked with typical acerbity, "they each died soon afterwards." She would probably have been a formidable actress, but she preferred to devote her life to her husband. This she did assiduously, with little verbal restraint, guarding him whenever possible from the stream of visitors seeking his patronage.

From 1959 Meuhin made his home in London. It was about this time that he began to widen his activities. He directed, and played regularly at, the Bath Festival (1958-68), the Windsor Festival (1969-72) and the Gstaad Festival (from 1956). At Gstaad he made a second home, and there he dispensed wisdom on a wide variety of subjects. For a while he had his own chamber orchestra, which he conducted and with which he appeared as soloist.

He also began to conduct many of the major symphony orchestras of the world. His achievements in this field have perhaps been underrated. Players responded warmly to his innate musicianship, and despite obvious flaws in his baton technique, his readings often attained a notable homogeneity and strength, though his repertoire was confined. He was associate conductor and president of the Royal Philharmonic Orchestra from 1982, and principal guest conductor of the English String Orchestra from 1988.

In the meantime he interested himself in Indian music and appeared in programmes with Ravi Shankar, the celebrated sitar player. Jazz was yet another enthusiasm, and he played and recorded in a hugely popular double act with the jazz violinist Stephane Grappelli.

In 1962 he founded the Menuhin School at Stoke d'Abernon in Surrey. There he insisted that students should be taught how to develop as rounded people, not just musicians. Pupils were trained as much in chamber music as in solo work. Many have gone on to important careers. Menuhin frequently held master classes at the school and it may well prove the most lasting monument to his generosity of spirit.

Menuhin's tone was rich and warm, his style overtly and spontaneously expressive, with just enough classical control for it not become in any way effusive. Through it, he communicated with composers: Bartok was overwhelmed by Menuhin's playing of his challenging music and composed his final major work, the Sonata for Solo Violin, especially for him; Walton also wrote a fine sonata.

Critics detected deficiencies both of spontaneity and technique in Menuhin's playing as his career progressed, and the violinist himself acknowledged that he had at several points in his musical life had to rethink his whole approach to his art. But no one could deny that he always enjoyed a special rapport with his audiences. As he grew older, his faithful and considerable public showed itself more than willing to make any allowances that might be needed for advancing years. Signs of technical fallibility, or of a certain loss of breadth in his playing, were more than compensated for by other, interpretative rewards.

Menuhin never lost his gift of commanding a hall's undivided attention with the spirituality of his interpretations. Well into his seventies, the now slight, even vulnerable, but wholly concentrated figure on the platform remained a potent focus of public acclaim.

Yehudi Menuhin was knighted in 1956 and appointed OM in 1987. In 1993 he was created a life peer. He is survived by Lady Menuhin and by their two sons, and by the son and daughter of his first marriage.

Maria Hollan

A life of handicap, good and ill fortune, and faith
September 29, 1999

Beyond her circles of friends in Britain, France and Hungary, few have heard of Maria Hollan. But through nine decades of handicap, poverty and misfortune she displayed a courage, confidence, simple piety and joie de vivre that never ceased to amaze and delight those around her.

She was born Maria Nagy de Felsoor, the daughter of a middling landowner in western Hungary. At the age of two she was crippled by polio, and though a German surgeon gave her back some mobility, she depended throughout her long life on sticks, crutches and unyielding determination.

At the age of 24 she married Erno Hollan, a landowner like her father and the son and grandson of men murdered in the brief Bela Kun Red Republic of 1919. The Depression drove him off his land to find work in Budapest. There she built on her Roman Catholic faith and her insatiable interest in other people a life that was to carry her through the vicissitudes of the next 25 years.

First war and then communism descended upon Hungary. While her husband fought in the Hungarian army, Maria Hollan and her two sons took refuge in the Benedictine monastery at Pannonhalma, not far from the estate on which she had grown up. After the war she got a job as a translator at the British Legation in Budapest, a job which in 1953 saved the family, if only by a whisker, from deportation to a village at the other end of the country. There she and other Hungarian staff brought British diplomats the whispers of rumour which alone in the Stalinist years added colour to the obligatory greyness of the press and radio.

In 1956, just before the revolution, Maria Hollan's husband died of lung cancer. Three months later her two sons fled to the West. So did many of her friends. But she stayed on, translating for the legation, teaching young diplomats Hungarian, a class enemy and self-confessed opponent of the Communist regime. Inevitably she came under pressure to report on the Legation's doings to the secret police.

All Western legations took the obvious precautions against Hungarian employees who were exposed to such pressure. In the British Legation Hollan never got beyond that carapace, never learnt a British secret; but over the years it became apparent how resolute was her resistance to secret police pressure. Her persecutors told her that she would lose her job and her flat, that she would never see her sons again, that they would drive her mad. Finally they gave her a choice between forced emigration and a worse fate. When in 1963 she left Hungary with her crutches and two pathetic suitcases in a British Legation car they asked her what she was doing, leaving her country in the company of imperialist spies.

There followed another surgical operation in the series which over the next 30 years were to keep Hollan more or less mobile. She got a job reading the Hungarian press for the Information Research Department of the Foreign Office. She got a flat and took up with old Hungarian friends in exile. A typical Sunday involved Mass at the Oratory and lunch in Richmond, bridge in Kensington and dinner in Highgate, all courtesy of London Transport and her indefatigable way with crutches.

She moved to Paris to be near her sons. She took up the same untiring round of activity: a visit here, Mass at every opportunity, and teaching the catechism to French children who started sceptically and ended with at least a modicum of her faith. She went to Mexico, Canada and South Africa to visit distant family. She went back to Hungary for religious retreats and thermal baths, returning with strong views on the Hungarian young, politics and society and the condition of the Church. She wrote a memoir of her life and advised the young on their love affairs and the middle aged on how to bring up their children.

Crippled, impoverished, widowed, exiled, she had every worldly reason for embitterment. Against these things she set her faith and her energy and her indomitable spirit, and lived happy and holy into her tenth decade.

Maria Hollan is survived by her two sons.

Maria Hollan, Hungarian émigré, died in Paris on September 22 aged 93. She was born in Hercegfalva, Hungary, on July 14, 1906.

Eva Neurath

"One of Hitler's gifts to Britain": bookseller, publisher and early feminist

4 January 2000

Eva Neurath, publisher, died in London on December 27 aged 91. She was born in Berlin on August 22, 1908.

Eva Neurath was one of Hitler's gifts to Britain. Fifty one years ago, together with Walter Neurath, another refugee who later became her third husband, she founded Thames & Hudson, a publishing house specialising in books about the visual arts. It now has the largest such list in the English language and is one of the most remarkable success stories in British publishing. It remains one of the few independent, family-owned publishers in Britain.

Born Eva Itzig as the youngest of five sisters into a financially secure, well educated and politically questioning family, she was brought up in a villa in Berlin Tempelhof. Her father manufactured buttons and her mother was a passionate socialist committed to women's rights. Eva early acquired some of her mother's uncompromising principles.

She left school at 14, not because of her own poor performance but as a protest at the expulsion of some of her friends. She nevertheless always regretted that this show of solidarity prevented her from studying at a university.

Eva's father died early, and her mother then married a solicitor employed by Ufa, the German film producer. While at school as well as later, Eva worked as an extra in several movies, the most famous of which was Faust, directed by F.W. Murnau in 1926. She also met the actress Pola Negri, who became a friend, and Ernst Lubitsch, the director.

But Eva's main work was for a bookseller, publisher and auctioneer. When she was 18, not long after she had been summarily fired for some misdemeanour, she married a former colleague,

Ernst Jutrosinski. The marriage lasted for little more than a year, but the couple remained close friends.

By then her mother, her private income destroyed by inflation, had opened what turned out to be a financially disastrous art gallery on the Kurfurstendamm. Eva meanwhile had found employment with Rosenbergs, another, more distinguished antiquarian bookseller. At the same time she came to know many of the outstanding figures in the Berlin cultural world, in the late 1920s experiencing a renaissance.

Small, vivacious and strikingly attractive, Eva Jutrosinski met her second husband, Wilhelm Feuchtwang, in 1932. An industrial adviser and patent broker, he was the son of the chief rabbi of Vienna, who objected to the proposed marriage until Eva agreed to convert to Judaism. With the wholehearted determination that characterised everything she did, she then maintained a strictly kosher kitchen in the Feuchtwang house on what is now Berlin's Ernst-Reuter-Platz.

Once the Nazis came to power, the dangers multiplied, though neither Eva nor her mother left anyone in doubt about their scorn for Hitler and his policies. When Feuchtwang was arrested in 1937, suspected of helping Jews to transfer funds abroad, his pregnant wife was terrified. Once released, Feuchtwang urgently considered emigration.

After the annexation of Austria in 1938 he and Eva left for Holland with their infant son Stephan. They had only ten marks between them and eluded the Gestapo by just five hours. They lived in Rotterdam for a year at the house of Feuchtwang's brother, the city's chief rabbi.

They then moved on to England, where Feuchtwang had business connections and where he was soon interned on the Isle of Man as an enemy alien. Eva, alone with Stephan, had to subsist on ten shillings a week. She had been close to starvation before – as a young girl in Berlin after the First World War – and now was again, on one occasion having to sell her carpet to buy food.

She was about to become a domestic servant when she received a visit from a recently released internee with a message from her husband. The visitor was Walter Neurath, the Austrian managing director of Adprint, a London book packaging company founded by another refugee. For Adprint Neurath had designed and produced the cheap but bibliophilic King Penguin series, inspired by the German Insel Bucherei, and had also devised a series of illustrated books called Britain in Pictures. He offered Eva Feuchtwang a job and by the end of the war she was head of Adprint's art department.

Until then, she would later explain, she had been a devoted wife frustrated by her lack of education and inability to realise her talents. Now for the first time she began to flourish. In 1949 she invested her savings – £150 – in a new publishing venture conceived by Neurath. He invested somewhat more and persuaded a printer and a firm of blockmakers to work initially for nothing. The name of the new publishers, Thames & Hudson, announced its intention to exploit the North American as well as the British market.

From the beginning it specialised in books about art, a subject then virtually ignored by English publishers. Following the lead given by Britain in Pictures, the reproductions were closely integrated with the texts. Thames & Hudson was also a pioneer in packaging and distributing books for American museums, and in co-publication deals with continental houses. The high costs of printing in colour were therefore shared, the same texts, translated into several languages, were printed in one location, and huge economies were made.

Thames & Hudson also introduced a series of remarkably cheap, uniform, lavishly illustrated, expertly written but accessible monographs that were among the earliest original paperbacks. Called the World of Art, the series has educated several generations of students and art lovers and is one of the reasons for the present popularity of the visual arts in Britain. The World of Art, always a mainstay of Thames & Hudson, now comprises more than 150 titles, some of them long since established as classics.

Walter Neurath was the driving force behind the firm's success, but Eva Feuchtwang's contribution was incalculably great, not least because she was the presiding genius of the art department, creating and developing an unmistakable house style. Her marriage to Feuchtwang continued for some time, though her partnership with Neurath soon extended beyond business. They married in 1953, three years after the death of Neurath's first wife, Marianne.

The Neuraths shared a beautiful house in Holly Terrace, near the summit of Highgate West Hill in North London, that contained a remarkable collection of works by Klimt, Schiele, Kokoschka and Ben Nicholson, and sculptures by Henry Moore. There were also paintings by Sidney Nolan and Arthur Boyd, about whose work Thames & Hudson published the earliest monographs. They, like

Moore and Kokoschka, became close friends, as did most of the other artists, critics, historians and archaeologists, who were the authors or subjects of Thames & Hudson publications.

When Walter Neurath died of cancer in 1967 his son Thomas became managing director but his widow's influence remained strong. Indeed, she remained the company chairman until her death. Although Thomas Neurath assumed responsibility for all commissioning and his sister Constance eventually took control of the art department, Eva was anything but a nominal member of the team. Even in her late eighties she continued to develop and control her own projects, bringing to them her extensive knowledge of art, especially modern, of book production, and the benefits of her innumerable international contacts.

In old age as in her youth, Eva Neurath was a disconcertingly charming, attractive and witty woman. Few could resist her requests or take offence at her criticisms, though some of her employees, especially her secretaries, often wished she was less dictatorial and prone to intemperate outbursts. Other employees, among them some of the most brilliant editors of their generation, often felt underconsulted, underpaid and underappreciated. Thames & Hudson, they felt, operated too much like a feudal fiefdom.

Eva Neurath worked at the firm until comparatively recently, her presence in the labyrinthine offices that, until last year, occupied a row of five shabby Georgian houses in Bloomsbury always signalled by her Bentley parked on the road outside, a disabled sticker (she suffered from poor eyesight for many years) discouraging the traffic wardens. When in London rather than at her house in Tuscany, she liked to go for lunch to the White Tower restaurant a few hundred yards away, driven there by her imperturbable chauffeur, Bill. She always took the same table that Walter Neurath did, usually entertaining existing and potential authors, for whom she would also sometimes cook dinner in her basement kitchen at Highgate.

Eva Neurath was married three times. She is survived by her son Stephan, her stepdaughter Constance, and her stepson Thomas.

Bernie Grant

Supporter of the dispossessed whose reaction to the Broadwater Farm riots brought him lasting notoriety

April 10, 2000

Bernie Grant's career was peppered with infamous outbursts, but easily the most notorious came after the Broadwater Farm riots of 1985 in which PC Keith Blakelock was murdered. The riots had been sparked by the death of a woman during a police raid, and Blakelock was trying to flee when he was set upon by up to 30 people armed with knives, swords and other weapons. In front of television cameras, Grant, as leader of the local council, proclaimed: "The youths around here believe the police were to blame and what they got was a bloody good hiding."

Douglas Hurd, then Home Secretary, branded him "the high priest of racial conflict", but Grant protested that he had simply been summing up the rioters' point of view. When he discovered more about the circumstances, he condemned the murder, but he always found it hard to escape the public odium that his first reaction had caused.

If he had not realised at first how inflammatory it was for a politician to appear to be taking the side of a violent mob against the police, he was certainly shocked, at a black Islamic rally a decade later, to be booed for saying "We are sorry a police officer lost his life". Some people, he found, had assumed that he endorsed their hatred and violence.

After ten years as a member of Haringey Borough Council (the last two as leader), Grant was elected to the safe Labour seat of Tottenham at the general election of 1987. This was the crowning moment of a career in which he had often asked uncomfortable questions and challenged those arrangements and assumptions which put the immigrant community in a position inferior to that of the rest of British society.

A year or so later Grant was sitting at the top table in a draughty hall listening as angry parents from the Broadwater Farm estate voiced their continuing frustrations. As the atmosphere grew more inflamed, Grant rose and calmly urged his audience not just to complain, but to become agents of change: "You didn't just vote for me to say how bad everything is," he told them. "You put me there to make things different." And in the years that followed the riots, he worked hard to improve relations between police and residents as "community policing" became the watchword of inner-city forces.

Nevertheless, he continued to attract opprobrium by supporting Winston Silcott, who in 1987 was convicted along with two other men of Blakelock's murder. In the absence of witness statements, the conviction was based on an alleged confession, but Silcott's lawyers said that the police notes had been altered. The case was referred to the Court of Appeal, which quashed the conviction in 1991, after the cases of the Birmingham Six and the Guildford Four had been overturned on similar grounds. Grant promptly called for the policemen involved to be prosecuted, and for a review of the criminal justice system. Silcott, however, remained – and remains – in prison, for the murder, on a different occasion, of Tony Smith, though he was later awarded compensation for wrongful conviction.

Grant was involved in several other cases involving racial minorities or immigrants, such as the death of Joy Gardner, who died from suffocation in 1993 when police gagged and bound her with adhesive tape while trying to deport her. Grant might be a firebrand on a political platform or in a television studio, but he was motivated by real concern and a sense of justice. He was kind and gentle in private, fervent in every cause he espoused – and pragmatic enough behind the scenes to be called upon in recent months to advise both the Prime Minister and Jack Straw.

Bernard Alexander Montgomery Grant – his name was a tribute to Britain's wartime desert generals – was born in British Guiana (now Guyana) where he was educated by Jesuits at St Stanislaus College, Georgetown. Arriving in Britain with his teacher parents in 1963, and with socialist views part formed by an uncle who was a president of the British Guiana TUC, he soon devoted himself to the issues of race.

He dropped out of an engineering degree at Heriot-Watt University, Edinburgh, when he discovered that its work experience scholarships in South Africa were offered to whites only, and he then became successively a railway clerk, a telephonist and, in 1978, a trade union official with NUPE.

He was an early member of the Workers' Revolutionary Party, and his leadership of Haringey earned him the embarrassed wrath of Neil Kinnock's regime, which was anxious to dissociate itself from the more extreme antics of the party. But Grant soon found that in local government he could change things. He told an interviewer in 1994 that "I soon had some real power and could make things happen for people".

His local constituency party deselected the veteran MP Norman Atkinson, so handing the safe Labour seat to Grant, and when he reached Westminster he became a member of the left-wing Campaign Group, along with Ken Livingstone, Tony Benn and Dennis Skinner. He also chaired the all-party group on race and community, and during his 13 years in Parliament he became a voice for the dispossessed and for his constituents.

As one of four black MPs to enter a House of Commons that had been all-white for 65 years, and as the first seriously to champion a racial as well as a geographical constituency, Grant arrived for the State Opening of Parliament each year in flowing African robes. In truth he looked no more bizarre than many of the other colourful characters who populate this auspicious annual occasion.

He soon found himself disenchanted with the workings of Parliament: "I quickly realised MPs haven't got any power at all," he said. "You have to beg people to do things for you, which are frustrating." Nevertheless, Westminster became a national platform for his perpetual indignation, and there was no shortage of causes for "Barmy Bernie" to rail about.

Whether or not the Labour Party was in government, Grant remained firmly in opposition: his own party was more racist than the Conservatives ("because the Tories are business people, travel abroad, eat the food of other peoples and tend to be much more worldly-wise"); making war on Saddam Hussein was "racially motivated"; and Tony Blair was warned that he could expect "severe difficulties" unless he moved away from his moderate manifesto.

His suggestion in 1995 that the government should allot £100,000 each to black Britons who chose to "return" to Africa or the Caribbean led to accusations that he had become a member of the most diehard "send-'em-back" school of racism. But Grant said that it was the very least a once imperial nation could do for those from the former colonies who had served it so well.

Although scornful of Britain's treatment of the subjects of the Empire, he was a staunch monarchist with a great affection for both the Queen and the Commonwealth – which he felt served Britain far better than the European Union. During the ill-judged and bad-tempered television debate Monarchy: The Nation Decides, his was a lone left-wing voice championing the House of Windsor.

And while some leftwingers might advocate a liberal approach to school uniform, school competition and school discipline, Grant was decidedly in favour of all three, often recalling with dewy eyes his childhood in British Guiana where he was educated in a smart blazer. He regretted sending his children to a state school where, he said, they received an "inferior" education.

Some of his interventions were more deeply felt than deeply considered. In 1997 as the Government dithered over its response to the volcano on Montserrat, Grant was stomping the foothills of the Caribbean island complaining about "betrayal" and "colonial injustice"; and when the Metropolitan Police Commissioner, Sir Paul Condon, reported that young black men make up the biggest single category of muggers in the capital, Grant was apoplectic in the face of the fact.

But recently, particularly as his diabetes and kidney failure took hold, Grant – like his friend Ken Livingstone – subtly shifted from hard man of the Left to caring man of the people. He became a milder, more accommodating figure, who by the end had all-but lived down his most ill-advised remark.

"People think I am just a police-hating, criminal-loving bad sort," he once said. "I have been called an uppity nigger. But I am not English. And in the Caribbean we have a different way of looking at things. I am outspoken and challenging."

Grant is survived by his second wife, Sharon Lawrence, whom he married in 1998, and by three sons from his first marriage.

Bernie Grant, Labour MP for Tottenham since 1987, was born in British Guiana on February 17, 1944. He died of a heart attack on April 8 aged 56.

Paul Hamlyn

Publisher, populist, plutocrat and philanthropist
September 4, 2001

Lord Hamlyn, CBE, publisher and philanthropist, was born in Berlin on February 12, 1926. He died in London on August 31, 2001, aged 75.

Paul Hamlyn was a publishing phenomenon. Though he did not start from rags, he achieved riches never previously dreamt of in the book publishing world, and he did it not by discovering great literary talents, but by establishing populist, good value series and imprints, which sold in their millions. Like the great showman William Foyle, he saw books as a commodity, and he piled them high and sold them cheap. By the time he had sold the companies, sometimes several times over, he was worth in excess of £200 million, yet by his own admission he was no bibliophile.

The unease he felt at being at once a lifelong socialist and hugely rich was in part mitigated by the generosity of the Paul Hamlyn Foundation, which was set up in 1987 with an initial endowment of about £50 million. Its main areas are education and the arts in Britain, and orthopaedic work in developing countries.

His generous donations became a particular focus of public attention at the beginning of this year when the Labour Party refused to name a donor who had provided it with two million pounds just before its own measures compelling parties to reveal their large benefactors became law. Opponents and the press assumed that Labour was cheating, but it turned out that Hamlyn had asked for the gift not to be publicised, someone had naively accepted, and Hamlyn had then been so gravely ill that it was impossible to ask his permission to reveal his name. When he found that his donation was becoming a public embarrassment, he promptly agreed to be named and his statement in which he said he was proud of his role in helping Labour was fashioned with such grace that it made the suspicions look unfounded and inept.

Hamlyn had been giving money to the Labour Party for years, but most of his donations elsewhere had been uncontroversial. He supported the Royal Opera House with £200,000 a year (from 1994), established a fund to support artists, and bought theatre and opera tickets for children who had never before attended a performance.

He had an introspective streak, and a dry, lugubrious sense of humour, not least at his own expense: he told one of his doctors that, whatever else might be wrong with him, he had a bad long-term case of MEM, or Middle European Melancholia. He saw money as merely an index of commercial success, and though he lived in some style, it often seemed that he was happiest when he could pack all he cared about into a suitcase.

Paul Bertrand Hamlyn was the son of a distinguished Berlin paediatrician, Professor Richard Hamburger (Paul changed his name in his teens to avoid the nickname "Sausage" at school), and the prosperous family home was filled with books – as well as a nanny, a cook and a pastry cook. But by the middle of the 1930s the ominous future for German Jews was clear. The family moved to Britain, and after the death of Paul's father in 1940 their financial circumstances were greatly changed.

Paul's elder brother, the poet Michael Hamburger, was able to go to Westminster School and Christ Church, Oxford, but when the war started in 1939 Paul was at St Christopher's School in Letchworth. He hated it. It was a Quaker school (his mother had Quakerish leanings), espousing vegetarianism and pacifism. He was a meat-eater and had no reason to feel pacific towards Nazi Germany. As soon as he had his matriculation certificate, and before he was 15, he left.

He immediately began to show his extraordinary energy and ingenuity. When, at 16, he became correspondence editor of Country Life, many of the incoming letters took on a new liveliness: he later admitted to writing them himself. Then, as an assistant at Zwemmer's bookshop, he was on good gossiping terms with the luminaries and eccentrics of wartime Fitzrovia. As a Bevin Boy (after a short spell with Samuel French, the theatrical publisher) he moonlighted from his job in a Monmouthshire pit as a part-time journalist for the South Wales Argus, as an excursion coach driver and as a weekend rep for a paperback publisher.

In 1948, with a legacy of around £350, he started his own bookshop in Camden Town. It was near to London Zoo where, the following year, the polar bear cub Brumas was to become the reigning star. Hamlyn's shop spread across the pavement and sold the zoo-bound public so many copies of a pictorial Brumas book that he was able to start as a publisher by setting up Books for Pleasure. It was a side-door entry, since the business was largely in remaindered books (there was then less competition and more profit in remainders), but it financed his entry into real publishing with the establishment of Spring Books and Hamlyn Books. By 1960 these enterprises were widely known, very successful, and already bore the essential Hamlyn hallmarks.

He did his printing where it was cheapest (and where disruptive union activity was least likely): then it was in Eastern Europe, later it was done, on a very large scale and with tremendous organisation, in the Far East. The titles, all nonfiction, were meticulously planned, targeted and vigorously marketed, not only to booksellers but to newsagents, specialist retailers, department stores and large chains such as Marks & Spencer.

Hamlyn's contracts with authors were seldom on a royalty basis, and he generally paid them a single flat fee. He worked very hard, sometimes twelve hours a day (and was still doing so a quarter of a century later, after he had become rich). And he was a demanding employer: if a crisis meant that he must work until after midnight, his staff had to do so too.

He saw the commercial need to cast his net wide and, together with EMI, he set up Music for Pleasure, selling cheap LPs and aiming to do for recorded music what Books for Pleasure did for the printed word. Then, in 1964, in Hamlyn's own phrase, "Cecil King seduced me", and he sold his business to IPC. He had not intended to sell what was a thriving operation, but King, then head of the huge group, offered £2.2 million. Hamlyn was still under 40, and millionaires were rare creatures in those days.

King also promised Hamlyn that, as chief of IPC's already extensive book-publishing sector, he could become the biggest publisher in the world, but the promise was never fulfilled, and the next six years proved frustrating. King, whom Hamlyn liked, was replaced by Don Ryder, whom he detested – and the feeling was mutual. Furthermore, IPC's ponderous bureaucracy was utterly alien to his decisive entrepreneurial temperament. When IPC bought Butterworth in 1968 he was put in charge of the company, but was ill at ease with a traditional legal publisher, and the appointment proved one of his rare failures.

He left IPC in 1970 and his friend Rupert Murdoch instantly recruited him as joint managing director of News International. Illness terminated this appointment (although he stayed on the News International board for another 16 years), and in 1972 he launched his most remarkable creation, Octopus Books.

It started small: his initial investment was only £10,000. It had the same rationale as the original Hamlyn Books, though now he subcontracted even more determinedly – he always declared himself to be an inefficient administrative manager of a large staff – and he persuaded several of his new managers to invest their money in their careers, even if it meant mortgaging their homes. (Two of them later found themselves worth about £6 million each.) Hamlyn worked and travelled for Octopus with all his old energy and zeal. The Bookseller dubbed him the Whizz Squid.

The small company grew and prospered. Within six years its pre-tax profit was almost three million pounds. A stream of acquisitions included Brimax, Websters and Bookwise, Mitchell Beazley, George Philip and some of the most famous imprints in the business: Heinemann, Secker & Warburg and Methuen – as well as Hamlyn Publishing. The purchase of Hamlyn Publishing (very cheaply, for it had fallen on hard times) gave Paul Hamlyn particular pleasure, since he had long been embarrassed by the widespread belief that he still controlled the then ailing company that bore his name.

When the Octopus Group went public in 1983, Hamlyn became nearly £40 million richer. And he became richer still in 1987 when Reed International, which had evolved efficiently from the clumsy IPC conglomerate of earlier years, bought Octopus for a reputed £530 million: he and various family trusts had always maintained financial control of the group, and he was said to have made £150 million personally.

Hamlyn joined the Reed board, playing a less active role in Octopus affairs, and by 1990 was its non-executive chairman. But he continued to be a significant force in the business, especially in major deals such as Reed's acquisition of 50 per cent of BCA, the largest (by far) of Britain's book clubs. He continued too to travel a great deal, particularly to India, combining pleasure with the books business.

He devoted himself, too, to the activities of the Paul Hamlyn Foundation, which really got into its stride when it moved to the 18th-century Sussex House in Hammersmith in 1989. By the early 1990s it was disbursing some £3 million a year. Its grants, in which Hamlyn took a strong personal interest, ranged from one million pounds to the Bodleian Library in 1989 to fifty pounds for a playgroup. In 1997 he pledged £900,000 to the British Museum to buy books to furnish the Hamlyn library, in the Round Reading Room.

Unsurprisingly, Hamlyn had his enemies, and some of those he had outmanoeuvred complained that he was a very sharp operator. Harold Macmillan, wearing his publishing rather than his political hat, memorably said: "We can't have the likes of Paul Hamlyn in British publishing."

But he also had many friends; indeed friendship was of great importance to his quick, mercurial nature. He learnt to enjoy his wealth, with much comfortable travel, substantial establishments in Provence, where he lived most of the year, and in London, Gloucestershire and Paris. But in addition to his large philanthropies, he was attractively given to small kindnesses. He was vain in that he greatly enjoyed being in the news because of some striking announcement or coup, but his vanity was small in relation to his achievement.

He was appointed CBE in 1993 and created a life peer five years later.

His first marriage, in 1952 to Eileen Watson, was dissolved in 1969. In 1970 he married Helen Guest, who survives him, as do a son and a daughter of his first marriage.

Ernst Gombrich

Art historian who wrote for the masses

November 6, 2001

Professor Sir Ernst Gombrich, OM, CBE, FBA, art historian, was born in Vienna on March 30, 1909. He died on November 3, 2001, aged 92.

One of those greatly gifted refugee immigrants to this country whose impact on cultural, scientific and social life has been out of all proportion to their numbers, Ernst Gombrich was an influential scholar of art history, as well as being familiar to the general public through his ever-popular outline history, The Story of Art. Since its first appearance in 1950 the book has been through 16 editions, selling more than six million copies and constantly being revised and updated in the light of new discoveries in art and advances in colour printing technology; it is one of the most successful and accomplished works of its kind.

Updating it was a task that Gombrich approached in all humility over the years. He delighted in the capacity which new printing processes gave his publishers to illustrate his insights to rising generations of art lovers, lay and student, who were then able to travel to the sites he named and test out his insights for themselves.

He eagerly welcomed new knowledge. His treatment, in the later editions, of the magnificent classical Greek Riace Bronzes, recovered from the seabed off southern Italy in the 1970s and now displayed – somewhat off the beaten track for the general traveller – in the National Museum at Reggio di Calabria, is characteristic.

Far from finding such a relatively recent discovery difficult or inconvenient to assimilate in a book which might have been thought to have set in its mould, Gombrich had no hesitation in declaring that these magnificent warrior figures added fundamentally to our view of what Greek art was capable of at the apogee of its inspiration. And in a large measure thanks to the treatment he gave them in the later editions of his book, the cryptically named Statua A and Statua B have taken their place alongside the Discobolus of Myron and the Hermes of Praxiteles in the iconography of ancient sculpture.

This was Gombrich the populariser – if, indeed, The Story of Art needs to be pigeonholed as such. Equally influential for art historians and students were his theoretical works, among them Art and Illusion, which took shape as the A. W. Mellon Lectures in the Fine Arts in 1956, and saw the light of day in book form in 1960. Together with the studies Gombrich gathered together in Meditations on a Hobby Horse (1963), it confirmed the arrival in the world of art history of an intelligence of the very first rank.

And yet Gombrich always liked to protest that he was "not very interested in aesthetics or art criticism, because so much of what people write is just an expression of their own emotions." His enterprise, as he saw it, was not to make qualitative judgments – he believed those emerged as the historical consensus of the well-informed – but to discover new facts and to squeeze from them new knowledge. "We must feed on fact, and on observation," he said.

Heritage and tradition were of paramount importance for him. In an age which has tended to place its emphasis on the individual vision, his emphasis was constantly upon precedent and the need for artists to learn their craft. Seeing, he argued, was a skill, and art is a training in perception. The artist learns what and how to see – as well as how to draw, paint or model – from his predecessors.

Gombrich was wary of pronouncements about "the Renaissance" or "Romanticism", and agreed with his friend Karl Popper that history was not an inevitable pattern, that things could have gone another way. For him art history was not about emotions and self-expression, nor about a succession of supposedly self-conscious movements, but was primarily a series of technical advances. Stylistic change was born of individual technical accomplishment: Giotto's realistic rendering of space, Uccello's understanding of perspective, van Eyck's mastery of oil painting.

Such developments gave artists a new medium, which could itself teach them to see in a new way. The artist, Gombrich maintained, "attends to things he can deal with; he attends to what his medium can yield. An etcher will not be interested in colour effects. That is what we call the style of an artist: his mode of attention."

Gombrich was very much a product of his native Vienna, and would probably have remained in Austria and Germany but for the rise of Hitler. Employed as a young research assistant at the Warburg

Institute, which re-established itself in England, he settled in Britain in 1936 and went on to enjoy a uniquely influential position not only in art-historical circles, but in philosophical and allied fields.

Ernst Hans Josef Gombrich was steeped in the intellectual life of Vienna which was shattered by the rise of fascism. His keen intelligence, like his deep love of music, was perhaps directly inherited. His father, Dr Karl Gombrich, was vice-president of a legal disciplinary council. His mother, born Leonie Hock, was a talented pianist and teacher who had been taught by Bruckner, was a friend of Freud and Mahler, and lived long enough to see her son become Slade Professor of Fine Art at Oxford.

Gombrich was educated at the Theresianum and then at Vienna University, where he studied art history under a series of illustrious teachers, including Julius von Schlosser. Although indebted to them, he would vividly recall their amusing, even absurd, quirks, as well as admitting to having been attracted to the lectures on psychology at least as much as to those on art. Psychology was to be the key to many of his later investigations.

Gombrich never had much patience with connoisseurship in the amateur tradition of attributing works of art to individual hands, and during his active life more and more was understood about how artists served apprenticeships and collaborated in studios. Nor was he content to be a narrowly professional art historian researching in archives or even – despite his long career at the Warburg Institute – in purely iconographical studies.

He may have begun with such studies, but he gradually shifted his focus to the study of ideas behind the images. He pursued these less in literary or social terms than in a broadly psychological context, tracing how we perceive them and how they may change. This approach proved significant and fruitful, resulting in work appreciated by philosophers, scientists, artists and educationists.

Gombrich's approach was based on detailed study of particular paintings, and he produced numerous straightforward, well-argued papers on aspects of art history, usually with a Renaissance emphasis. Almost his earliest published work was an exemplary article which appeared in 1934 on Giulio Romano's activity at the Palazzo del Te, in Mantua, constructed as a house for the lover of Federico Gonzaga.

In 1936 Gombrich joined the Warburg. In that year, too, his first book, an English history of the world for children, Weltgeschichte fur Kinder, appeared, the approach of which partly anticipated

The Story of Art. It received a second edition in 1985. In 1940, in collaboration with the psychoanalyst Ernst Kris, he produced a book on caricature.

During the Second World War Gombrich worked in the BBC monitoring service, an experience to which he was to ascribe his rapid acquisition of the flawless English that was to characterise his writings. The daily chores of translating, writing and checking for six strenuous years, were, he said, entirely beneficial in that regard. At the end of the war one of his tasks was to write the note that announced to Churchill that Hitler was dead.

When The Story of Art made its first appearance in 1950 it was immediately recognised as a remarkable achievement, providing – with unobtrusive scholarship and jargon-free simplicity – a coherent account of art through the ages for a wide range of readers. Gombrich was a master of lucid English prose, and succeeded in explaining complicated developments and ideas clearly. The book is not a mere summary, but an argument, beginning with the first words: "There really is no such thing as art. There are only artists."

Inevitably an historical survey achieved in so concise a compass had its limitations, some of which were to do with Gombrich's own: he did not seek fully to engage with non-Western art; he took a rather old-fashioned view of Mannerism; and his view of the modern period, especially Abstraction, is somewhat in the nature of a postscript.

After The Story of Art, Gombrich's fame and career accelerated. In 1950 he was elected Slade Professor at Oxford, a post he held until 1953. It was an experience he found not entirely congenial and he contrasted it with his treatment as Slade Professor at Cambridge, 1961-63. In 1956 he became Durning-Lawrence Professor in Art History at University College London, and in the same year he gave the Mellon Lectures in Washington about the history of artistic progress towards Naturalism. The lectures were published in 1960 as Art and Illusion, a book which confirmed his reputation as a highly original thinker.

Art and Illusion investigates the means by which artists convince us that their marks on paper or canvas look like a person or a landscape – how the illusion works – and argues that "to draw an unfamiliar sight presents greater difficulties than is usually realised". The artist cannot just draw what is before him, and only with a great struggle can he see what he is not already accustomed to seeing. The book was much praised and indeed received in some circles with almost mystic enthusiasm. Gombrich extended the discussion further in The Image and the Eye (1982).

In 1959 Gombrich became Director of the Warburg Institute and Professor of the History of the Classical Tradition in the University of London. His occasional lectures and articles were collected in a series of volumes, of which the first, Meditations on a Hobby Horse (1963), won the WH Smith Award. As a visiting lecturer and contributor to conferences, Gombrich was much in demand, particularly in America. He gave the Wrightsman Lectures in New York, taking pattern and design as his theme. In 1970 he published a biography of Aby Warburg, founder of the Institute. That pious task had long occupied him, and caused him some struggles.

By the time of publication of Tributes (1984), Gombrich seemed pessimistic about the future for humanism as he conceived it. He tended to see himself as a lone surviving defender of values shared and inculcated by those he commemorated in the book.

Publicly and privately, Gombrich carried his considerable eminence with almost excessive modesty, always courteous and approachable and interested in the work of others. Faintly smiling, faintly pachydermatous in a greyish suit, he might be seen eating a frugal lunch at the Warburg, or slipping quietly into a seat at a concert or art-historical congress. But while his behaviour seemed tacitly to convey scholarly equality, and rebuke pretension, he held his own views with firmness, even sharpness, keeping in check an impatience bordering on arrogance.

His softly lisping conversational urbanity could be spiced by caustic observations on people and behaviour. The range and depth of his knowledge made him a formidable opponent, especially for those who wished to generalise about aesthetics. "If you try to formulate a principle for beauty in art, somebody can show you a counter-example," he once said.

He lived modestly in a terraced house in Hampstead, surrounded not by pictures but by musical scores. He never collected art, saying that the best was available to him in the National Gallery.

Gombrich was a fellow of many learned societies and the recipient of a host of academic honours. He was elected a Fellow of the British Academy in 1960, appointed CBE in 1966, knighted in 1972 and, finally, appointed a member of the Order of Merit in 1988.

Ernst Gombrich married, in 1936, Ilse Heller, a pianist who had been a pupil of his mother's. They had one son, Richard, who is himself a distinguished scholar. His wife and son both survive him.

W. G. Sebald

German novelist whose work took literary
England by storm

December 17, 2001

W. G. Sebald, German author and scholar, was born in Bavaria on May 18, 1944. He died in Norfolk on December 14, 2001, aged 57.

W. G. Sebald was one of the most remarkable literary talents to have emerged in recent times; he was also one of the most baffling and peculiar.

Born in Germany, but resident in Britain for almost forty years, he pursued a distinguished academic career as a literary scholar, and was well into his forties by the time he began to write the deeply idiosyncratic works of imagination that made his name. Though he wrote in German, his reputation at the time of his death stands perhaps even higher in the English-speaking world than it does in his native land.

The first of his works to be translated into English, The Emigrants, was hailed by Susan Sontag as "an astonishing masterpiece" when it appeared in 1996; Sebald, she said, was the "contemporary master of the literature of lament and mental restlessness". The second, The Rings of Saturn, was pronounced the Book of the Decade by The Irish Times. Vertigo, the third to be translated but written first, showed how the foundations of his extraordinary vision had been laid. And when Austerlitz was published in English earlier this year, readers and critics were quick to concur with the verdict their German counterparts had reached a few months before: this was his magnum opus, and Sebald, in Michael Ondaatje's description, was "the most interesting and ambitious writer working in Britain today".

In the first chapter of The Rings of Saturn there is a vivid account of the work of the 17th-century English author and physician Sir Thomas Browne. It might be applied with equal justice to Sebald himself. He "wrote out of the fullness of his erudition, deploying a vast repertoire of quotations and the names of authorities who had gone before, creating complex metaphors and analogies, and constructing labyrinthine sentences that sometimes extend over one or two pages, sentences that resemble processions or a funeral cortege in their sheer ceremonial lavishness. It is true that, because of the immense weight of the impediments he is carrying, his writing can be held back by the force of gravitation, but when he does succeed in rising higher and higher through the circles of his spiralling prose, borne aloft like a glider on warm currents of air, the reader is overcome by a sense of levitation. The greater the distance, the clearer the view: one sees the tiniest of details with the utmost clarity. It is as if one were looking through a reversed opera glass and through a microscope at the same time."

His books are allusive, elaborate, visionary and dense. Their mood is muted, elegiac, with a sardonic edge – too easily unremarked – to lighten the pervasive gloom.

Like most German writers of his age – he was born in 1944 – Sebald was conscious of writing always in the shadow of his country's Nazi past. But his approach to the crimes of his parents' generation was unusually oblique. He was unconvinced by what he called the "official culture of mourning and remembering" instituted in Germany in the decades after the war, and unmoved by the work of older German writers who tried to deal directly with the Third Reich and the Holocaust in their work. Instead he gathers history's scraps, fragments of recollection, the detritus that marks the passage of individual lives. He shows how the present is touched by the past, and how we reshape the past in bringing it alive.

He shows how we try to remember. Max Ferber in The Emigrants studies Tiepolo reproductions in a book. "I sat looking at those pictures with a magnifying glass, trying to see further and further into them. And little by little that summer day in Wurzburg came back to me."

But memory is a difficult, distorting thing. As someone else in the same book says: "It makes one's head heavy and giddy, as if one were not looking back down from the receding perspectives of time but rather down on the earth from a great height, from one of those towers whose tops are lost to view in the clouds."

Sebald's work moves seamlessly between history and invention; memoir and myth; fantasy, travelogue and reportage. Boundaries are constantly blurred. Among the fictional characters there are many real names, including that of W. G. Sebald. From time to time an odd, unclear, uncaptioned photograph will punctuate the text. There are very few paragraphs. To read these books is to embark, like their protagonists and narrators, on a journey with no clear end in view – and without a map. But the journey, for the most part, is exhilarating and surprising, and it is hard to stop. The end, when we get there, turns out to be a kind of knowledge – of the past, of the present, of ourselves – that we might not otherwise have had.

Winfried Georg Maximilian Sebald was born in 1944 in the Bavarian village of Wertach im Algau, into a family he described as "conventional, Catholic, anti-communist, working-class". His father, who had joined the army in 1929 and rose through the ranks to become a captain, was taken prisoner in France towards the end of the war. He returned from captivity only when Max (as he would always be known to friends and colleagues) was three; he was to remain a remote figure, finding work in another town and coming home at weekends.

Sebald's greatest childhood influence was his grandfather, Josef Egelhofer, "an exceptionally kind man" with whom he went for long walks in the country, and whose death when the boy was 12 came as a terrible blow.

From the Gymnasium at Oberstdorf, he went to Freiburg University, studying literature for two years, before pursuing further studies in French-speaking Switzerland. He would remember the years in which he grew up as a time when the recent past was never discussed. The realisation that the defendants on trial in the 1960s for wartime atrocities were people just like his parents and their neighbours brought home to him for the first time the enormity of what had gone on. It made him determined "to know what had happened in detail, and to try to understand why it should have been so".

From 1966 he spent two years as a language assistant at the University of Manchester, and returned there in 1969 for a further year after a brief career as a schoolmaster in St Gallen. In 1970 he was appointed to a lectureship in modern German literature at the University of East Anglia, where he was to remain for the rest of his career, advancing to a chair of European literature in 1986. "I've lived here for thirty years," he said recently of Norwich, "but I don't feel in the least at home."

That rootlessness – and the quest for its opposite – was a theme both of his literary work and of his research. An important focus of his academic studies was Austrian literature, and its preoccupation with Austrian identity, which he surveyed in two collections of essays, Die Beschreibung des Unglucks. Zur osterreichischen Literatur von Stifter bis Handke (1985) and Unheimliche Heimat (1991). He also wrote monographs on the Wilhelmine satirical dramatist Carl Sternheim and on Alfred Doblin, the pioneer of Expressionism and author of Berlin Alexanderplatz, as well as editing a volume of essays on German theatre of the 1970s and 1980s. In 1998 he returned to the themes of identity and belonging when he published Logis in einem Landhaus, a study of some favourite writers associated with the Swiss and South German provincial landscape he left behind when he moved to England, among them Gottfried Keller, Johann Peter Hebel, and Robert Walser.

A more controversial book appeared in 1999. The title essay in Luftkrieg und Literatur was based on a lecture delivered in Zurich in 1997, in which Sebald accused postwar German writers of ignoring almost entirely the wartime devastation of their country's cities and civilian populations in Allied air attacks. He asked why this subject should have come to be regarded as taboo, and what might happen – to Germans' understanding of themselves and of their terrible recent past – if it were not. His questions caused consternation far beyond literary circles. Another essay in the same volume gave a venomous account of the conduct under Nazism of Alfred Andersch, one of the pillars of German literature of the immediate postwar years, whose Sansibar oder der letzte Grund remains a popular set text in almost every German school; this, too, aroused hostility in the land Sebald had left behind.

This provocative critical reckoning with Germany's literary tradition carried the weight it did because its author, in self-imposed exile, was by then one of German literature's most internationally successful exponents. The works that had made him so began in the late 1980s when, he once said, the increasing bureaucratisation of British higher education began to take much of the pleasure out of his professional life. In 1988 he published Nach der Natur: Ein Elementargedicht, a triptych of reflections in rhymeless verse on nature and its destruction. Schwindel. Gefuhle appeared in 1990 (in English as Vertigo, 2000), interweaving the narrator's travels in Italy with those of Kafka, Casanova and Stendhal.

But it was with Die Ausgewanderten (1992; The Emigrants, 1996), an exploration of the fate of a group of Jews who escaped the Holocaust, and Die Ringe des Saturn (1995; The Rings of Saturn, 1998), a disorientating pilgrimage through East Anglia at its most grim, that he found his distinctive voice. With Austerlitz (in German and English 2001), whose protagonist was sent, as the child of Czech Jewish parents, to Britain on a Kindertransport from Prague, he consolidated a reputation already secure, and promised a great deal more. For Years Now (December 2001) is a book of 23 short texts (the first he had written in English) with images by the artist Tess Jaray.

Sebald, who in 1989 was founding director of the British Centre for Literary Translation at UEA, was fortunate in his own translators. He had exacting standards in these things, and Michael Hulse (Vertigo, The Emigrants and The Rings of Saturn) and Anthea Bell (Austerlitz) rose quite magnificently to their daunting task. On the whole, Sebald once said, he preferred his English readers; the Germans wrote him "very odd letters".

Max Sebald is survived by his wife, Ute, and by his daughter, who was badly hurt in the road accident in which he was killed.

Martin Esslin

**Writer and broadcaster who brought modern
European drama to the British**

February 27, 2002

Professor Martin Esslin, OBE, writer and former Head of BBC
Radio Drama, was born in Budapest on June 8, 1918. He died in
London on February 24, 2002, aged 83.

A fugitive from Nazism who arrived in Britain in 1940, Martin
Esslin made an immense contribution to the understanding of
modern European drama in the English-speaking world, through
his activities in a variety of spheres: authorship, production,
teaching and broadcasting.

Within three years of Bertolt Brecht's death in 1956, he had
written a study of the dramatist which is still indispensable for
an understanding of its subject. His book The Theatre of the
Absurd (1962) coined a term which almost instantly entered the
language to become an unavoidable definition of the drama of such
playwrights as Eugene Ionesco and Jean Genet and their spiritual
heirs. Among these was Harold Pinter, whom Esslin came to know
well, writing a study of his work which went through a number of
editions, expanding as it did so.

Having been involved in broadcasting in various capacities
almost from the moment of his arrival in this country, he was,
between 1963 and 1977, the enormously erudite Head of BBC
Radio Drama. His 14 years' stewardship constitute a golden age
of radio drama, a period of uncompromising high seriousness in
which he championed such "difficult" playwrights as Beckett was
thought to be, in a mass medium, and made them more generally
intelligible to the English mind. Thereafter, in a career of prolific
authorship which continued to illuminate drama criticism with his
insight, Esslin was for two quarters annually from 1977 to 1988,
Professor of Drama at Stanford University.

Martin Julius Esslin was born in Budapest in the summer of

1918, with the Austro-Hungarian Empire on the verge of defeat and extinction. His parents sent him to be educated at a gymnasium in Vienna, from where he went on to read English and philosophy at the University of Vienna. He also studied theatrical direction at the Reinhardt Seminar of Dramatic Art in Vienna.

Prospects of a career in the theatre were rudely curtailed in March 1938 by Hitler's annexation of Austria. Joining a Jewish exodus from the country, Esslin fled first to Brussels, where he spent a year, before escaping for a second time, as the German Army rolled into the Low Countries and France.

Esslin made his way to London where the BBC's recently born German Service was taking shape under Hugh Carleton Greene. There, Esslin joined a remarkable band of emigres, which included the actor Marius Goring and the singer Lucie Mannheim. "Stringing" from his Californian retreat, Thomas Mann also contributed commentaries for transmission by the BBC to Nazi Germany.

The emigres working for the BBC German Service had to steer a careful course between the demands of "official information" about the war, and a desire to report as truthfully as possible what was happening. There was also room for some dramatically creative use of characters to engage the imagination of listeners in Nazi-occupied Europe and allow a satirical commentary on the war.

Esslin worked as a producer and scriptwriter for what became the BBC's European Services until 1955, when he became head of European Productions. There, he inherited the mantle of a department which had broadcast Anouilh's plays in English long before they became West End successes. This principle he extended to the playwrights of the Theatre of the Absurd (to which at that time he had yet to give a name). Ionesco's Rhinoceros, actually had its world premiere in an English translation commissioned by the BBC before the play was staged in Paris (and long before Laurence Olivier appeared in it at the Royal Court).

In 1961 Esslin was appointed Assistant Head of Drama (Sound), and two years later Head of Drama (Radio). There, alongside a diet of such well-established popular soaps as Mrs Dale's Diary and The Archers – progeny, it has to be said, that could bring a blush to his cheek – he set himself to extend what he saw as a National Theatre of the Air, using the three BBC networks of that era, to produce hundreds of plays a year.

His own favourite was The Third Programme (now Radio 3) which, in those days before it became principally music channel, he saw as an ideal vehicle for transmitting serious, innovative drama. Under Esslin, the Third became one of Beckett's most devout champions, producing work from him on several dozen occasions. Younger figures such as Harold Pinter and Tom Stoppard were also writers for whose work, with its tormented mental landscapes, radio's stark simplicity was an ideal medium. Vaclav Havel, in a later age to become famous as President of a Czechoslovakia liberated from the Soviet yoke, was another European playwright whose work was first heard in English through BBC broadcasts.

This trail-blazing did not, of course, ignore the classics of European drama. Well aware that many of his avant garde playwrights had had their own first experience of Chekhov or Ibsen from radio broadcasts in English, Esslin made sure that the works of these, too, received regular airings.

Meanwhile, Esslin had, in 1959, published his first book. Its title, Brecht: A Choice of Evils, addressed the problem of the dual nature of this politically controversial figure. As Esslin put it: "Brecht was a Communist; he was also a great poet. But while the West liked his poetry and distrusted his Communism, the Communists exploited his political convictions while they regarded his artistic aims and achievements with suspicion."

In the case of Brecht Esslin saw the mysterious life of language itself as the playwright's salvation, producing, an autonomous ethic that rose above any propagandist intention the dramatist might have had. "He (Brecht) wanted to arouse the critical faculties of his audience, but only succeeded in moving them to tears...he wanted to make his theatre a laboratory of social change – and had to see it strengthen his public's faith in human nature. He sought to spread the cold light of logical clarity – and produced a rich texture of poetic ambiguity."

Esslin was to return to Brecht in his later writings. In the essay Bertolt Brecht (1969) he pointed out that Brecht was still known outside Germany largely for his plays. Esslin explored the then little translated poems, essays and stories and hazarded the heretical opinion that posterity might find the true Brecht in his poems, rather than in his dramas.

Meanwhile he had published the pathbreaking The Theatre of the Absurd, which remains his best known book to the general theatregoer. Focusing on the work of Beckett, Ionesco, Adamov and Genet, it dilated on its thesis that their plays were not intended to work out a drama in the conventional sense, but to "communicate a pattern of poetic images". At the beginning of The Theatre of the Absurd, Esslin tellingly contrasted the confusion felt by those critics who first saw these plays on stage, with the rapturous reception given to a production of Waiting for Godot by the inmates of St Quentin prison in 1957. The book went through a number of editions in successive years, broadening its scope to include discussion of the surreal political works of Slawomir Mrozek, Havel and other Soviet bloc writers.

The Peopled Wound: the plays of Harold Pinter appeared in 1970 and was to go through five editions, the last as Pinter the Playwright (1992). In the writing of it, Esslin was given access by the playwright to early poems and suppressed material to produce a work that was strong in its sensitivity to Pinter's use of language. Among Esslin's other works were Artaud (1976), The Age of Television (1992) and The Field of Drama (1987), and he edited the Illustrated Encyclopaedia of World Theatre (1977).

Among Esslin's many honours from around the world were the title of Professor, conferred by the President of Austria (1967); an honorary doctorate from Kenyon College, Ohio (1978); and the Ehrenkreuz fur Kunst und Wissenschaft, first class (1998) from Austria. He had been appointed OBE in 1972.

Martin Esslin married, in 1947, Renate Gerstenberg. He is survived by her and by a son and daughter.

Stewart Steven

Editor with drive, chutzpah and determination
January 20, 2004

Stewart Steven, Editor of The Mail on Sunday from 1982 to 1992 and of the Evening Standard for three years thereafter, brought to British popular journalism a rather old-fashioned kind of genius. He made his way in Fleet Street the hard way.

He believed in old-style scoops, and occasionally they got him into trouble. He was a down-to-earth journalist, not an Oxbridge-educated editor, yet he took both his papers into political, cultural and artistic territory you did not find elsewhere in the tabloids. And he made a great deal of money for the House of Harmsworth.

Stewart Steven was born in 1935, the son of a Jewish businessman refugee from Hitler's Germany and his Christian German wife. His father died when he was 9; the family business faded under an inattentive uncle; his mother died when he was 17.

Steven was left, the middle child of a penniless orphan family of three, with few friends and fewer roots in Britain, and nothing at all to turn to in the Germany that they had fled.

Steven's parents had converted in Britain to Roman Catholicism, and put him to a Catholic education in Wimbledon and at Mayfield in Sussex. He found the experience profoundly antipathetic, complaining ever afterwards of the snobbery, philistinism and anti-Semitism he encountered. Certainly, the schoolmaster who reported to his widowed German mother "I am convinced that Stewart is not playing a straight bat" seemed to make little effort to communicate with others unlike himself; but, oddly enough, love of and skill at cricket was one of the few assets that Steven carried away from his English public school.

He needed a job – any job provided it was not in the City, towards which his uncle pointed him. He tramped the length of Fleet Street in the traditional style and found himself lowly jobs on the Manchester Guardian and the Oxford Mail. He had no school-of-journalism qualifications for the trade, and throughout his life straightforward spelling was not his strong suit. But he brought to successive jobs curiosity, an eye for oddity, chutzpah and sheer determination, and by the time he was 26 he had made his way, with a two-year diversion into National Service, to writing parliamentary pieces for a features agency. At 28 he was covering Westminster for provincial papers in the West Country, at 29 he was on the Daily Express, and at 32 was its foreign editor.

Whenever, then and later, Steven's friends turned to discussing him, real affection was blended with something more quizzical. He had a gift for friendship that extended beyond the journalistic and political worlds he cultivated most. He brought generosity of spirit to his work. Throughout his life he read widely, broadening the horizons his schooling had failed to extend. He held on to his left-of-centre views despite working for High Tory newspapers. He brought the usefully sceptical eye of the outsider to British institutions in need of more than a lick of paint. All these things his friends valued.

There was more scepticism about some other things. He could listen; but he preferred to talk, more loudly and longer as he grew older and a little deaf. He had a portentous air about him, shading into pomposity. "My very good friend" became a catch-phrase, and when it was attached too often to a man of rising importance, eyebrows arched on the faces of his friends. And there was amusement about his scoops that went wrong, as when he discovered Martin Bormann in a jungle in Brazil or uncovered comprehensive but unproven wrongdoing at Rover's forerunner, the old British Leyland.

But none of these quirks checked Steven's steady advance as a journalist, or lost him the deep affection of his friends and colleagues. His five years as foreign editor of the Daily Express built his reputation as a journalist and a manager of journalists, and when in 1972 he was headhunted by the Harmsworth papers, he went to the Daily Mail as assistant and later associate editor. He stayed there for ten years, and his career might well have run out of steam there.

But in the early 1980s Harmsworth turned to the creation of The Mail on Sunday.

Things went wrong for the man appointed to run it; a crisis loomed and catastrophe threatened; Steven was drafted to put things right. In a long burst of sustained brilliance, he did so. He drove his journalists as hard as he drove himself. He cashed all his cheques of friendship around Fleet Street and Westminster. In his first three spectacular years as its Editor he made The Mail on Sunday a brilliant success, with a unique position on the borders between popular and broadsheet national journalism.

Steven fought hard and worked hard to build his career as a journalist, but he found time for other things. Wide reading and self-confidence made of him something of a light-hearted polymath. He enjoyed his own cooking, and still more that of the best restaurants in London. He turned friendships into journalism, and journalism brought him more friends.

And he wrote three books, none of them remarkable but each of them successful.

Operation Splinter-Factor uncovered a complicated plot of West against East in the early Cold War. The Spymasters of Israel drew on his contacts in that country, who may have been encouraged to spill beans to him more generously by his uncritical support for its policies, a support that won him the reputation among his friends of Mossad's best unpaid agent of influence in London. And The Poles, an easy-reading dissection of Poland and its people, wove together skilfully everything he learnt about them from his Polish wife and her Polish friends, in Warsaw and exile.

It was going to be difficult to cap his success at The Mail on Sunday and Steven, who earlier in his career had taken three years off his life, announced that come what may he intended to retire at 60. He gave every indication of wanting to see out his time at the paper he had created, but a reshuffle pressed. It pointed Steven towards the Evening Standard. At first he resisted: a London paper after a national, an evening paper which, like such papers everywhere, had to struggle against declining demand; and, for himself, daily grind after the more leisurely pace of weekly publication. But the logic of the changes was compelling. ("They kept wheeling in more barrow-loads of money".) Steven became Editor of the Evening Standard and, as his driver told him, "Guv'nor of London".

He set himself to earn the sobriquet, and he brought all his journalistic experience and talent to the job of giving the paper a distinctive voice about the capital. It increasingly cultivated the arts, and Steven built useful friendships in these new worlds. It campaigned for investment in London. It flung itself into quirky little campaigns, like the continued admission of motor vehicles to the narrow streets of Soho, and major ones, such as the saving of St Bartholomew's Hospital. It defended unpopular causes, such as John Major's reputation. Above all, artists of every kind recognised him as an impassioned and effective advocate of their interests. Entirely sure of himself at last, Steven had the courage to go his own way, pick fights and define new issues for Londoners' attention.

And he rode out, unruffled, what might have been the last great Steven disaster in journalism. In 1995 he commissioned an article on the Labour Party from Bryan Gould, a Labour politician who had recently taken himself off to an academic life in New Zealand. A piece arrived by fax. When Gould saw it he totally failed to recognise it. Eventually the truth emerged. The piece came not from a man who had turned his back on the British Labour Party, but from the precocious son of a Tory Cabinet minister. Gould's fax, coming in later, had been put aside unread. To come out of the mess with dignity required all of Steven's chutzpah, but it left no stain on his reputation, only a last affectionate reminder of the messes that he had got himself into in his youth.

Leaving the Evening Standard, Steven spent some rather unsatisfying months trying as Editor to restore the fortunes of Punch, but he stuck by his determination to enjoy the leisure that his journalistic career had denied him. He had a villa in Cyprus and a country house in Wiltshire, which his friends found an incongruous possession for a man who had asked: "What is the country for?" He wrote a weekly and much respected column for The Mail on Sunday. He had an ailing wife to care for. By going as he did, he made sure of going out on the crest of the wave, circulation worries left for his successor at the Evening Standard to cope with.

And in retirement he had the time, as chairman of the National Campaign for the Arts, to continue to promote the artistic causes which as an editor he had made his own.

In 1965 Steven married Inka Sobieniewska, once a professional pop singer and for much of her life a painter of considerable ability. They seemed an unlikely couple, he voluble and ebullient, she quietly uncommunicative, but they brought each other comfort, support and good companionship. They had no children, but she brought him a son from a first marriage. They both survive him.

Stewart Steven, journalist and newspaper editor, was born in Hamburg on September 30, 1935. He died in London on January 19, 2004, aged 68.

Lady Mary Henderson

Greek war heroine and grande dame of British diplomacy
January 24, 2004

In a full and fascinating life, Lady Henderson was a Greek brought up in England, a Red Cross nurse in Greece during the Second World War, sentenced to death by the Gestapo, covered the Greek civil war as a correspondent and lived as a British ambassador's wife in the grand style in Bonn, Paris and Washington. She also became a leading figure in the fashion world, instrumental in promoting international recognition for the British fashion industry.

Mary Henderson looked petite, tiny and frail. But she was tough enough to survive an SS prison camp, the rigours of life as a war correspondent, and to handle the full-time job running Britain's top embassies. She always made a point of wearing British designer clothes, in her own style, reminiscent of a Victorian governess, with a high neck, long sleeves and a long skirt. But this puritanical look, all her friends remarked, was offset by the twinkle in her eyes.

Mary Xenia Cawadias was born in Athens in 1919. Her father, Professor A. P.Cawadias, was doctor to the King of Greece. When Greece became a republic in 1924, he joined King George II in exile in London and set up home in Wimpole Street – next door to the famous Barretts' house -and became British citizens.

She and her brother, Henderson wrote in her memoir Xenia, were brought up by their English nanny "to love all things British; to believe that the English (and in particular Byron) were blond Gods that could do no wrong while the Germans were wicked murderers". But she felt profoundly foreign at Queen's College for Girls in Harley Street and never found an answer to the question of whether she was Greek or British. Her Greek name, when read out, always produced giggles at school: Xenia, in fact, is Greek for "very foreign".

When she was 20 her mother took her for a holiday in Athens, where they were trapped by the war. Mary trained as a nurse for the

Greek Red Cross and dealt with war casualties from the Albanian
front. During the famine that followed the German occupation she
ran a soup kitchen for children but was eventually arrested by the
Gestapo for helping British servicemen. She was held in solitary
confinement and then in a camp awaiting execution until she was
released on the eve of liberation.

After the war she became a correspondent for Time and Life
magazines, covering the brutal Greek civil war and its appalling
atrocities. During that period she met and married a young British
News Chronicle correspondent Stephen Barber and returned to
England. "Our marriage lasted a very short time," she said in her
memoir. "It was a mistake, we were not suited to each other. In the
end I walked out."

She returned to Athens to report on the civil war and towards its
end met a young British diplomat Nicholas Henderson. They were
married in 1951 in the Greek Orthodox Church in Bayswater, and
Mary Henderson began her long diplomatic career.

After Vienna, Santiago, Warsaw and Bonn, Sir Nicholas and
Lady Henderson were posted to Paris where, on one occasion, they
brought over a large part of the Chelsea Flower Show – flowers and
machinery – and set it up in the embassy garden.

At the end of the Paris posting the Hendersons retired from
the Foreign and Commonwealth Office, but a few weeks after the
couple had moved to their cottage in Berkshire, Margaret Thatcher
recalled him to take over the Washington embassy in 1979.

There, their engagements were scheduled six months in advance,
with luncheons and dinners for 30 or 40 people held three times
a week. Their grand Lutyens residence was always full of guests.
"It was more like running an hotel than a country house," Mary
Henderson said. "I suppose I'm just old-fashioned. I'm Nicko's
wife and this is my job." Many of the embassy meals were taken
from her Paris Embassy Cookbook. "I am basically a cook," she
once said.

"After all, all Englishmen marry their cooks."

During their stay in Washington Mary Henderson redeco-
rated their residence the most elegant in the capital – at little cost
to the taxpayer. Fifteen rooms, bedrooms, the main ballroom,
drawing rooms, the library and halls were restored free of charge
by top British interior designers, including David Hicks and John
Stephanidis, with wallpaper and curtains provided by British firms,
including that of her close friend, the late Laura Ashley.

British firms were encouraged to contribute to the project as a permanent showcase for British design. But the grand opening party for the newly refurbished residence, intended to be a major occasion in the diplomatic year in Washington, had to be abridged because it coincided with the Falklands war.

At the end of their Washington tour, Mary, with Roy Strong, Jean Muir and Caroline Charles, formed part of a group to co-ordinate British designers, the fashion industry and the Government. She began by arousing Mrs Thatcher's interest in the project and holding sparkling parties at Downing Street for the British fashion world. For the first time the Government was persuaded to help to subsidise British Fashion Week and particular emphasis was placed on supporting young designers. Today Britons head French fashion houses and British fashion has received worldwide recognition. "She brought glamour and international knowledge and funding to our industry and brought politicians, celebrities and designers together," said Caroline Charles.

She was an adviser on the British Fashion Council and was presented with its highest honour, the Hall of Fame Award. She was appointed OBE in 1988.

Lady Henderson was born on March 29, 1919. She died of pneumonia on January 22, 2004, aged 84.

Maurice Wilkins

Co-discoverer of the double-helix

October 7, 2004

Maurice Wilkins, CBE, FRS, biophysicist, was born on December 16, 1916. He died on October 5, 2004, aged 87.

Maurice Wilkins shared the 1962 Nobel Prize for Physiology or Medicine with Francis Crick and Jim Watson, nine years after their discovery of the structure of DNA. But while Crick and Watson enjoyed the limelight, Wilkins did not. A diffident and private man, he preferred to stay in the shadows, and his contribution to the remarkable discovery of the double-helix DNA structure – the molecule that genes are made of – is relatively little known. Few colleagues ever got to know him well.

In 1953 Wilkins was working at King's College London, where he and his group used X-ray diffraction methods to measure the angles, bonds and orientations of the DNA molecule. At the same time, their friendly rivals, Crick and Watson, were pursuing their DNA research at the Cavendish Laboratory at Cambridge.

Crick and Watson were familiar with the X-ray work at King's, and it was from this data that they, with remarkable biochemical and biological insight, derived the double-helix model and saw its biological significance. Papers describing the results of the two groups appeared side by side in the science magazine Nature in April 1953. Wilkins's group then spent eight years demonstrating that the model was right.

The award of the Nobel Prize to Crick, Watson and Wilkins followed in 1962, but was not an unblemished triumph. Controversy soon arose, mainly about the role in the discovery of the structure of DNA of one of Wilkins's colleagues at King's, Rosalind Franklin. Using X-ray techniques, in which she was particularly gifted, Franklin had taken what was then the clearest X-ray diffraction photograph of the structure (the famous Photograph 51), clearly showing that it was a helix.

It was with the aid of this and of Franklin's unpublished data that Crick and Watson were able to work out the structure of DNA. Franklin did not know to what extent they used her data, and was probably not even aware that Watson had seen the photograph. But Franklin herself was the first to realise that there are two forms of DNA.

In March 1953, however, she left Wilkins's team and went to work with John Desmond Bernal at Birkbeck College, London. Like Franklin and Wilkins, Bernal was an X-ray crystallographer. In 1958, after five years of research with Bernal, Franklin died of ovarian cancer at the age of 37, four years before the Nobel was awarded.

Wilkins, Crick and Watson were later accused of exploiting Franklin's work, and the story is often told as an example of the unfair treatment of female colleagues by male scientists. Undoubtedly the three should have clearly acknowledged that they could not have discovered the structure of DNA without Franklin's data, and although much scientific work is collaborative, they were aware that a Nobel Prize was in the offing.

Wilkins himself commented: "Undoubtedly Rosalind's contribution to the DNA structure was considerable, but not necessarily in a different category from those of other workers in our lab." Others believe that this understates Franklin's contribution.

Maurice Hugh Frederick Wilkins was born at Pongaroa, New Zealand, in 1916, the only son of Edgar Henry and Eveline Wilkins of Dublin. His father was a medical doctor who had gone to New Zealand in 1913, but in 1923 he obtained a job as a school doctor in Birmingham and the family returned to England.

Wilkins went to Wylde Greene College and then to King Edward's High School in Birmingham. While at school he was a keen astronomer, using telescopes, including one using a 9.25in (234.95mm) concave mirror that he had made in his own workshop.

His interest in optics continued long into his professional life.

He won a number of scholarships that covered most of his university expenses, allowing him to study physics at St John's College, Cambridge, graduating in 1936.

He chose St John's because its staff included especially eminent physicists such as Mark Oliphant. Surprisingly, he achieved only a lower second in Part II of the Natural Science Tripos. Perhaps he spent too much time at the University Socialist Society and on other non-academic activities.

He was, for example, active in the Cambridge Scientists' Anti-War Group. Because of the threat of war with Germany, the Government issued gas masks to every British citizen. The Anti-War Group studied the masks and helped to have them improved. Meanwhile, the Spanish Civil War and the rise of Fascism persuaded Wilkins to join the Communist Party, which was then much in vogue in Cambridge.

Because of his poor degree, Wilkins could not get a postgraduate research position at Cambridge, but he had become interested in the phenomenon of thermoluminescence and wanted to explore it.

This interest had impressed his tutor, Oliphant, who put him in touch with John Randall, who had worked at GEC on luminescence. So Wilkins joined Randall's research group at the luminescence laboratory in Birmingham – he was extremely lucky to find a post doing exactly the research he wanted to do.

Thermoluminescence arises when an electron, for example, passing through a regular crystal becomes trapped in an irregularity in the crystal. If the crystal is then warmed, the electron will jump out and emit light. Electrons can stay in deep traps for a very long time, and archaeologists use thermoluminescence to date objects. Crystals may also emit light spontaneously after absorbing energy, a process called phosphorescence.

During the Second World War, Oliphant also ran a group at Birmingham working on the atomic bomb, which included the brilliant nuclear physicists Rudolph Peierls and Otto Frisch. Wilkins joined this group, working on how to evaporate uranium metal. The idea was to use evaporation and diffusion to separate out the uranium isotope needed to fabricate the atomic bomb (uranium 235).

In 1944 it was decided that this group, including Wilkins, should move to the cyclotron laboratory at the University of California at Berkeley to work on the Manhattan Project, the American programme to develop the atomic bomb.

Wilkins's attitude to the development of nuclear weapons was at the time similar to that of other scientists working on the project. They were convinced of the need for the Allies to develop the bomb before the Germans did (a view held particularly strongly by the many German refugees on the project). But some of them changed their opinions when Hiroshima and Nagasaki were destroyed, and became increasingly in favour of nuclear disarmament and international control of nuclear energy. Wilkins himself became increasingly concerned about global security as the Cold War developed.

At the end of the war Wilkins rejoined John Randall, who now had a biophysics group at St Andrews University, to study biological problems from a physical standpoint. The group found it hard to get funding in Scotland, however, and moved in 1946 to King's College London, where Wilkins began X-ray diffraction studies of DNA and collagen: the first step along the road to the double-helix model. And as the new science of molecular biology was invented, the group took a world lead under Randall's guidance.

Wilkins was elected a Fellow of the Royal Society in 1959, and the next year, two years before their Nobel Prize, he, Crick and Watson were awarded the Albert Lasker Award, given to attract attention to work that helped the understanding of serious diseases using novel methods.

From 1970 to 1978 Wilkins was the director of a Medical Research Council unit in the biophysics department at King's (where he was Professor of Biophysics, 1970-81), researching into membrane structure.

He remained, though, a scientist with broad interests. In the mid-1960s he became president of the British Society for Social Responsibility in Science. The first meeting of this radical group took place at the Royal Society in London, the august centre of the scientific establishment. Of particular interest to Wilkins was the role of scientists in the development of biological and chemical weapons.

He was an active member of the Pugwash movement that organised conferences on science and world affairs. Pugwash was particularly effective during the Cold War, when its conferences were attended by very influential eminent scientists from both the US and the Soviet Union.

In the 1980s there was a surge of public interest in the anti-nuclear movement and Wilkins was active in writing and lecturing on the dangers of nuclear war and on the consequences of testing nuclear weapons in the atmosphere.

During his retirement he wrote his autobiography, The Third Man of the Double Helix (2003). His interest in science and world affairs never left him.

Wilkins was appointed CBE in 1963.

He was twice married and is survived by his widow, Patricia, and four children.

Joseph Rotblat

Nuclear scientist who turned his back on nuclear weapons

September 2, 2005

Professor Sir Joseph Rotblat, FRS, Nobel Prize for Peace 1995, president of the Pugwash Conferences on Science and World Affairs, was born on November 4, 1908. He died on August 31, 2005, aged 96.

Although Joseph Rotblat had a distinguished career in physics he will be remembered more for 60-odd years of his life which he spent working for nuclear disarmament.

He was the chief organiser of the Pugwash conferences on science and world affairs. The destruction of Hiroshima and Nagasaki – by the atomic bombs which he helped to develop on the Manhattan Project – convinced him that nuclear weapons should be abolished, and he worked tirelessly for this end.

He also made considerable contributions to nuclear and medical physics. But he received the high recognition he so richly deserved for his scientific research and for his work for disarmament only in his later years, when he became a Fellow of the Royal Society and a Nobel laureate.

Joe Rotblat was born in 1908 in Warsaw, the fifth child of seven. His father, Zygmunt, was a businessman and until the First World War the Rotblat family was prosperous. After the war, however, the business failed and the family became very poor. Rotblat became an electrician. His ambition was to become a physicist, however, and after studying at night he was awarded a masters degree in physics in 1932 at the Free University of Poland and then became a research assistant in the Warsaw Radiological Laboratory.

In March 1939 he went to work at Liverpool University, invited by James Chadwick, the physicist who discovered the neutron, an important step in the discovery of the fission process which led to the development of the atom bomb.

His main work was on the energy of neutrons emitted during the fission of uranium nuclei. In August 1939 Chadwick offered Rotblat the Oliver Lodge Fellowship.

Tragically, he was unable to get his wife Tola out of Poland before the Germans invaded on September 1, 1939, and she died during the war.

By 1941 Chadwick's team at Liverpool had established that an atomic bomb was theoretically possible. At the beginning of 1944 Rotblat went with the Chadwick group to work at Los Alamos, near Santa Fe, New Mexico, the home of the Manhattan Project to develop the atom bomb.

By late 1944 it was clear to American Intelligence that the Germans would not develop an atom bomb. As soon as he discovered this, Rotblat quit the Manhattan Project, the only scientist to do so for reasons of conscience. He left Los Alamos under a cloud. Chadwick was not pleased that a Briton was the first to leave; and there was also a security complication.

Rotblat had learnt to fly while at Los Alamos and left the laboratory without the security people knowing. They suspected that he might fly to Poland and give away secrets about the atom bomb. The Americans, regarding him as a security risk, refused to give him an entry visa for years.

Rotblat had worked on the bomb because he was afraid that the Germans would produce one first. He saw no reason to continue when he knew that they would not.

Moreover, he discovered that there was a hidden political agenda for the Manhattan Project – nuclear weapons were to be part of the looming power-political struggle between the US and the Soviet Union.

He was appalled when the atomic bombs were dropped on Hiroshima and Nagasaki killing some 250,000 people. In his opinion, it was not necessary to use them against the two cities.

By the time the bombs were used, Rotblat was back at Liverpool University as a senior lecturer in the physics department and director of research in nuclear physics. Perhaps as a reaction to his work on the atomic bomb project, he became increasingly interested in the medical uses of nuclear energy. In 1950 he moved as a medical physicist to St Bartholomew's Hospital Medical School to be Professor of Physics. He stayed at Bart's until he retired in 1976.

In the medical school Rotblat worked on the effects of radiation on living organisms, specifically studying ageing and fertility effects. He soon became interested in the health effects of radiation from the radioactive fallout produced by the atmospheric testing of nuclear weapons.

Of particular concern to him were the hazards of the bone-seeking radioactive isotope strontium-90. His aim was to determine safe levels of exposure to ionising radiation. Though he was keen to publicise radiation hazards, he was particularly careful not to exaggerate the risks.

In 1955 Rotblat analysed the fallout from an American nuclear test at Bikini Atoll in the Pacific, deducing that it was a three-stage hydrogen bomb – he called it a fission-fusion-fission bomb – which had a particularly large explosive yield and released a vast amount of radioactivity into the atmosphere. He published his results in a scientific journal, infuriating the Government, which wanted information about nuclear weapons to be kept strictly secret.

His tendency to upset the Establishment may well explain the reluctance of the Royal Society to make him a Fellow, an honour he did not receive until the beginning of 1995.

In November of the same year he was awarded the Nobel Peace Prize, shared with the Pugwash conferences, the organisation of scientists which Rotblat was instrumental in establishing in the mid-1950s.

Pugwash evolved directly from the "manifesto" drawn up in 1955 by Bertrand Russell and Albert Einstein. Russell wrote to Einstein that "eminent men of science should draw the attention of world leaders to the impending destruction of the human race" in a nuclear war. The manifesto was signed by an international group of extremely eminent scientists; among them Frederic Joliot-Curie, Linus Pauling and Hideki Yukawa as well as Rotblat. Rotblat, then the vice-president of the British Atomic Scientists' Association, was well known to Russell. The Russell Einstein manifesto called for a conference of scientists to discuss nuclear disarmament and the abolition of war.

The first Pugwash conference was held in July 1957 and funded by Cyrus Eaton, a Canadian tycoon, president of the Chesapeake and Ohio Railroad, on the condition that it met at Eaton's home in Pugwash, Nova Scotia (hence the name of the organisation). Twenty-one international scientists, mainly physicists and one lawyer, from ten countries, East and West, attended, many of them famous enough to have direct influence with their governments.

The 1957 conference took place at the height of the Cold War.

At that time it was the only significant high-level contact between East and West. It was also the first time that senior scientists discussed political issues arising from the application of science, specifically the application of nuclear physics to the development of nuclear weapons.

Since 1957 at least one Pugwash conference has been held each year. All in all, there have been more than 200 general conferences and specialist work-shops involving participants from some 60 countries. Rotblat attended almost all of them.

Pugwash has avoided publicity and is, therefore, not well known, but there is no doubt that it was influential in, among other things, achieving agreement on the 1963 Partial Test Ban Treaty; establishing contacts between the US and Vietnam in the late 1960s; the negotiation of the 1972 Biological Weapons Convention; and in the discussions leading to the negotiation of the 1972 Anti-Ballistic Missile Treaty.

Rotblat must be given credit for these remarkable achievements. He was the first secretary-general of Pugwash and became its president in 1988. He also wrote several histories of Pugwash.

When relations between the superpowers improved during the 1980s the influence of Pugwash waned, although it has remained significant.

Soon after he left Los Alamos Rotblat realised that most natural scientists do not grapple with the major ethical issues resulting from the applications of science and that, although this is most clearly illustrated by the activities of military scientists, it also applies to natural scientists working in many non-military fields.

He argued that the lack of ethical concern among scientists contributes to a serious and consistent misuse of science and technology, bringing into question the integrity of scientists and helping to explain why they are too often regarded with suspicion and distrust.

Rotblat used statistics to support his argument. There are around 2.5 million research scientists and engineers in the world. He used to emphasise that, of these, about 500,000 work only on military research and development. If only research physicists and engineers, those at the forefront of technological innovation, are included, more than half are working for the military, improving existing weapons and developing new ones. And these are the best of the bunch, generally with higher salaries and much larger funds for research than their fellows in civil research. Considerably more funds are given to military research and development than civil research and development receives.

It was a great disappointment to him that fewer than 5,000 scientists have attended the Pugwash conferences – a fifth of one per cent of research scientists.

Although Rotblat was most aware of the misuse of nuclear physics, in his later years he became concerned about the possible military use of biological science, particularly genetic engineering. He argued that genetic engineers may well develop the ultimate in genocidal weapons. While nuclear physicists and engineers were responsible for developing yesterday's genocidal weapons – the nuclear weapons – tomorrow's genocidal weapons will, he predicted, come from the work of biologists.

In recent years Rotblat became increasingly concerned about developments in nuclear weapons policies that, he thought, are putting the world in increasing danger of a nuclear conflict. He was particularly worried about recent developments driven by the current US administration, though other countries appear to support these major policy changes. He mainly opposed the policy to use a nuclear weapon in a pre-emptive strike against a non-nuclear nation.

The general public does not, he argued, seem to be aware of these increasing dangers. To raise this awareness, he gathered together leaders of different non-governmental organisations working in this field and created a weapon of mass destruction awareness programme. The programme was launched in London on September 21 last year by Rotblat and the former Soviet President Michael Gorbachev.

Rotblat's dedication to Pugwash and the energy he put into the organisation amazed all who knew him. The way he combined Pugwash with his scientific work, about which he was similarly motivated, was extraordinary. Although he travelled extensively on Pugwash business, he did not miss one of his lectures for the first bachelor of medicine course at Bart's, which he delivered with great enthusiasm from 1949 until he retired in 1976.

In addition to numerous papers on nuclear physics and radiation biology, Rotblat wrote nearly 30 books, most on various aspects of the control of nuclear weapons and the prevention of war.

Apart from his FRS and Nobel prize, Rotblat received numerous awards and honorary doctorates in many countries. He was appointed CBE in 1965, received the Albert Einstein Peace Prize in 1992 and was knighted in 1998.

Zaki Badawi

Muslim leader who worked for dialogue with other faiths
January 25, 2006

Few men have done as much to reconcile Islam with modernity as Zaki Badawi, the founder and principal of the Muslim College in London. And few men have played such a crucial role in attempting to find a harmonious balance between the beliefs, culture and values of Islam and secular British society. Indeed, that almost two million British Muslims are today able to define themselves as such owes much to the vision of the Egyptian-born scholar who saw, early on, that the many Muslims who settled in Britain from different parts of the Islamic world would, one day, form a significant strand of British society – which happened to be Muslim.

For years, Badawi was the unofficial – and almost lone – spokesman for Muslims in Britain who had no visible figurehead or institutional structure. Appointed in 1978 as chief imam of the London Central Mosque as well as director of the Islamic Cultural Centre, he used these influential positions in the capital to call for an Islam that fitted comfortably with British values, so that younger generations, brought up and educated in this country, would find no conflict between their faith and their civic identity as British citizens.

To him, this meant an Islam that was inclusive, moderate, tolerant and without the rancour or hostility that marked attitudes to Western values prevalent in some of the more zealous sects of Arabia and the Middle East. He therefore devoted his life in Britain to building bridges – of faith, of dialogue and of scholarship. It is thanks largely to his pioneering work in the 1990s in helping to establish a forum for the three Abrahamic faiths – Christianity, Judaism and Islam – and his tireless, behind-the-scenes work in reaching out to British society and institutions that Britain has fared so much better than other European nations with Muslim minorities in integrating its Muslim citizens. But for Badawi,

Britain might have fared far less well in avoiding the social alien-
ation that has marked relations between Muslims and the rest of
society in France.

Equally, however, Badawi was an outspoken voice in upholding
Muslim dignity and the true values of his faith when these came
under attack. This was never more crucial than in the aftermath
of the September 11 atrocities in America. And when many
other leading Muslim scholars were reluctant to speak out to
condemn violence or denounce terrorism, he wrote an article
for The Times in which he insisted that taking revenge on the
innocent was abhorrent to Islam. He gave a warning that no
society was immune from violence, and the worst was one which
donned the garb of religion. But he said the Koran emphasised
that those who disturbed the peace of society and spread fear
and disorder deserved the severest punishment that could be
imposed.

His denunciation of violence and extremism was forcefully
repeated again last year, when he joined religious leaders in
commemorating the victims of the London bombings and in
calling for tolerance and calm. Again, his words, among others,
may have helped Britain to avoid any widespread and violent
backlash against Muslims across the country.

Born in Cairo in 1922, Badawi studied at al-Azhar University,
where he claimed to have gained his rebellious streak. "I have
always refused to be deferential, even to heads of state," he told
a journalist in January 2003. "Irreverence is part of my Islamic
culture, of my training at al-Azhar."

It did nothing to harm his studies: after an undergraduate
degree in theology, Badawi gained a master's degree in Arabic
language and literature and the King Faruq First Prize for best
postgraduate student. After gaining his doctorate, he returned to
teach at al-Azhar before coming to Britain for the first time in 1951.

He gained a degree in psychology from University College
London, followed by a doctorate from London University in
modern Muslim thought.

He then spent several years in South-East Asia, setting up the
Muslim College of Malaya and taking teaching posts in Singapore
and Kuala Lumpur. He took up professorships in Kano and Zaria,
Nigeria, and in Jeddah. He returned to London as a research
professor for the Haj Research Centre of the King Abdul Aziz
University in Saudi Arabia.

Badawi first came to grips with the British way of life, and the challenges it held for Muslims, in 1978 when he took the post of director of the Islamic Cultural Centre (ICC), while also serving as chief imam of the London Central Mosque in Regent's Park. He helped to establish the Shariah Council, to reconcile conflicts between Islamic and British law. He found it incredible that most imams would not – and could not – preach in the language of their adopted country, and he was the first Muslim to make this criticism clear.

He doubted, too, that priests or teachers could reach out to young British Muslims as if they were on home soil in Pakistan or Bangladesh, and was quite sure they should not try. As British Muslims became third- and fourth-generation citizens, he felt certain that the cross-pollination of ideas needed a new, Westernised approach, and an awareness and respect of all faiths, in order to make sense of it.

The prospectus of the Muslim College, which he established in 1986 to train imams in the new approach, and where he served as principal, states that the training of "traditional" imams "is not always sufficient to deal with the cultural environment of modern Western Europe and the USA, nor with problems arising from interaction with Western societies".

Perhaps most infuriating to fundamentalists was Badawi's firm belief in the idea of British Muslims, with British as a badge of honour, a social and cultural designation, not a mere branch of one contiguous caliphate. "Within a couple of generations Muslims will lose their cultural baggage. Indian and Pakistani ways will disappear. They will adopt Western cultural values, and the whole community will be brought together as British Muslims," he said.

A dislike of "cultural baggage" was at the heart of Badawi's rebellious streak. He campaigned against female genital mutilation, insisting that it was an outmoded cultural, not religious, practice with no causal link to Islam.

He stated that the fatwa had become overused, and that those who proclaimed them usually had no divine sanction. "Since Ayatollah Khomeini issued his against Salman Rushdie, everyone has opened a fatwa shop," he said.

Badawi incurred the wrath of Britain's imams in 1989 when he stated that, much as he disliked his book, should Rushdie knock at his door with the youth of Bradford at his heels, he would certainly give him sanctuary. He wished to restore the idea, lost in the Iranian Revolution, of loving the sinner, hating the sin.

Naturally, Badawi's belief in a type of Islam both acceptable to and supportive of Western society made him an "Uncle Tom" character to many imams. He seemed to represent the face of Islam that liberal, middle-class Britain hoped to do business with.

He was certainly an antidote to the gloom of 9/11 and the London bombings. Badawi, in explaining the religion's ability to adapt, would often refer to its golden age, its absorption of other faiths and its role in preserving the Classics. Such reasoned Islam, between mosque and minaret, he hoped would come to prominence in Britain.

Badawi prepared 38 articles on financial management with respect to Muslim law. In Britain, where most people maintain an enduring faith in the property market, Badawi's work in establishing sharia-compliant or "halal" mortgages may prove the most binding part of his work to bring the next generation into the fold. At the Islamic Real Estate Finance conference in London in July 2003, Badawi explained how Muslims could take advantage of his schemes, backed by the Treasury, to own property in Britain or overseas.

In 1997 Badawi established, with Sir Sigmund Sternberg and the Rev Marcus Braybrooke, the Three Faiths Forum – "To encourage friendship, goodwill and understanding amongst people of the three Abrahamic monotheistic faiths in the UK and elsewhere". He was vice-chairman of the World Congress of Faiths and director/trustee of the Forum Against Islamophobia and Racism (Fair). He was a founder-trustee of the Festival of Muslim Cultures, and it was his vision for UK Muslims to take a more prominent role that inspired the festival, which was launched this month.

Yet Badawi, given to the celebration of compatible faiths rather than a grudging cognisance of "people of the book", remained a maverick – albeit an increasingly important one.

Turned back from JFK Airport by US authorities in July last year, Badawi showed pity rather than anger. "They were very, very embarrassed and I felt sorry for them." He said, adding: "America is a lovely country. There is no reason why it should behave like that." Badawi had joined Iqbal Sacrani and other leaders of the faith to denounce the perpetrators of the London bombings eight days earlier. Their points of agreement were relatively few, however. Sacrani's recent statement that homosexuality is "not acceptable" and the Muslim Council of Britain (MCB) boycott last year of the Holocaust remembrance ceremony will give many cause to miss a peacemaker who would, wherever possible, give words of support and, where not, keep his own counsel.

In private, Badawi was jovial, warm and hospitable. He enjoyed nothing more than a friendly, reasonable debate on the values of Muslims in Britain today and the challenges of reconciling Islam and modernity in Britain and across the wider Muslim world.

He was, however, saddened by the growth of extremist sects and their appeal for many young, disillusioned Muslims. And he blamed the Government and press for listening to the self-publicists who, he believed, were trying to impose their leadership on the Muslim community in Britain.

Partly this was because he found that his own moderation was increasingly under attack from younger, more assertive leaders, and partly it was the natural resentment of an older man for those who, he believed, had elbowed him out of the limelight.

But he relished his own acceptance into British society (he was a member of the Athenaeum) and the recognition he was accorded by other scholars and academics. Even in old age – which was certainly not visible in his face – he was active in writing, lecturing and preaching. He was glad that many of his causes, especially the demand that imams should be properly trained and speak good English, were finally recognised by the Government. The MCB, which now represents the main umbrella group of British Muslim organisations, was planning a ceremony to honour his scholarship, faith and role as a pioneer in British-Muslim relations. But he died before any such proposal could be advanced.

He was appointed OBE (hon) in 1998 and KBE in 2004. He is survived by his wife, Maryam, and by a son and a daughter.

Zaki Badawi was born on August 11, 1922 and died on January 24, 2006.

Charles Forte

From milk bar to catering empire

March 1, 2007

In 1935 Charles Forte opened a milk bar in Upper Regent Street, London, with £500 drawn from his savings and another £3,000 borrowed from his father and a business contact. From that modest start, he became one of the most successful entrepreneurs of the postwar era, with a business empire that ranged across hotels, restaurants, theatres, coffee shops, pubs, motorway service areas, airport and airline catering, amusement parks, piers and confectionery.

Always a bold entrepreneur, Forte moved into a completely different league in 1970, when he merged his company with Trust Houses to form Trust Houses Forte (later Trusthouse Forte). With assets in the region of £120 million, the new group was one of the largest hotel and catering businesses in the world.

After fighting off a hostile bid from Allied Breweries, Forte maintained a tight grip on the business for more than two decades. When, in 1992, he finally stood down as chairman in favour of his son, Rocco, he was 84 years of age.

Appointed life president, Forte enjoyed his honorary title for just three years.

In 1996, after one of the most ferocious takeover battles of the decade, the Forte group was acquired by Granada for £3.9 billion.

The eldest of four children, Charles Forte was born in 1908 in Monforte Casalaticco, Italy. At the age of 4, he was sent to join his father, Rocco, in Scotland, where he had opened a small cafe in Loanhead, near Edinburgh. He attended Alloa Academy, where he became head boy, and then boarded at St Joseph's College, Dumfries.

At 17 he joined the family business, which now comprised a chain of ice-cream parlours and cafes, both in Scotland and along the South Coast of England. He learnt the ropes in a restaurant

196

in Weston-super-Mare. By 1929 he was manager of the Venetian Lounge in Brighton.

It was his father, he later told The Times, who shaped his business philosophy: "He had all those principles that now seem old-fashioned. Basic things that are so essential – about hygiene, about always being honest to customers and staff, about working hard and not being extravagant."

In 1934 Forte read a newspaper article about an Australian who had opened a milk bar in Fleet Street. Intrigued, he went to London to take a look and then approached the owner, Hugh Macintosh, with a business proposal – make him a partner and he would boost the bar's profits by adding sandwiches, ice-cream sundaes, pastries and a coffee machine. Macintosh was not prepared to depart from his original concept, however.

Undeterred, Forte scraped together enough money to open the Meadow Bar in Upper Regent Street, next to Boosey & Hawkes. By 1940 he owned eight such establishments in London as well as a central catering business to supply them, and was being described in the press as "the milk bar king".

After Italy's entry into war as an Axis power in June 1940, Forte, still at that time an Italian citizen, was interned on the Isle of Man. But he was released after three months, and was able to resume his business activities.

His company was to expand swiftly after 1945 as he capitalised on the opportunities presented by growing consumer spending power and the public's desire for higher standards of food and entertainment. He acquired a string of properties in Piccadilly, including Rainbow Corner, a former Maison Lyons, which he bought with a £30,000 loan from Prudential Assurance. By leasing back part of the property to himself at a rent of £4,000 a year and letting the rest to the Canadian Government for £8,000 a year, he produced an income of £12,000 on a £30,000 investment. In 1950 he bought the site of the Criterion Theatre for £800,000. Within six years he was able to boost the Criterion's turnover from £80,000 to £500,000.

In 1951 Forte won the contract to provide catering facilities at the Festival of Britain. He was later granted concessions at a number of airports, including Heathrow and Gatwick, and he won contracts from numerous European airlines to provide in-flight food.

Forte bought the Cafe Royal in 1954. Four years later he

acquired his first hotel, the Waldorf, in the Aldwych. At the end of the decade, he began to accumulate service station concessions on Britain's burgeoning motorway system.

After going public in 1962, the business would expand through the purchase of more hotels at home and abroad, and the acquisition of the chocolate manufacturer Terry's of York and the Kardomah cafe chain.

A hands-on, details man, Forte ran his companies on simple lines from the centre, with careful financial control. His boardroom philosophy, he declared, was to "satisfy our customers, increase our profitability, rear initiative, provide excellent working conditions and act with integrity at all times".

In 1970 the Forte group merged with Trust Houses, which controlled about 200 hotels, including such London institutions as Grosvenor House, the Hyde Park Hotel, Brown's and the Cavendish. It also held large stakes in two Travelodge companies, giving it a strong presence in both North America and Australia.

Before to the deal was struck, it was understood between Forte and Trust Houses' chairman, Lord Crowther, that Crowther would hold the same position at the new group, but would step down after a year in favour of Forte, who would initially serve as deputy chairman. Soon after the merger was completed, however, it became clear that Crowther did not see this understanding in that light. When challenged, he claimed that there was no enforceable contract and that he had merely expressed "an intention".

The tension between the two sides of the business increased still further as differences of operating culture emerged. In contrast to the Forte group, which had always relied on human contacts, discussion and personal supervision, Trust Houses had been run on highly bureaucratic lines. Whereas the staff in Trust Houses' HQ left work at 5.30pm, Forte's central management was accustomed to working late hours.

These problems were further exacerbated when Allied Breweries launched a £128 million takeover bid for THF that split the board and caused huge animosity.

Forte's response was swift, fierce and effective. Already the owner of by far the largest single share of the equity, he borrowed £2million to outbid Allied for shares in the market. Making adroit use of the media to promote his case, he then rallied support from friends, employees and other shareholders to secure the rejection of Allied's offer.

Having won control of the board of THF from Crowther, Forte became chief executive, a role he occupied until 1978, when he became executive chairman. Three years later he became non-executive chairman, a move that prepared the way for the succession of his son Rocco (now Sir Rocco).

In 1981 Forte launched a bid for the Savoy Hotel group but this was rejected. He later tried again, and after spending £38 million, he ended up with 69 per cent of the Savoy's equity but – owing to the group's unusual share structure – just 42 per cent of the voting capital. In 1989 he would finally acknowledge defeat and make peace with the Savoy's board and its chairman, Sir Hugh Wontner.

After his retirement as chairman in 1992 Forte continued to maintain a close watch on the business. Then, when Granada made its offer for the Forte group, he acted as his son's principal adviser. This time around, however, he found himself outflanked by another masterful manipulator of the media, Gerry Robinson, the Granada chief executive, who made much of the fact that he, too, was a self made man. During the course of a bitter war of words, the Fortes landed a few notable blows of their own, but THF failed to win the all-important support of a number of institutional investors, and was taken over by Granada, the £3.9 billion tender leaving the Forte family with about £350 million.

Forte's autobiography, *Forte*, published in 1986, portrayed a proud, passionate man who was utterly devoted to his family. It contained much humour and irony, its most memorable sections undoubtedly being those that were concerned with settling (or trying to settle) old scores, most notably with Trust Houses' Lord Crowther and the Savoy Hotel group's Sir Hugh Wontner.

Forte was knighted in 1970. He accepted a life peerage from Margaret Thatcher's Government in 1982, having turned down a peerage many years earlier when it had been offered on the proposal of Hugh Gaitskell of the Labour Party, then Leader of the Opposition.

Charles Forte married, in 1943, Irene Chierico. He is survived by her and by their son, Sir Rocco, and five daughters, one of whom is the interior designer and hotelier Olga Polizzi.

Charles Forte was born on 26 November, 1908. He died on 28 February, 2007.

Michael Hamburger

Modest man who gave his life to translation, literary criticism and poetry

June 11, 2007

Michael Hamburger, OBE, poet, critic and translator, was born on March 22, 1924. He died on June 7, 2007, aged 83.

The poet, critic and translator Michael Hamburger was a key figure in English and European letters for more than 60 years.

An original, questioning temperament with a meticulous sense of the responsibilities of language, he earned the respect of writers of several contrasting generations. As a translator he had particular success in introducing the work of Holderlin and Paul Celan to English readers, but the authors he served with unfailing sensitivity ran the stylistic and historical gamut from Buchner to Rilke and Trakl, and from Goethe to Enzensberger and Grass.

Michael Peter Leopold Hamburger was born in 1924 in Berlin. His father, Professor Richard Hamburger, was a Jewish paediatrician with literary interests whose own father had introduced ideas from the French avant-garde into Germany. His mother, born Lili Hamburg, a Polish Quaker, was a member of a prominent banking family.

Childhood friends in Berlin included the brothers Clement and Lucian Freud. Soon after Hitler became Chancellor in 1933 the Hamburgers moved to Britain. Richard Hamburger had to retrain in Edinburgh before settling in St John's Wood, North London. There he managed a limited general practice, after developing Hodgkin's disease, from which he died in 1940.

Michael Hamburger was one of four children. His renegade younger brother Paul was to become the publisher and philanthropist Lord Hamlyn. Michael was an academic success at George Watson's school, Edinburgh, and Westminster School (where he was a contemporary of Tony Benn), before winning an exhibition in Modern Languages at Christ Church, Oxford, in 1941, having taken the entrance exam a year early to save his mother his school fees.

His wartime degree was interrupted by military service but, nursing the literary ambitions which he had held since before his father's death, Hamburger published his first book of poems, translations from Holderlin, in 1943 at the age of 19.

His characteristic reticence was displayed when it took a direct order from his commanding officer in the infantry for him to accept an invitation to read from the poems at the Poetry Society. The original poems that appeared in his first two collections, Flowering Cactus (1950) and Poems 1950-51, drew on the rather inflated poetic diction that was current in the immediate postwar period, but already demonstrated Hamburger's individual tone and preoccupations. This was particularly true of the longer poem, From the Notebook of a European Tramp, whose narrator wanders through a devastated Europe of bombed cities and displacement camps, noting:

"I still tried to live like other men and not to know

That all we lived for had already died."

From 1948 Hamburger had attempted to live the life of a freelance writer and translator. He associated with some of the leading literary figures of the time, including Edwin Muir, Kathleen Raine and Robert Graves, with whom he stayed in Majorca. He even passed as sufficiently bohemian to be introduced to the notorious Aleister Crowley.

During this period he also met Ann Ellen File, the poet Anne Beresford, whom he married in 1951. The birth of their first child persuaded him of the need for regular employment, and he became an assistant lecturer in German at University College London, where his professor would introduce him as a journalist, on the grounds that his academic efforts were more concentrated on his articles for The Times Literary Supplement than on the thesis he was supposed to complete as a condition of his post. He moved to Reading in 1955, first as lecturer and then reader in German, and his writing on German literature completed during this period was collected in Reason and Energy (1957) and Prophecy to Exorcism (1966).

Hamburger left Reading in 1964, again having earned the antagonism of a professor – this time for the presumption of driving a second-hand Daimler. He took a series of temporary appointments in the US, which allowed him to devote at least six months of the year to full-time writing.

The peripatetic lifestyle may have strengthened his literary work as he became open to the more concrete expression of the objectivist strand in American poetry, but it had a disastrous effect on his personal life, leading to the temporary breakdown of his marriage and a psychological crisis.

It was at this crisis point that Hamburger found his distinctive tone as a poet, particularly in the sequence Travelling, which was extended twice after its first publication and finally completed in 1976. In this poem, his free-moving, ruminative lyricism is both philosophical and minutely sensitive to the natural world:

"And I moved on, to learn
One of the million histories
One weather, one dialect
Of herbs, one habitat
After migration, displacement
With greedy lore to pounce
On a place and possess it,
With the mind's weapons, words,
While between land and water,
Yellow vultures mewing,
Looped empty air
Once filled with the hundred names
Of the nameless, or swooped
To the rocks, for carrion."

The desire "to pounce on a place and possess it" expressed itself in another area of Hamburger's life – gardening. First in Reading, and in a much more ambitious way when he and Anne Beresford settled in Suffolk after their remarriage, he preserved rare varieties of apple trees by growing them from seed.

Two prose classics derive from this period of Hamburger's career: The Truth of Poetry (1969), a compelling critical study of European poetry from Baudelaire on, and his vivid, quirky autobiography, A Mug's Game (1973), revised as String of Beginnings (1991).

His retirement to Suffolk also saw some of his most significant achievements as a translator, particularly his masterly version of the notoriously complex poems of Celan, published in 1988 and 1995.

He received numerous awards, not least for the distinction and dedication with which he worked to make the riches of German literature accessible to English-speaking readers. His translations twice won the Schlegel-Tieck Prize, and he was awarded the Goethe Medal (1986) and the European translation prize (1990).

He was appointed OBE in 1992.

Three years later he published his Collected Poems, followed by the sequence Late (1997) and a further collection, Intersections (2000). Despite this activity, Hamburger felt at odds with the contemporary poetry scene, particularly with what he saw as a decline in serious literary reviewing. In his book The Rings of Saturn, W. G. Sebald, another German author who had settled in East Anglia, recreated a visit to Hamburger in Suffolk, picturing jars of preserved fruit in a pantry behind Jiffy bags stacked for re-use as part of an epiphany of the writer's lonely struggle, in which he saw himself and Hamburger as twin souls.

Hamburger was to outlive his younger admirer, whose long poem After Nature he translated for posthumous publication in 2002.

Hamburger's 2002 volume, From a Diary of Non-Events, was a celebration of the strengths of the "anti-poetry" of minimal rhetorical gesture, whose postwar development in several European languages had been treated in The Truth of Poetry.

The events of the year 2001, including the foot-and-mouth epidemic, his golden wedding, the death of his brother Paul and the attack on the World Trade Centre, were subsumed to the cycles of nature. His was a poetry of restitution, moving from global conflict and dualities of identity to the recurring rhythms of a threatened natural world to which he was minutely attentive.

"And here once more on a sun-dappled patch
Cleared of ground elder roots
One twenty-five-year-old cyclamen corm, exotic,
Kindles two hundred flowers
Against an almost overshadowing yew,
Blackness that has not killed but sheltered it."

He is survived by his wife and two daughters and a son.

Clement Freud

Broadcaster, restaurateur, maverick and wit

April 17, 2009

For more than four decades Clement Freud was one of Britain's most versatile and enduring personalities. Famed for his lugubrious, whiskered visage and deadpan wit, he was at various times a club proprietor, cooking correspondent, restaurant reviewer, sporting correspondent, amateur jockey, Liberal MP, long-time journalist, and television and radio broadcaster. He was known to millions of Radio 4 listeners as the dry and articulate regular contestant on the comic panel game Just a Minute.

He was still appearing on the programme up to his death, and his final appearance has yet to be broadcast.

The last of three sons born to Ernst and Lucie Freud, Clement Raphael Freud was born in Berlin in 1924 (on "twentyfourfourt-wentyfour" as he used to say). The grandson of the psychoanalyst Sigmund Freud, Clement remembered his grandfather fondly and bore his famous name largely with resigned dignity. His older brothers are the artist Lucian Freud and Stephen Freud, who until recently was the proprietor of an ironmonger's shop in Marylebone.

The family moved to Britain in 1933 and Clement was educated at Dartington Hall, and then St Paul's. (Sigmund Freud and his immediate family did not leave Vienna until 1938, settling in London where he died in 1939. His four sisters remained in Vienna and died in concentration camps.) Clement left school at 16 and was apprenticed as a cook at the Dorchester.

Towards the end of the war he was called up into the Army, serving in the Royal Ulster Rifles and finishing his martial stint, thanks to his fluency in German, as a liaison officer at the Nuremberg trials. It was a grim period in his life which he was loath to speak about except in lighthearted tones.

After the war he returned to catering, opening the Royal Court Theatre Club, above the Chelsea theatre. Here, for £10 a week, he engaged such unknown artists for cabaret shows as Rolf Harris, David Frost, Jonathan Miller and Dudley Moore. It was here that he cut his teeth as a performer, introducing each act with his trademark mordancy.

In 1956 he got his first break in Fleet Street, becoming a sports writer on The Observer. By the mid-1960s he was writing in numerous places on various matters: humorous articles for the News of the World; cookery for The Observer; and sports writer for the original Sun. His byline also appeared in countless magazines, and by 1967 he was believed to be the highest-paid journalist in the country, earning about £30,000 a year.

As with all things in his life, he was a very competitive journalist, though at times too competitive. He broke his leg while trying to learn how to ski for a magazine article, and once had to be rescued after taking an RAF survival course in the Bavarian Alps, during which he got frostbite.

In the early 1970s he went into politics, and was selected by the Liberals to stand as MP for the Isle of Ely, Cambridgeshire, in a 1973 by-election.

When it was announced that he would stand for the seat, the sitting Conservatives took it as a joke, though they were chastened after Freud won, especially since the Liberals had not even stood there in the 1970 general election.

Freud placed a £1,000 bet on himself, his winnings being two years' salary for an MP.

As a celebrity MP – albeit a hardworking one for his constituency and the Liberals' spokesman on education, the arts and broadcasting – Freud regularly featured in the headlines for his outspoken views and at times unorthodox behaviour. In 1980 he made a speech in the Commons calling for better wine to be served at the Houses of Parliament; in 1981 – against government protocol – he was caught using House of Commons writing paper to try to raise money for the Liberal Party; and when the Northern Ireland Secretary Jim Prior ruled out the hanging of terrorists, Freud suggested that they might be lynched instead.

He also got into trouble for gambling at the Playboy Club in 1981 while he was a director of the club, thereby contravening the Gaming Act. The court heard how Freud had called bets on the roulette wheel even as the ball dropped, and on every occasion the bets were accepted. His son Matthew remembers that his fourth birthday party was held at the club, Bunny Girls and all.

A long-time correspondent for the Racing Post, he liked a flutter, managing to win £10,000 from the 1987 Greenwich by-election (shortly before that year's general election) which was won by the Social Democratic Party candidate Rosie Barnes.

As a result of the Playboy Club affair, Freud was dropped from Beefeater's lucrative gin commercials; though he had already become a celebrity in the 1970s, starring alongside Henry the bloodhound (who with his fixed stare and droopy eyes he strangely resembled), advertising dog food in television commercials.

Known to his friends as Clay or Clem, he was not always the most agreeable of men. Claiming that it gave him an allergic reaction, he was fiercely against smoking, and was known to stick his head behind curtains at dinner parties in protest at other people smoking cigarettes. He could on occasions be less than good tempered and as an MP he got through ten secretaries in eight years.

He was eventually ousted by his constituents (now in the seat of Cambridgeshire North East) in the 1987 general election. Although he was compensated that year by a knighthood, he was reputedly unhappy not to be elevated to the peerage and threatened to stand in the 1988 Kensington by-election as an independent Liberal against the official Social and Liberal Democrat candidate.

There were other fallouts, most notably with his brother Lucian. They had not spoken since they were very young, because, according to Clement's daughter Emma, Lucian had bet his brother that he could beat him in a race to Green Park. "When Clem ran off, Lucian then started shouting: 'Stop thief! He's stolen my money'." Clement was so angry that he never spoke to him again. (When Lucian was once asked when it was that he fell out with his brother he replied: "I never fell in with him.") In fact, betting on anything and everything proved to be a trait of all three Freud brothers.

Matthew believes that from their early teens onwards hardly a day went by when the brothers weren't putting money on a horse. But they remained wary of each other and although, when young, they often frequented the same coffee bar in Marylebone High Street they always sat at separate tables and would try to arrive at different times.

Freud once challenged Sir Hugh Fraser that he was the better horseman and beat him in a private race to win £1,000.

In his post-parliamentary career, Freud consolidated his position as a celebrity, returning to journalism most notably as a diarist for

The Times. Naturally, his column embraced dining out. In a Soho restaurant he asked for a bowl of chicken broth. "I have washed up in better and hotter liquid," he observed laconically.

He was also a contributor to The New Yorker, Punch and, right up to his death, The Sun. He appeared in a chef's capacity on many a television programme, and, since his first appearance on it in 1968, remained a stalwart on Just a Minute.

In 1990 he was commissioned by British Rail to design the fillings for its new sandwiches, which bore his signature, and that year he also played himself in the BBC's production of the Kingsley Amis thriller The Green Man.

He wrote many books, mostly on gastronomy, including No-one Else Has Complained (1988) and The Book of Hangovers (1981). A children's book, Grimble (1968) attracted a fan club of 150,000 or so for a time. Freud wrote it for his children in the first instance and later narrated it on BBC Television's Jackanory, completing the broadcast by cooking a simple recipe.

He won the annual award of the Guild of Professional Toastmakers for best after-dinner speaker of 1973, and was from 1974 to 1980 Rector of the University of Dundee. He was Rector of the University of St Andrews from 2002 to 2006. In 1969 he was winner in his class in the Daily Mail London to New York Air Race and in 1971 he won line honours in the Cape Town to Rio Yacht Race.

In 2006, at the age of 82, having recently been fitted with titanium and plastic knees, he set about climbing "the three peaks": not Ben Nevis, Scafell and Snowdon, but Parliament Hill, Primrose Hill and Notting Hill.

"Regardless of the surgeon's promise that I would be able to dance the tango by Remembrance Day, I am still pretty lame," he wrote in The Times.

"When propositioned recently by a woman to 'come upstairs and make love', I had to explain that it was one or the other." Nonetheless, he managed to plant an "I was here" flag on all three summits in one morning.

His autobiography, Freud Ego, was published in 2001. He listed his recreations in Who's Who as racing, backgammon and pétanque.

Freud was a playful, nonconformist and contrary man who got an impish pleasure from confusing people with his sharp intellect. Nicholas Parsons, the chairman of Just a Minute, was often the butt of his withering barbs.

His pet hates included cigarettes, scent and Dr Scholl's sandals. Matthew Freud believes that his father became such a success because he was driven to prove that he was more than just the grandson of a famous man.

Clement Freud was married to Jill Raymond in 1950. He liked to refer to her as his "first wife" – "to keep her on her toes". The marriage was a happy one. He is survived by her and their three sons and two daughters, who include the television presenter Emma Freud and the public relations executive Matthew Freud.

Sir Clement Freud, journalist, broadcaster, cook and former MP, was born on April 24, 1924. He died on April 15, 2009, aged 84.

Ralf Dahrendorf

Brilliant sociologist and ubiquitous politician
June 19, 2009

Ralf Dahrendorf was prominent in public life in Britain as well
as in his native Germany, not only as an outstanding authority
in sociology and related disciplines but also as an influential man
of action, in his roles as party spokesman and minister in Bonn,
European Commissioner in Brussels, head of two famous educational institutions in Britain, and active member of the House of
Lords.

Ralf Dahrendorf was born in Hamburg in 1929, the son of the
Social Democrat politician Gustav Dahrendorf, an anglophile,
and Ralf and his younger brother, Frank, were both given English
names.

The circumstances of Dahrendorf's boyhood in wartime Berlin
were turbulent and even tragic. In July 1943 all four of his grandparents perished in the massive British air raids on Hamburg. A
year later his father, who had been involved with other leading
Social Democrats in the background of the plot to assassinate
Hitler, was sentenced to prison, and was released only when the
war ended. Meanwhile, the young Ralf Dahrendorf, who was
a member of a discussion and reading group organised by an
anti-Nazi teacher, was arrested and imprisoned in a concentration
camp to the east of Berlin. Here he witnessed among other things
the exceptionally brutal execution of a Russian prisoner of war for
stealing some margarine.

Dahrendorf was freed in the general confusion accompanying
the Russian advance on Berlin. Here, as the life of the city was
being re-organised, the Russian authorities made him responsible
(although he was only 16) for transport and food distribution in
one of the urban districts. His father accepted a position in charge
of power supply in the Soviet Zone but fell out with the Russians
and succeeded, with British help, in getting his family to Hamburg.

This came just in time to save them from persecution by the author-ities, as Gustav Dahrendorf was one of the Social Democratic leaders who resisted the forcible merger of their party with the Communists, to form the "Socialist Unity Party" of the Soviet Zone. In Hamburg, in the British Zone, Ralf Dahrendorf came to know some of the leading officials of the Control Commission, including Robert Birley, Professor T. H. Marshall and Noel (later Lord) Annan. This began a connection with Britain which was to last the whole of his life: he was deeply impressed by a visit to the Anglo-German discussion centre at Wilton Park early in 1948, and when he entered the House of Lords in 1993, Noel Annan was one of his sponsors.

In 1947 Dahrendorf began his studies of philosophy and classics at Hamburg University. His doctoral dissertation, completed when he was 22, was concerned with the concept of justice in the thought of Karl Marx, and was soon published as his first book, Marx in Perspective. In the same year, 1952, he came to the sociology department of the London School of Economics, where T. H. Marshall was now a professor, and where his London PhD, on the nature of the unskilled labour force, marked his transition from philosophy to sociology. His fellow-graduate students at "the School", who included A. H. ("Chelly") Halsey, David Lockwood, Ronald Dore, Jean Floud and Asher Tropp, were attracted to American sociology because it then firmly believed in itself and in its capacity to become a science. However, they continued at the same time to see some value in Marxism, even in those days of the alleged "end of ideology". The intersection of these two preoccupations resulted in their characteristic quasi-Marxist revisionism within the transatlantic corpus of sociological theory of the time: the "functionalism" of Talcott Parsons, they argued, overrated harmony and value consensus in society, and underrated the importance of power-relationships and of conflict. A criticism of this view is the main concern of Dahrendorf's Class and Class Conflict (German edition 1957, English translation 1959), one of the books which established his reputation as a sociologist.

It may be said that he owed his rapid rise to academic promi-nence partly to the fact that, when German intellectual life was being revived in the post-Hitler years, in a world dominated by America, in sociology as in other areas, he was one of the first of the rising German generation to acquire confident familiarity with the new centres of activity, such as the Centre for Advanced Study in Palo Alto, California, where he spent the academic year 1957-58.

His career progressed rapidly. Junior appointments in Frankfurt and Saarbrücken were followed by professorial posts in Hamburg, Tübingen and Konstanz. At Konstanz (a newly founded university, called by some "the Sussex of Germany"), he was the first dean of the social science faculty.

Two other themes became prominent in his life and work. One was the influence of the political liberalism of Karl Popper and of the economic liberalism of Milton Friedman, which he was later to record in his BBC Reith Lectures of 1974, The New Liberty.

This commitment to liberalism manifested itself when he entered German politics in the 1960s not as a Social Democrat like his father, but as a liberal, a member of the Free Democratic Party. In his writings, too, he saw the need to go beyond the "social-democratic consensus", and to face the problems engendered by the very success of that honourable tradition. His view, significantly, was that in the modern world liberty was more at risk than equality.

The other prominent theme in Dahrendorf's life at this stage was the personally felt problem of the proper relationship or balance between fact and value, scholarship and politics, thought and action.

It was in a way ironical – since his political views moved mildly to the right – that his life continued to be based firmly on the essentially progressive concept of the unity of theory and practice, and a determination that the world be not only understood, but also changed.

The outward manifestation of this resolve was a rapid progression in public life, from an advisory post on education policy with the Baden-Württemberg Land government to membership of the Land parliament (1968-69) and of the national executive committee of the Free Democratic Party (1968-74).

As a prominent spokesman for reformist liberalism, Dahrendorf was highly influential in preparing his party, and also the German electorate, for the move to the left which came in 1969, when the "social-liberal" coalition led by Chancellor Willy Brandt took office after a substantial victory at the polls. Dahrendorf, himself elected to the Bundestag, was immediately appointed by his party leader Walter Scheel, the new Vice-Chancellor and Foreign Minister, to the post of Parliamentary Under-Secretary for Foreign Affairs.

After a few months in office in Bonn he moved on, in July 1970, to become one of the two German members of the European Commission in Brussels. Here he was responsible for the Community's foreign relations until January 1973 (when his post was taken over by his new British colleague, Christopher Soames) and then, until October 1974, for research, science and education. During his four years in Brussels, Dahrendorf made an important contribution to the European Community's progress, thanks to the lively and enterprising way in which he carried out part of a commissioner's functions, namely the devising, negotiating and executing of new policies.

Sometimes this meant the development of closer relations with countries of the Third World, and sometimes the achievement of mutual recognition of academic and professional qualifications between the Community's member states. On the other hand, he was clearly impatient with the more bureaucratic duties of his Brussels post (in 1971 he caused a stir by publishing pseudonymous articles in a German weekly, criticising the Community's ways of working), and in 1974 he returned to the LSE, this time as its director.

He later admitted to having been influenced by the opinion of his close friend, the US historian Fritz Stern, that this appointment "would fit very well with your biography". Dahrendorf took over from Sir Walter Adams at a difficult moment in the LSE's history.

The student turbulence of the Adams period, which might have deterred others from accepting the post, had in fact abated, though Dahrendorf displayed tact, patience and physical courage (as he had done in Germany in the troubled 1960s) in dealing with some students who still persisted in histrionic dispute. Under his leadership the school now faced the problems arising from the financial stringency of the 1970s and 1980s, notably the effect on student numbers of the Government's raising of the fees charged to those from abroad, a sizeable proportion of the LSE's enrolment.

In some ways, his directorship tended to be cautious rather than adventurous: it would probably have been hard for him to promote new initiatives, against internal opposition, at a time of financial retrenchment when there was little room for manoeuvre.

In one controversial episode, his proposal in 1976 to create at the school a centre or institute for policy studies, he gave way to the strong opposition of some of the senior professors, who argued that such an innovation would be contrary to the LSE's principles of independent academic inquiry, even though others regretted that he did not fight harder for his proposal.

During the the Labour Government of 1974-79 Dahrendorf was close to the country's centre of power, but this ceased to be the case when the Conservatives under Margaret Thatcher returned to office in 1979. One feature of his style of leadership at the LSE was that, although he was constantly travelling in Britain and abroad – lecturing, broadcasting, serving on a royal commission or some other body, and generally enhancing LSE's public reputation – he was always ready to give detailed attention to really important issues facing the school, such as professorial appointments or financial problems .

His life-long commitment to the LSE, even after he left the directorship, was demonstrated in many ways. When he was elevated to the peerage in 1993, he chose the title of Baron Dahrendorf, of Clare Market in the City of Westminster, and in later life he affirmed that his favourite book, among all those he had published, was his monumental history of the LSE, written to mark its centenary in 1995. In 1984, after a decade at Houghton Street, Dahrendorf returned to the sociology chair in Konstanz which he had left for a political career in 1968, and it seemed for a time that he was likely to re-enter German politics as well.

He remained active in journalism and broadcasting, and he continued to preside over the educational foundation linked to the Free Democratic Party, the Friedrich Naumann Stiftung.

However, his links with the English-speaking world remained strong too. He was an active member of the boards of the Ford Foundation and the Ditchley Foundation, and he gave vigorous support to the Constitutional Reform Centre established in London in 1985.

Dahrendorf's friends found it hard to believe that he would remain permanently in Konstanz, and it was no surprise when, after spending the year 1986-87 at the Russell Sage Foundation in New York, he became Warden of St Antony's College, Oxford, in succession to Sir Raymond Carr. He then spent ten years guiding and developing the fortunes of a still-young academic institution which, despite its extremely high international reputation, suffered from an acute lack of resources. Funds were raised, new buildings were erected and the reputation of the college, as a world-class centre for international and comparative studies, was further enhanced. At the same time Dahrendorf was playing an increasingly influential role on a wider stage. He adopted British nationality in 1988 (so that the honorary KBE to which he had been appointed in 1982 now made him formally "Sir Ralf"), and in 1993 he was appointed a life peer.

In his early years in the Lords he took the Liberal Democrat whip, but as time went by he came to feel less committed to any party line, and became a cross-bencher. Over the years he contributed to the deliberations of the Upper House in many ways: one of his most significant roles was that of chairman, for several years, of the Lords' Select Committee on Delegated Powers. He also held directorships in the fields of industry and banking, and continued to produce an impressive stream of books on contemporary affairs, notably on developments in the new Europe which emerged after the end of the Cold War.

Dahrendorf will perhaps be remembered in two ways in particular: first, as the internationally renowned thinker and man of action whose achievements were recognised by decorations and honorary degrees from a great number of countries; and second, in Britain, as the German-turned-Briton whose contributions to British thinking and policy on social affairs, as a BBC Reith Lecturer, television commentator and parliamentarian, were arguably greater than those of any German since Bismarck's ideas shaped the social policy of Lloyd George. Dahrendorf married first, in 1954, his LSE fellow-student Vera Bannister, by whom he had three daughters, and second, in 1980, Dr Ellen de Kadt. His is survived by his third wife, Christiane, and his three daughters.

Lord Dahrendorf, KBE, director of the LSE, 1974-84, and Warden of St Antony's College, Oxford, 1987-97, was born on May 1, 1929. He died on June 17, 2009, aged 80.

Squadron Leader Mahinder Singh Pujji

Fighter pilot over France, North Africa and Burma

September 28, 2010

A graduate in law from Bombay University, Mahinder Singh Pujji was already a qualified pilot by the time war came in 1939, and he volunteered for RAF service the following year. Coming to the UK for further training, he saw service as a fighter pilot in sweeps over France and in North Africa, in both of which theatres he was involved in intense action.

He was subsequently posted back to India where he flew ground attack and reconnaissance operations over the jungles of Burma, participating in air operations over the strategically important battle for Kohima. Pujji ended the war as a squadron leader, having been awarded the Distinguished Flying Cross. After nearly 20 years living in India he settled in Britain in the mid-1970s.

Mahinder Singh Pujji was born the son of a senior government official in Simla, India in 1918, the former hill station in the Himalayan foothills which then served as the summer capital of the Indian Empire. He read law at Bombay (Mumbai) University, learning to fly at Delhi Flying Club, where he qualified as a pilot in 1937. Before the war he was working for Shell Oil as a fuelling superintendent.

Volunteering for RAF service in 1940, he was one of the first batch of 24 Indian pilots who were posted to Britain for operational training that summer. Like his contemporary Ranjan Dutt (obituary, November 6, 2009), who subsequently became an air vice-marshal in the postindependence Indian Air Force, Pujji distinguished himself on this first course and, like Dutt, was selected as a fighter pilot.

As a Sikh, he was determined not to be deflected from wearing the turban, which is mandatory to the religion although at first this was deemed by authority to be unsuitable headgear for an RAF officer and impractical for a fighter pilot. However, it soon became accepted that the RAF cap badge could be affixed to it without prejudice either to his performance as a pilot or to the dignity of the service, and Pujji wore his turban both on the ground and on operations until the end of the war.

He later claimed that the turban had helped to prevent him suffering serious impact injuries when he crash-landed after his plane was badly damaged in a dogfight over the Channel. "There was blood pouring from my head, but that six feet of wound cloth which makes up my turban saved me from worse impact injuries," he said.

His first posting was with 253 (Hyderabad) Squadron, operating Hurricanes, with which in the spring and summer of 1941 he flew fighter sweeps by day and night from bases in southern England over occupied France. He was next posted to 43 Squadron in which he served as a flight commander on fighter sweeps and intruder sorties.

In 1942 he was posted to North Africa where he flew American-built Tomahawk fighters in the intensive air battles which raged over the ground forces in the Western Desert. Pujji was shot down and wounded, and spent time in hospital in Cairo, before returning to the front line. In his dogfights with the fighters of the Luftwaffe, his final tally was two Messerschmitt Me109s shot down and three damaged.

He was next posted to India where he was assigned to the North West Frontier and flew Lysander and Hurricanes on army co-operation and reconaissance sorties over Afghanistan and Waziristan. As he recalled, it was hazardous work over inhospitable terrain with a certain and horrible death awaiting any pilot who fell into the hands of the ferocious Hoor tribesmen.

Pujji's next two tours of the war were served in Burma, where he flew "Hurribombers" – as Hurricanes used in ground attack and armed reconnaissance operations were styled. These were with No 6 and then No 4 Squadron, which soon became known as "the eyes of the 14th Army", which, under its commander General William Slim, was involved in dislodging its Japanese opponents from Burma.

One of Pujji's most notable reconnaissance feats was to locate a force of 300 West African troops under American command, who had become detached and lost in the jungle. All American attempts to locate them had failed and RAF help was sought.

Flying low over the jungle, Pujji had to circle the clearing in whose fringes the troops were hiding from the enemy, scribble a message on a notepad on his knee and drop it accurately. When the Americans, following his co-ordinates, failed to find the lost troops, Pujji's report was called into question. It was not until he personally led an American Lightning fighter to the spot that he was vindicated. He was awarded the DFC for his Burma services.

After the war Pujji remained in India and after independence in 1947 had a busy career in Indian civil aviation as an administrator and air traffic controller. He continued flying himself and set many gliding records.

In 1974 he came to England, settling in London where he managed a hotel. In East Ham, where he made his home, he was in retirement an active member of many voluntary groups. In October 2000 he was made an honorary Freeman of the London Borough of Newham. He later moved to Gravesend, Kent, and a biography, *For King and Another Country*, was published earlier this year.

A popular and frequent figure at veterans' events, he was always a prominent guest at such events as Black History Month at the RAF Museum, Hendon, in 2003 and the opening of the RAF Museum's Diversity of the Royal Air Force exhibition in 2009.

Squadron Leader Mahinder Singh Pujji, DFC, wartime fighter pilot, was born on August 14, 1918. He died on September 18, 2010, aged 92.

Lucian Freud

Brilliant painter and prolific lover
July 22, 2011

Throughout the 1980s the reputation of Lucian Freud grew steadily nationally and internationally, and since the death of Francis Bacon in 1992 he was widely recognised as the greatest living painter. He was certainly the leading figure in what has been called the school of London – named on the model of the École de Paris, and, like that, consisting largely of immigrant artists rather than natives.

But leadership of such heterogeneous assemblage should not be taken to imply the existence around Freud of any significant body of disciples, let alone pupils. As a painter, Freud was always the cat who walked by himself. His bold, flamboyant style of realistic painting, heavy with impasto, was essentially his own invention, for the most part sublimely unconcerned with fashionable practice: even when minute realism in painting came back into vogue his whole manner of applying paint to canvas was the direct antithesis of the photographic smoothness aimed at by hyperrealists.

With hindsight it is possible to see connections between Freud's mature style and that of the "unsparing" portraits and nudes that Stanley Spencer was painting in the 1930s, but it is dubious whether this indicates influence or merely likemindedness. Similarly, apparent links between Freud's work and that of late German academic painters like Lotte Laserstein – much remarked on when Laserstein had her first ever one-woman London show at the age of 89 in 1987 – are most likely quite coincidental.

Though Freud was originally German, born in Berlin the son of Sigmund Freud's youngest son Ernst, he and his family, including his brothers Clement, the writer, broadcaster and former MP, and Stephen – moved to London when he was 10, on Hitler's accession to power in 1933. Already, in his time at the Franzosisches Gymnasium in Frankfurt, he had marked himself out as a compulsive draughtsman. Clearly he had the makings of a juvenile prodigy to more people than just his adoring, artistic family. When he found artistic expression for his second great passion, horse-riding, by sculpting a stone horse at the age of 15, his father was sufficiently impressed to take it to the Central School of Arts and Crafts. More significantly, the school was sufficiently impressed to admit him immediately.

Freud was not only artistically but also socially precocious. During the two years he spent at the Central School he was living mostly in a studio in Fitzrovia and getting to know all sorts of notables and influential people on more or less equal terms. His family indeed seems to have been amazingly willing to let him run his own life on his own terms, and when he decided, on the advice of someone casually met in a café, to exchange the Central School for the East Anglian School of Drawing and Painting in Dedham, Essex, no one raised any objection.

The school was at that time run by Cedric Morris and his life-partner Lett Hains. At this time Freud was painting in what at a glance seems to be a rather Primitive style, though closer inspection suggests a surprising sophistication of approach. Morris himself was something of a primitive in his style of painting, but provided his pupils with a liberating influence and the confidence to paint and draw just the way he felt, however eccentric it might seem.

At Dedham Freud was the star pupil, and remained so even after he had contrived to burn the place down with a carelessly disposed cigarette end. (That, at least, is the legend, and the school certainly was destroyed by fire in July 1939.) Freud stayed on with Morris, living and painting in Morris's own home. In 1941 he enlisted in the Merchant Navy, but was invalided out in a few months. For the time being he went back to Morris, who was now at Hadleigh in Suffolk. Here he did many of those meticulously detailed drawings, making a certain stiffness and awkwardness into a deliberate effect of style, which remain his first widely known and appreciated works.

By 1943 Freud was back in London, painting and drawing in what was already unmistakably his own style, in which needle-sharp perceptions of reality were laced with an element of surreal-istic bizarreness and a spikiness and preoccupation with death which allied him (unwillingly, it would seem) with the contem-porary school of British Neo-Romantics, with one of whom, John Craxton, he shared a studio for a couple of years.

It was in such company that Freud had his own earliest significant public showings: with Julian Trevelyan and Felix Kelly at Lefevre in 1944; with Trevelyan, Craxton, Colquhoun and MacBryde at the same gallery in 1946; and with Craxton at the London Gallery in 1947. By 1954 he was considered important enough to share the British Pavilion at the Venice Biennale with Ben Nicholson and Francis Bacon, but, curiously, he does not seem to have had any notable one-man shows until he joined Marlborough Fine Art's stable of artists in 1958.

Freud taught at the Slade School of Art from 1948-58. The Duke and Duchess of Devonshire were early patrons, hanging his paintings at their home, Chatsworth House, Derbyshire.

During the 1950s Freud's style had evolved considerably. His early style aimed at a hard, smooth finish concealing all evidence of individual brush-strokes. In this style he painted a number of his most famous works, including the one-breast-bared *Girl with a White Dog* (1951-52), the faintly surreal *Interior in Paddington* (1951) and the 1952 portrait of Francis Bacon which was notoriously stolen from the Berlin National Galerie version of Freud's 1988 touring retrospective. (One can see why Herbert Read then dubbed him "the Ingres of Existentialism".)

But by the end of the 1950s he had moved on to something very like his mature style: much more evidently painterly, with the forms of the nudes upon which he increasingly concentrated boldly sculpted in a heavy impasto. It was as though, in terms of the 20th-century German art with which he seemed increasingly to align himself, he had moved from a typical Neue Sachlichkeit exteriority to an almost Expressionist subjectivity, involving an emotional charge which could no longer be contained within hard edges and crisply delineated forms.

There has seldom been any argument about Freud's extraordinary technical skill, or the individuality of his vision. On the other hand, the quality of his vision and the nature of his attitude towards his subjects have provoked a lot of argument and positive hostility. A frequent complaint has been that his nudes – especially the female nudes – are lacking in any sense of compassion or even of warm sensuality, presenting the bodies of his subjects very much as meat on a slab.

Those who fancied their skills at amateur psychoanalysis often brought to bear the skimpy evidences of his secretive but much talked-about private life, seeing in the paintings clear signs of the rooted misogyny that his grandfather, Sigmund Freud, considered to be the mark of compulsive Don Juanism. (Freud did not make much secret of his womanising and apparent need to impregnate as many as possible of his casual contacts: he acknowledged various illegitimate children, and some sober estimates put their number at more than 30.)

The charges levelled against Freud of uglification and derision were not necessarily diminished or convincingly countered as time went by, and his contribution to the National Gallery's series of Artist's Eye selections in 1987 seemed to offer corroboration that this was the way his taste worked: every single piece he selected from the gallery's permanent collection, whether famous or normally tucked away in the reserves, had enough elements of ugliness or grotesquerie to make it clear that these were a strong element in their appeal. But as Freud gradually assumed modern-classic status, the chorus of doubts was stilled, and his art was marketed by his regular dealer, James Kirkman, with unusual skill, major works even appearing one at a time, in an atmosphere of reverence, like the magnum opus of some Victorian master.

It was no doubt partly because of this that Freud became in the 1970s a sought-after portrait painter. He began with several portraits of his mother, painted in his new "unsparing" style, but went on to paint many public figures – perhaps most famously Lord Goodman – to universal admiration. He was particularly successful with male sitters, partly at least because his later portraits tended to be images of power rather than pulchritude, his penchant for concentrating on the warts actually contributing to the (to the masculine ego) generally flattering effect. He also painted several double portraits of men-only nude or semi-nude couples – and a famous nude one of his regular male models with a pet rat – as well as a group of works inspired by Watteau.

He painted several of his daughters naked. He also sometimes took time out to paint landscapes, usually unlovely scenes of urban desolation glimpsed from the windows of his studio in Paddington, and the occasional still-life, like his *Two Plants* (1977-80), to remind people that his almost Pre-Raphaelite skills as a draughtsman remained unimpaired.

Flesh fascinated Freud and in 1990 he began painting a series of unsparing nude portraits of Leigh Bowery, a risqué performance artist who was decidedly fat. "I found him perfectly beautiful," Freud said later. After Bowery died of Aids in 1994 Freud turned to "Big Sue", Sue Tilley, a 20 stone Jobcentre employee who by her own account said that Freud got value for money because "he got a lot of flesh".

Benefits Supervisor Sleeping, his ruthless portrait of her lying vast and naked on a sofa, cupping one bosom, was sold at auction in 2008 for £23 million, then a world record price for a work of art by a living artist, supposedly to the Russian plutocrat Roman Abramovich. Some years earlier Tilley had offered a print of her portrait given to her by Freud to bailiffs seeking to recover a £700 unpaid debt. They laughed and took her electric kettle instead.

At the age of 70 Freud turned his merciless gaze on himself and executed a warts-and-all self-portrait, standing, brush in hand, naked apart from an incongruous pair of hobnailed boots.

Far gentler on the eye was his nude portrait of the waiflike model Kate Moss which he executed after reading that it was her ambition to be painted by him. Another model, Jerry Hall, then Mrs Mick Jagger, also posed for him naked, and pregnant. Those who kept their clothes on included Andrew Parker-Bowles, the former husband of the Duchess of Cornwall, in *The Brigadier* – seated in unbuttoned Household Cavalry jacket and medals, florid of face and full of stomach – and, most famously, the Queen, whom Freud portrayed in an uncompromising portrait of her face which inevitably caused much controversy in the media and led to accusations of treason in some quarters.

"I paint what I see, not what you want me to see," he once said. Flattery was not in his vocabulary. Perhaps those of his subjects to whom he was kindest were animals, whippets in particular, lying sleekly, innocently alongside a naked human being. And there is a magnificent painting of a horse's backside in *Skewbald Mare*, which he used to observe being ridden at a riding school near his home in Holland Park. As a one-time race-goer and gambler, Freud was something of a connoisseur of horses.

If throughout most of his career he chose force rather than finish, raw energy rather than refinement, these seemed legitimate choices, dictated by his own personality and vision rather than by fashion. When the world came round to him, it was on his own terms, which was probably the only way he would have it.

As the 20th century drew to a close and the 21st began, Freud remained sublimely indifferent to the modern movement in art and its break with paint on canvas, confidently ploughing his own furrow with his inimitable figurative paintings in oil. Like his old friend and drinking companion Francis Bacon, Freud's idiosyncratic portraits – candid almost to the point of cruelty – bore all the recognisable and distinctive hallmarks of a very particular author. His examinations of the human form, executed with a pathologist's clinical eye for detail, were unmistakably by him. But unlike Bacon's images of tortured and restless humanity, Freud generally presented his sitters in repose and tranquillity. He was a slow, painstaking worker who would alleviate the tedium of the long hours he required of his sitters by reciting poetry to them and providing them with excellent food and drink.

Restrospective exhibitions of his work were held in London, Washington, Paris, Berlin, Barcelona, Los Angeles, Venice, Dublin, Copenhagen and The Hague among other cities.

His pictures commanded high prices. Just last month his painting *Woman Smiling*, a portrait of his former lover and mother of four of his children Suzy Boyt, painted in 1959, was sold at auction for £4,745,000.

He was appointed a Companion of Honour in 1983 and a member of the Order of Merit in 1993.

In addition to his various less regular liaisons Freud was married twice. By his first wife, Kathleen, otherwise Kitty Godley, the daughter of Jacob Epstein, to whom he was married from 1948 to 1952, he had two daughters. His second marriage, to Lady Caroline Blackwood, daughter of the 4th Marquess of Dufferin and Ava, also lasted four years, 1953-57, and was childless. She died in 1996.

In his eighties the enigmatic Freud was still immensely attractive to women, young women too, and Emily Bearn, a journalist in her twenties, was among several who became close to him for a time. She is thought to be portrayed sitting submissively at his feet in *The Painter Surprised by a Naked Admirer* (2005).

Freud is survived by many children.

Lucian Freud, OM, CH, painter, was born on December 8, 1922. He died on July 21, 2011, aged 88.

Basil D'Oliveira

England cricketer whose exclusion from a tour of apartheid South Africa in 1968 hastened that country's long exile from international sport

November 21, 2011

The career of Basil D'Oliveira was proof of C. L. R. James's dictum "what do they know of cricket who only cricket know?" Beyond his achievements on the field he became, just as importantly, an embodiment of cricket's wider social and racial context at a time when his country, South Africa, and the international community, were split by apartheid.

Although good enough to get into South Africa's Test side, as a Cape coloured, or person of mixed race, he was not allowed to. Under apartheid, the team was for whites only. Eventually, frustrated by this lack of opportunity, he decided to make his career in England and soon proceeded, by way of the Worcestershire county side, to the England team.

In the autumn of 1968 England were scheduled to visit South Africa and D'Oliveira was a strong candidate for the touring party. But the year did not run smoothly for him. He played in the first Test of the summer against Australia, but, despite a defiant second innings of 87 not out in an England defeat, he was surprisingly dropped for the rest of the series.

Then, on the eve of the fifth and final Test at the Oval, Roger Prideaux, one of the original selections, dropped out through illness and D'Oliveira was recalled. He made the most of his unexpected opportunity, scoring a magnificent 158 in England's first innings and taking a crucial Australian wicket just when it looked as though the weather would cheat England of victory.

His place on the tour of South Africa seemed a formality but when the team was announced he had been left out. Immediately there were accusations that the side had been picked on political, not cricketing, grounds. Pressure from the South African Government, which had intimated that D'Oliveira would not be acceptable, was denied. Doug Insole, the chairman of selectors, said that there were better players.

D'Oliveira heard the news after hitting a century for Worcestershire. He was so distressed that he broke down and was allowed to leave the match and go home. But, though devastated by his omission, he maintained an impeccable dignity and avoided saying anything that might further inflame the situation.

Some MCC members, led by the Rev David Sheppard, a former Test batsman, accused the club of placating the South African authorities in order to preserve the tour and there were angry exchanges. They put down a motion of censure on how the MCC had handled the matter. The club received more than 1,000 letters of protest.

The story then took another unforeseen twist. In an echo of the Prideaux episode, Tom Cartwright was forced to pull out of the tour through injury and D'Oliveira was drafted in. In cricketing terms this was illogical. Cartwright was mainly a bowler and D'Oliveira was principally a batsman. Having offended liberal opinion the first time round, the MCC seemed determined to do the right thing this time.

This gave John Vorster, the South African Prime Minister, the excuse he had been looking for. He called D'Oliveira "a political cricket ball" and said that he would not receive a team "forced on us by people with certain political aims". The MCC had no option but to cancel the tour and England did not play South Africa again until after apartheid was abolished in the early 1990s. The row played an enormous part in hastening South Africa's isolation from international sport.

So D'Oliveira never played Test cricket in the country of his birth, though there was belated compensation for him when South Africa hosted the Cricket World Cup in 2003 and he was invited to take part in the opening ceremony. It was at Newlands, the Test ground in Cape Town from which he had been banned as a player. Walking awkwardly after two hip operations, he was given a warm reception by the multiracial crowd.

The son of a tailor and prominent club cricketer, Basil Lewis D'Oliveira was born in Cape Town in 1931. He was educated at Roman Catholic schools and had ambitions to be a doctor but family circumstances decreed that he left school at 15 and found a job. He joined a printing company and, though barred from doing the less menial jobs, which were reserved for whites, it gave him secure employment and a steady income.

His talent for sport, football as well as cricket, soon became apparent and the company encouraged him. Facilities for non-whites were primitive. As a boy D'Oliveira played cricket on cobbled streets and even after he joined St Augustine's, a leading Cape Town club, the "ground" was a piece of wasteland from which stones and other debris were removed on the day of the match. The pitch was a large mat, heaved into position by members of the team. Before he came to England, D'Oliveira had rarely played on grass.

D'Oliveira was a self-taught cricketer who overcame the handicaps of poor pitches and the absence of nets or coaching to become a heavy-scoring batsman and useful seam bowler. For his works side, at the age of 19, he made 225 in under 70 minutes out of a team total of 236 and in a club match he took nine wickets for two runs. By the time he went to England he had made more than 80 centuries.

The peak of his achievement was captaining a non-white South African team in matches against a side of Kenyan Asians but these "Tests" were far from the real thing and eventually, in despair, he wrote on impulse to John Arlott, whose distinctive Hampshire voice had become familiar through his commentaries. D'Oliveira's imploring letters, written in green ink on cheap notepaper, found a sympathetic response.

Arlott, who had covered the MCC tour of South Africa in 1948-49 and been disgusted by the treatment of its non-white people, was determined to help. He sounded out John Kay, cricket correspondent of the Manchester Evening News, about D'Oliveira's chances of playing as a professional in the Lancashire leagues. Normally such opportunities fell only to established Test players, but when Middleton were suddenly left with a vacancy after the withdrawal of the West Indian, Wes Hall, they decided to take a chance on D'Oliveira.

He was offered a contract at £450, but would have to pay his airfare. Friends, white and black, clubbed together to raise the money. His first few weeks in Lancashire were miserable.

The weather was cold and wet, he took time to master the slower English wickets and missed his wife and small son whom he had had to leave behind in South Africa. But by the end of the season he was ahead of even the great Garry Sobers in the league averages.

After further successful seasons with Middleton, Tom Graveney suggested he tried county cricket and he joined Graveney at Worcestershire. Worried that his age might be a handicap, he took three years off it. In 1964 he hit a century for Worcestershire against the touring Australians and the year after, his first full season, he scored more than 1,500 runs and took 35 wickets. In 1966, having taken British citizenship, he was chosen for England.

In his first Test, against the West Indies at Lord's, he was unluckily run out for 27, but he scored two fifties in his second and 88 in the next, with four sixes including a straight hit against Hall, one of the fastest bowlers in world cricket. In 1967 he made the first of his five Test centuries against India, but one of his finest innings was 114 not out on a crumbling wicket in Pakistan on the tour which replaced the aborted trip to South Africa.

D'Oliveira was a composed batsman who started an innings watchfully and accelerated once he taken stock of the pitch and bowling. He had a short backlift but, thanks in part to strong forearms, hit with great power. A speciality was a sweep so fine that it barely eluded the wicketkeeper. His bowling was deceptive, no more than medium pace but with enough swing and wobble to surprise batsmen who were well set. He was a notable breaker of stands.

D'Oliveira's success in the first-class game is all the more creditable because it came so late. He was 34 when he first played Test cricket and he continued playing regularly for Worcestershire until he was 47. His record was impressive enough: he averaged 40 in his 44 Tests, and scored more than 19,000 runs with 45 centuries in all matches, but he had lost the years when most cricketers are at their peak.

He played his last Test in 1972 when he was approaching 41 but some of his more memorable innings were still to come. In 1974, while helping Worcestershire to another county championship, he made his highest first-class score: 227 against Yorkshire at Hull. His determination to bat on to a large score was fired by remarks about his colour from a Yorkshire bowler.

Two years later, in the Benson & Hedges final against Kent at Lord's, he tore a hamstring while fielding. Although unable to move his feet, he scored a remarkable 50 which threatened to turn the game. In his final season he took on the Somerset and West Indies fast bowler Joel Garner and scored a quick half century, which included a hook for six. As news of his impending retirement spread, he was applauded at cricket grounds around the country.

After retirement he stayed with Worcestershire as the club coach and eventually saw the team he had nursed win two consecutive championships. Never having been coached himself, he preferred a pragmatic approach, long on encouragement and short on technical dogma. He continued to live in Worcester, in the house he had first bought there, and in 2004 a new stand at the county ground was named after him. He had been suffering from Parkinson's disease for several years.

A new generation became aware of the significance of his story in 2004 when a magnificent biography by the political commentator Peter Oborne won the William Hill Sports Book of the Year prize.

D'Oliveira is survived by his wife Naomi, whom he married in 1959, and their two sons, Damian, who also played for Worcestershire, and Shaun. Damian is a member of the coaching staff at Worcester and Basil D'Oliveira's grandson, Brett, also plays for the club. Basil D'Oliveira was appointed OBE in 1969 advanced to CBE in 2005.

Basil D'Oliveira, CBE, cricketer, was born on October 4, 1931. He died on November 19, 2011, aged 80.